FANNY & JOHNNIE CRADOCK
(BON VIVEUR)

The
Cook Hostess'
Book

EDITED BY ANN HAZLEWOOD
ILLUSTRATED BY VAL BIRO, F.S.I.A.

THE
COOKERY BOOK CLUB
LONDON

ISBN 0 00 435153 3

This Edition published 1971 by
The Cookery Book Club
St. Giles House, 49/50 Poland St., W1A 2LG
By arrangement with Messrs. Wm. Collins Sons & Co. Ltd.

Printed in Great Britain by
Collins Clear-Type Press

CONTENTS

AS WE FOUND IT NECESSARY TO REFER TO A NUMBER OF RECIPES ALREADY PUBLISHED IN THE *Cook's Book* AND THE *Sociable Cook's Book* (PUBLISHED BY FONTANA) WE MARKED THE FORMER WITH A * AND THE LATTER WITH A †

OUR METRIC CONVERSION CHART PAGE 29 TO PAGE 33 WAS FIRST PUBLISHED BY *The Daily Telegraph.*

We are grateful to the Gas Council for providing the following chart showing comparative temperatures:

GAS MARK	APPROXIMATE ELECTRICAL TEMPERATURE
1/4	240°F
1/2	265°F
1	290°F
2	310°F
3	335°F
4	355°F
5	380°F
6	400°F
7	425°F
8	445°F
9	470°F

To Mary Lee Fairbanks
Nonpareil of hostesses

one · RUN IT LIKE A BATTLE

We owe to Mrs. Douglas Fairbanks the *Ultima Thule* on being a hostess. She said, the morning after the coming-out ball which she gave for her daughter Daphne, "It was all marvellous but then let's face it, I ran it like a battle."

All parties should be run like battles. Hostesses should be like great generals, visionaries who can see the outcome and the triumph and then work back from their visions of success and pre-plan in such a way that their minds are clear and their spirits high when the actual fray commences.

It seems to us, looking back over a lifetime of parties given by us, by our parents and their parents that nothing is more stupid than parties which the host and hostess cannot enjoy to the full themselves. Our aim throughout this book on contemporary cooking and hostessry is above all to share a pattern for pleasure—even if it does mean some preliminary labour. This only becomes a nightmare when harrassment and flustering intervene with the awful dawn speculations on what has been forgotten, overlooked, left to the over-full last minute. None of which can happen if you plan . . . properly . . . and from the beginning.

Anyone who is giving parties today, is inevitably understaffed, overtaxed, beset, bedevilled and bewildered by the appalling cost of living and driven hairless by the spirit of slop-through and slap-up which seems to pervade this country like a malignant paralysis of ambition and endeavour. Their capabilities *must* stretch to the uttermost to contend with these prevalent evils.

No one could be more aware of them than we are at the moment of writing. Anyone who has had over fifty assorted workmen in their home, on and off for a bitter, searing year of restoring, re-decorating and renewing knows to just what extent the labourer has become unworthy of his hire . . . with . . . *cela se voit* . . . a few glowing and notable exceptions. In the past, an unsatisfactory housemaid was one who swept the dust under the carpets. Now

the analogy holds good for almost every service for which we
have to pay; from the grocers whose (unpunctual) deliveries bear
no resemblance to the orders given; and the telephone which is
constantly out of order though no deductions are made for this
dis-service; to the jobbing gardener who turns over the weeds
(growth uppermost) or the supplier of little gilt chairs who takes
large chunks out of the walls against which he stacks them and
walks pads of mud on to the parquet as his booted feet go uner-
ringly across this and off the carefully laid drugget.

Moaning to one's women friends ensures a lonely future.
Taking hell out of yourself because of it only increases the lines on
your face; but accepting it as the national norm; planning and
budgeting to contend with and over-ride it all; learning to laugh
at it and stubbornly refusing to let it break your spirit is a daily
exercise which any woman who runs a home and opens her door
to friends **must do.**

In the preceding paragraphs we have rid ourselves of all these
accumulated resentments because we want you to know before
you read a single recipe or even study our proposed plans,
quantity lists and party suggestions that we have a most genuine
and profound respect for any wife and mum or busy career
woman who entertains today. We never cease to marvel at the
resourcefulness which enables so many to look their problems in
the eye and cut them stone dead . . . and by so doing to ensure that
there is more pleasure in going to a party now than ever there was
for our forebears, many of whom had means, staff, leisure and
opportunity on a scale which will probably never come again.
In short we "take off all our hats to you" (as Mr. Aage Thaarup
once said to us) before we start and now let us see what we can
contribute that some of you do not know already.

The *modus operandi* is identical for a bridge tea, a ball for three hundred or a family picnic on the beach. All are improved by being run like battles with the kitchen as the Battle Ground and the weapons your *batterie* of equipment, pots and pans, telephone and enough paper to make innumerable lists.

Battle orders in this establishment, which is very much a home but as tranquil as Paddington station on a Bank Holiday at peak rush hour, are drawn up whenever a new proposal is mooted. We will give you a cross section from our own:—

Two hundred and twenty guests, with Press and Television Camera crews as well, for the launching of a new book.
Eight to a business luncheon and trainees and staff to feed in the kitchen as well.
A grandchild's fourth birthday party.
Seven hundred and twenty food colour pictures to be photographed in seventy-two consecutive weeks, all the cooking and garnishing to be done between other jobs.
A display table of tested examples of what can be made with an about-to-be-launched new food product.
Supper in the garden for sixty.
Sixteen to a fork luncheon.
A gardening weekend ahead and twelve hungry mouths to feed and no time for cooking.
The Vicar to tea on Wedensday and *mise en place* for cooking television on the same day.
Dinner for fourteen and the "daily" with her right hand in plaster.

For each and every one of these our first moves are constant and must always include jobs to be done—or there will not be any money to pay for the parties! First we make lists and clearly these are variable, but in the main they include:—

1. Number of guests.
2. The menus.
3. The accompanying drinks.
4. Table arrangements listing the glasses, plates, bowls, knives, forks, cloths and decorations required for chosen menu and wines.
5. Every item to be cooked and the relevant garnish.
6. The order of cooking and when it is a big party the sub-divisions:

   (a) items which can be made well in advance and stored without deterioration; (b) items which will refrigerate for several days, such as *roux*, *velouté*, *Béchamel*, mayonnaise and *Espagnole* sauces, confectioners' custard and butter cream; (c) items which can only be made two days beforehand; (d) items which can only be made the day beforehand; (e) items which have to be made on the day—like *choux* paste which is otherwise inedible.

If there are more than one or two of these last included, *the whole menu must be revised* at this early stage because the cook hostess who gives herself a lot of cooking on the day of a party wants her brains tested! She has other things to do.

The kitchen draft of the menu is then married not only to the list of plates, cutlery etc. but also to the dishes on which each item will be served. This enables you to check the garnish for each item and to ascertain precisely what will be needed. Only then can the final shopping lists be tackled. If it is a big party, these too must be sub-divided. There is nothing more calculated to bring on high blood pressure, a migraine or a *crise de nerfs* than a mad foray to the telephone to find out why such-and-such has not been delivered on THE day or to leave all and bolt for the nearest shop to buy something which has been completely forgotten! Try to ensure that everything is safely in the house twenty-four hours ahead of THE day or perhaps in most cases we should say THE evening.

This is the key to success. It is the flutterings, fussings and maniacal little dashes to buy this and that which make havoc of a cook hostess's work and wear her down till she feels she is standing on her ankles; or as Sir Archibald MacIndoe said once—about a weary waiter, "He hadn't any feet left, they were just the bottom of his legs turned up."

Once the lists are made and broken down into their separate

compartments, *the evidence will show for itself way ahead of panic time whether or not the proposed plan is too demanding and there is far too much work to be done on one day and practically nothing on another.* When this happens, scrap and start again until your plan shows you that you *can* embark on your venture, secure in the knowledge that while it may be hard work, it is *not* more than you can reasonably encompass without reducing yourself to a jittery wreck by the time your guests arrive.

Because *"l'homme propose, Dieu dispose"* and however well organised you are, some extraneous demand upon your time will crop up if you are blessed with a normal family pattern! So leave room for it and always over-estimate rather than under-estimate the time you will need in your kitchen, reception room and bedroom to make yourself presentable at the last "Well now, there's nothing more I *can* do" moment. Say to yourself, very firmly indeed, "The cook, host or hostess who leaves it all to chance expends more adrenalin in fear and agitation than ever the methodical one will do cooking and presenting an elaborate and demanding meal which has every detail planned."

Then we suggest you come to terms with what you are, madam, so that you can appreciate yourself in your twentieth century role.

three · **MRS. JEKYLL AND MRS. HYDE**

We think you are either Mrs. Jekyll and Mrs. Hyde or Mr. and Mrs. Jekyll and Hyde or the Misses Jekyll and Hyde. In the former role you may very well get flour on your nose as you brush a strand of hair out of your eyes and dash to the telephone or snatch Junior's grubby little paw out of the spin-dryer. You may well have an apron over your jeans, have no time to go to the hairdressers and do mayhem to your hands somewhere between the window box or herbaceous border, the sink, the paintpot, the potato peeler and the silver polishing; but by some alchemy you are capable of turning yourself into a groomed and smiling hostess who looks as if she does not have a care in the world and whose nails are impeccably varnished—although the job was probably done a few moments before the party came in and while exhorting the children to get back into bed at once and withdrawing your husband's missing socks from the linen cupboard by your teeth! (Wet nail varnish!)

Whatever the cost, you bridge the transition, somehow, but at least you have the consolation of knowing that it is no longer necessary these days for anyone to practise the genteel deceits so necessary to Miss Matty and her sister when they registered surprise at the appearance of the sponge fingers which they had made themselves that morning.

Even when we were children the conventions remained that it was extremely ill-bred to make comments, however, praiseworthy, about the cooking. Not so today, if you can contrive to produce an outstanding pudding or a particularly unctuous soup, you can be sure that it will be noticed, praised and almost certainly there will be some—er—restrained hinting during the powdering session after dinner concerning the possibilities of Liz, Susan or Jane getting their hooks on the recipe! You can also accept that the conventional norm for dinner parties is three courses and you will be regarded as remarkable if you produce more. If as Mrs. Jekyll you have made beautiful coffee in the morning and left it to re-heat *au bain marie** for Mrs. Hyde to serve in a trice, you will be regarded as a pearl above women.

As there is a very great deal more to all this, let us examine a little in greater detail some of the things which Mrs. Hyde could not endure that Mrs. Jekyll had left undone for her. It is Mrs. Jekyll who plans meals in such a way that Mrs. Hyde barely leaves her guests at all and, when she is devoid of any help whatever, Mrs. Jekyll sees to it that the first course is pre-prepared in such a way that it need only be either set in position a few moments before the meal or dished up in seconds and taken in. She also chooses a main course which can take care of itself in the oven with a little carefully calculated pre-timing and even if she is offering a cheese board in the classical and correct position—*after the main course and before the pudding*—this is in dining room position with the pudding—for, of course, with only one pair of hands this will be a *cold one*! Mrs. Jekyll's liaison with Mrs. Hyde throughout is such that it would be unthinkable for Mrs. Hyde to leave her guests while she cleared away or washed up. Mrs. Jekyll will do that later or the next morning for nothing is more dreadful than employing any of the three alternatives: to absent herself; to place the guests in the awful position of having to offer help or suffer agonies concomitant with their helping clear up when they do not know where anything goes or because Mrs. Jekyll may not have left the kitchen as *point device* as it might be!

Nor, when Mrs. Jekyll knows that she is going to have tem-porary help, does she rely upon the spoken word for her instruc-tions. She *writes it all down* so that if something has to go into the oven, come out of the steamer or be warmed through at a parti-cular moment it is listed and timed, not at 7.45 this, that or the other because guests can be late or your assessment of the time taken by a course be inaccurate for some reason or another. Better we suggest such timing estimates are done something like this . . . Written Instructions Example.

Mrs. Sims: When Henry takes in the main course, take the ice cream pudding out of the freezer (it is already dished up and covered with foil), remove the foil and leave on the kitchen table until Henry is ready for it. The coffee is standing in water in the meat baking tin over a low light; just rinse the coffee pot with boiling water from the kettle (set ready for you), leave 1 minute, pour away, take out the vanilla pod—it's a long black thing—but don't throw it away; pour in the coffee from the first panful, put it on the coffee tray—everything else is ready—and let Henry take it through to the drawing room as soon as you hear us leaving the dining room. Then when I ring for Henry, he will bring the empty pot back and you can fill it up again, as before, and for the men when they join us.

Even this is not quite enough. Mrs. Hyde will be dressed and ready about ten minutes before she expects her first guests. Then she can run over the list with Mrs. Sims *et al* so that Mrs. S. can ask any questions that arise from Mrs. Jekyll's notes. Mrs. Jekyll then checks her counter list for Henry or whoever else is involved and sees to it that each one dovetails. Finally, she whips round the rooms which are to be used, has a final check to see that nothing has been forgotten and is free *to enjoy her own party*.

four · AREAS OF CONFLICT

No definitions that we could achieve could guarantee to embrace the varying patterns of all of you. The best we can do is to itemise the extremes and leave the permutations and combinations to each individual. Roughly speaking, you fight out a party on three fronts: with storage facilities, over what the millions of clubs up and down the country call "floristry" and in kitchen. No one needs to be reminded by us that the house in general and the rooms of entertainment in particular will have to be made clean and tidy.

The privileged few have a flower room; the less fortunate have a cupboard under the stairs for containers and a corner of the kitchen table for the work. The amount of squirrelling, i.e. hoarding, which can be done is not only a matter of expenditure but also of space, so while the dream is of a deep freeze, vast refrigeration and a bone-dry and airy store room where long-keeping stocks of all descriptions may be shelved, hung and hoarded away in cupboards, we must just accept the validity of the quote, "Man does what he must at the point where he stands." The same may be said of kitchens and only those who have saved up for years, are newly weds or have had a sudden windfall can afford to scrap everything and embark from scratch upon the kitchen of their dreams.

Even so there are far more houses in Great Britain where the basic kitchen areas are so deplorably planned in the first place that it needs a genius to adapt their shapes to ideal kitchen conditions. All we can hope to do is to tell you that we have moved into an old house where by the simple means of removing the only plywood wall in the building, we were able to achieve the best basic kitchen area that has ever come our way. In all fairness we must add that we did have a windfall which enabled us to do some of the things that we have longed to do for many, many years.

Our first determination was that we would finish with cooking with our faces to the wall and come right out into the open, as is done in every chef's kitchen throughout the centre of the gastronomic world—FRANCE. Canopied by air extraction and strong lighting we work, we must admit, in a much larger cooking block than the average housewife would ever need; but the principle— scaled down to small kitchen areas—is, we submit, worthy of mention.

We have designed a block with a concrete base 4 ft. wide and 8 ft. 6 ins. long. In it we have four cookers back to back and *topless*. We just wheedled the manufacturers to remove all four tops with their incorporated grills and smacked them up against the walls so that we can now grill at eye level with a separate working surface underneath them which, of course, covers free-standing storage cupboards below.

We have done the same cupboard storage top-surface working unit treatment with the cookers themselves; but instead of having permanent tops we have made these removable to slot into the box of our window *banquette* in the kitchen meal bay. Thus we are able to slide off a top and use a cooker, dumping onto the working surface left and right, or lift off the laminated plastic working surface tops at will and reveal chopping boards and marble blocks for pastry work immediately beneath them. These in turn form the roofs to our cupboards which have sliding runners with metal hooks on so that we can hang 5 copper pans to a cupboard and therefore, having a runner in each of 6 cupboards, can accommodate 30, with all the side walls around the floor area for storing other kitchen equipment. In explanation of the size of our kitchen we hasten to add we sit down a minimum of 16 to luncheon every working day quite apart from visitations from our vast families.

To justify what we consider the only really practical kind of island unit, it must be situated with one side in such close proximity to a double sink and a double drainer and wall cupboard above that you only have to swing round and not take one single pace in order to dump stuff in the sink, get water from it or reach wines, seasonings, flavourings, colourings, herbs, sauces *et al* from wall cupboards. We are obsessed after many years in the kitchen with the value of saving time and motion, hence the lunacy of having a large kitchen table plonk in the middle of the room so that you are going round it like a blue-based fly every blessed day, all day long. We go *through* 4 draw-leaf, rectangular, laminated plastic topped tables which close up to a mere 2 ft. 4 ins. × 2 ft.

We are not alone in being cook addicts although because we do so much professional as well as personal work, we do tend to have more of everything than is needed in the average home. Therefore we respectfully submit that anyone who has a large collection of ornamental icing pipes, an assortment of little bottles of harmless vegetable colourings and of flavourings cannot really want to search through the lot and scratch about behind the rows for whichever it is that is totally concealed by everything else. Johnnie measured the area of the shelves in our cupboards. He then made additional ones in ply and affixed a narrow beading all round the edge of each so that they are like very shallow trays. They can be painted or covered with suitably coloured or patterned Fablon which is very strong and equally easy to keep clean. Then when you want something, you merely pull the tray out, see the item you want, take it and simply push the tray back again.

Instead of trays, cut 1″ thick blocks of wood for icing pipes. Hammer in 3″ nails all over the surface 1½″ apart. Invert each pipe over a nail and there they stay—ready for instant selection, easy return and thus the total elimination of more scratching about.

We cannot withold the irrelevant addition that we were so enamoured of ourselves because this was such a help, that we did exactly the same thing for cotton reels and thereby disposed of cats' cradles in the work basket, to say nothing of being able to choose the colour, fabric in hand, without disturbing a single reel until the right one is picked out.

Give yourselves extra working space by having a "lid" of laminated plastic made to slip over your cooker when it is not in use. Slide it away down the side of the cooker when using the hot plate.

IF you have a big kitchen, you might like to copy our utensils trolley—but if you do, remember to take off the wheels that are supplied when you buy. These have a crab-like tendency in action, and are terribly hard to steer. Instead, get four of the big hospital type rubber wheels, have these fixed on securely and the trolley will roll about with the minimum of pressure. Then screw cuphooks to the topmost trolley-bar and from these hang whisks, slices, ladles, spiders, perforated spoons, tin openers and skewers.

Keep all special kitchen knives, wooden spoons, plastic scraper-spatulas, canelle knives and Parisian cutters on the top tier. Use the second shelf for spices, vinegars and seasonings, and the bottom one for kitchen foil, greaseproof, wax paper, paper icing bags, pencils, trussing string and such others. Then you can wheel your concentrated *batterie de la cuisine* around with you at much saving to leg and labour.

Make sure your seating is comfortable. A good sit down between labours is inadequate on either a stool or a section of a bench. If a dining alcove is incorporated see that the banquettes are thoroughly well padded and have small firm cushions for those who have a tendency to backache.

Spend your absolute limit on lighting. You do not have to switch everything on at once, but working in a bad light is lethal to your eyesight and totally inadequate for any kind of the fine work which is so often necessary.

Make your kitchen tablecloths as gay and bold as possible. Go for single sets of plates and bowls rather than for a dinner service —then you can ring the changes on the old and the new, the Danish and the French, the classic and the ultra modern.

As soon as you can afford it, install air extraction. Those sweet aromas which prompt the impractical to splash out bits of death-less prose about the lovely cooking smells of this and that are much more likely to be Nauseous Ponks when they escape the kitchen and go sweeping through the house.

Make sure you have a proper shelf for cookery books. Their place is either in the kitchen or beside your bed and cookery writers would do well to remember this when publishing vast coffee-table books of great splendour which are too big to be of any practical use. Above all be certain of list-paper and pencils close at hand. It is strange but true that if you make a list and then leave it behind when you go shopping, the act of making it will imprint the items on your mind. Time spent at counters mutter-ing, "Now *was* there anything else, I wonder!" is time wasted— and that is a luxury none of us can afford.

A kitchen is a workshop—a studio—a genius's lair. There is no possible justification for any arty-crafty prettying-up which interferes in the slightest degree with the work done in any kitchen. It always irritates a serious cook to see those glossed-up colour pictures in which every available space is exquisitely arranged with *objets d'art*, as if the kitchen were a showroom and the working surfaces the display areas.

Ceilings, windows and their embrasures and wall panels which are not taken up with storage or unit space can be used for decoration. Colour schemes can be as gay and brilliant or as smooth and gentle as the cook desires; but it is he or she who should be consulted at every stage of kitchen-building; not some itsy-bitsy girlsy-boysie who is dotty about Blue John (this month) and fills purple-coloured shelves with exquisite blue bits whose sole function thereafter is to attract dust and create unjustifiable work.

Of course the shape of the room will to a certain degree predetermine the position of the major items; but there is no excuse for refrigerator and/or deep freeze being placed at the opposite end of the room from the sink and cooker.

Nor should the labourer at the sink be expected to look out upon a gloomy expanse of mouldering brickwall. We had just such a wall at one end of the old kitchen in our previous home. The blank wall, a sinister, falling-leaf collector shaped like a trough, was only 3 ft. from the window. We distempered it annually in white and highlighted in turquoise a cluster of besom, rake, hoe, trowel, leaf-rake and pitchfork which we pinned to the white wall like a giant spray. A similarly whitewashed trug placed centrally and filled with hearts tongues, which will grow anywhere withstood manfully the assaults of ten detestable English winters.

Where anything will grow upwards, pin a bit of trellis to the painted wall and induce climbers to brighten it up still further. For a north facing wall use one of the white and pink or silver-tipped *Hederas* (ivies); a tough old *Lonicera Henrii* (evergreen) or Japanese Quince and Forsythia. If one window happily faces south, plant the evergreen clematis which has either white or pink flowers in spring, *C. Armandii Alba* or *Rosa* and tangle in with it a *C. Fargesii* with its charming buttercup flowers right through October, and stuff in seeds of both green and purple *Cobaea Scandens* (annual in our climate) and *Tropaeolum Speciosum* which hangs little flames from its trailers all summer through. You spend a great part of your life in your kitchen. So do we. It behoves us to make it as pleasing to US in every respect as space and income permit. Be selfish about it and be mulish with any so called kitchen planners who are not also *Very Experienced Cooks.*

five · PREACHING TO THE CONVERTED

Please turn to our acknowledgement at the front of this book if you want to know where this chart first appeared or indeed wonder why the original version is already hanging in your or a friend's kitchen. We reproduce it here because there is the faint possibility that in some households other than our own, books lose themselves less rapidly than nice little conversion charts put up in handbag size.

Many years ago we horrified a group of English experts by announcing, "All our cookery source books are French." Our statement was greeted with a disapproving chorus of "Fancy translating all those kilos into ounces." Working on the basis of a flat 28 grammes to one ounce—ignoring the odd decimal points—we have stubbornly persisted with this "chore", unconsciously arming ourselves against the now imminent national change-over.

Of course the mathematicians are right when they give exact translations to the last decimal point; but we think the average housewife would go hairless trying to achieve this every time she wanted a quick conversion of, say, 2½ ozs. flour, 4 ozs. castor sugar, 1¾ ozs. butter and 2½ fl. ozs. milk.

Our Way, the conversion would be 70 g., 112 g., 49 g. and 8 cl.
The Mathematicians Way, the conversion would be 70·8617 g., 113·3784 g., 49·6030 g. and 8·52 cl.

CONVERSION TABLE—SOLIDS

A KILOGRAMME is sub-divided into grammes.
COMMON ABBREVIATIONS: kg. = kilogramme; g. = gramme.

Ounces into Grammes

¼ oz.	= approx.	7 g.	3 ozs.	=	,,	84 g.
½ oz.	= ,,	14 g.	4 ozs. (¼ lb.)	=	,,	112 g.
¾ oz.	= ,,	21 g.	5 ozs.	=	,,	140 g.
1 oz.	= ,,	28 g.	6 ozs.	=	,,	168 g.
2 ozs.	= ,,	56 g.	7 ozs.	=	,,	196 g.

8 ozs. (½ lb.)	=	,,	224 g.		25 ozs.	=	,,	700 g.
9 ozs.	=	,,	252 g.		26 ozs.	=	,,	728 g.
10 ozs.	=	,,	280 g.		27 ozs.	=	,,	756 g.
11 ozs.	=	,,	308 g.		28 ozs. (1¾ lbs.) =		,,	784 g.
12 ozs. (¾ lb.)	=	,,	336 g.		29 ozs.	=	,,	812 g.
13 ozs.	=	,,	364 g.		30 ozs.	=	,,	840 g.
14 ozs.	=	,,	392 g.		31 ozs.	=	,,	868 g.
15 ozs.	=	,,	420 g.		32 ozs. (2 lbs.)	=	,,	896 g.
16 ozs. (1 lb.)	=	,,	448 g.		33 ozs.	=	,,	924 g.
17 ozs.	=	,,	476 g.		34 ozs.	=	,,	952 g.
18 ozs.	=	,,	504 g.		35 ozs.	=	,,	980 g.
19 ozs.	=	,,	532 g.		35¾ ozs.	=	,,	1000 g.
20 ozs. (1¼ lbs.) =		,,	560 g.					(1 kg.)
21 ozs.	=	,,	588 g.		A scant 9 ozs.	=		¼ kg.
22 ozs.	=	,,	616 g.		A scant 18 ozs.	=		½ kg.
23 ozs.	=	,,	644 g.		A scant 27 ozs.	=		¾ kg.
24 ozs. (1½ lbs.) =		,,	672 g.					

CONVERSION TABLE—FLUIDS

A LITRE is sub-divided into millilitres, centilitres and decilitres.

1 LITRE = 10 decilitres = 100 centilitres = 1,000 millilitres.

½ LITRE = 5 decilitres = 50 centilitres = 500 millilitres.

¼ LITRE = 2·5 decilitres = 25 centilitres = 250 millilitres.

COMMON ABBREVIATIONS: l. = litre; dl. = decilitre; cl. = centilitre; ml. = millilitre.

Fluid Ounces into Millilitres

1 fl. oz.	= approx.	28 ml.		19	,,	=	,,	532 ,,
2 fl. ozs. =	,,	56 ,,		20	,,	=	,,	560 ,,
3 ,,	= ,,	84 ,,		21	,,	=	,,	588 ,,
4 ,,	= ,,	112 ,,		22	,,	=	,,	616 ,,
5 ,,	= ,,	140 ,,		23	,,	=	,,	644 ,,
6 ,,	= ,	168 ,,		24	,,	=	,,	672 ,,
7 ,,	= ,,	196 ,,		25	,,	=	,,	700 ,,
8 ,,	= ,,	224 ,,		26	,,	=	,,	728 ,,
9 ,,	= ,,	252 ,,		27	,,	=	,,	756 ,,
10 ,,	= ,,	280 ,,		28	,,	=	,,	784 ,,
11 ,,	= ,,	308 ,,		29	,,	=	,,	812 ,,
12 ,,	= ,,	336 ,,		30	,,	=	,,	840 ,,
13 ,,	= ,,	364 ,,		31	,,	=	,,	868 ,,
14 ,,	= ,,	392 ,,		32	,,	=	,,	896 ,,
15 ,,	= ,,	420 ,,		33	,,	=	,,	924 ,,
16 ,,	= ,,	448 ,,		34	,,	=	,,	952 ,,
17 ,,	= ,,	476 ,,		35	,,	=	,,	980 ,,
18 ,,	=	504 ,,						

UNORTHODOX AND AMERICAN MEASURES
CONVERSION TABLE

1 level teacup flour	= 5½ ozs.	= 154 g.
1 ,, breakfast cup flour	= 6½ ,,	= 182 g.
1 ,, teacup castor sugar	= 7½ ,,	= 210 g.
1 ,, breakfast cup castor sugar	= 10 ,,	= 280 g.
1 ,, teacup rice	= 6½ ,,	= 182 g.
1 ,, breakfast cup rice	= 9½ ,,	= 266 g.
1 ,, teacup breadcrumbs	= 3½ ,,	= 98 g.
1 ,, breakfast cup breadcrumbs	= 4¼ ,,	= 119 g.
1 ,, teacup butter	= 7½ ,,	= 210 g.
1 ,, breakfast cup butter	= 11 ,,	= 308 g.
1 ,, teacup olive oil	= 7 ,,	= 196 g.
1 ,, breakfast cup olive oil	= 10½ ,,	= 294 g.
1 ,, teacup icing sugar	= 5¼ ,,	= 147 g.
1 ,, breakfast cup icing sugar	= 8½ ,,	= 238 g.
1 ,, teacup golden syrup/black treacle	= 11½ ,,	= 322 g.
1 ,, breakfast cup syrup/black treacle	= 15½ ,,	= 434 g.

All measures are for rounded spoonsful

1 tablespoon icing sugar	= ½ oz.	= 14 g.
1 ,, castor sugar	= ¾ oz.	= 21 g.
1 ,, pieces or soft brown sugar	= 1 oz.	= 28 g.
1 ,, flour	= 1 oz.	= 28 g.
1 ,, butter	= 1¼ ozs.	= 35 g.
1 ,, spice	= ¼ oz.	= 7 g.
1 ,, flaked almonds	= ¼ oz.	= 7 g.
1 ,, cornflour	= ½ oz.	= 14 g.
1 ,, barley	= 1 oz.	= 28 g.
1 ,, ground rice	= 1 oz.	= 28 g.
1 ,, potato flour	= ¾ oz.	= 21 g.
1 ,, semolina	= 1 oz.	= 28 g.
1 ,, French cooking salt	= ¾ oz.	= 21 g.
1 ,, table salt	= 1 oz.	= 28 g.
1 ,, black pepper	= ½ oz.	= 14 g.
1 ,, drinking chocolate	= 1 oz.	= 28 g.
1 ,, glucose	= ¾ oz.	= 21 g.
1 ,, Indian tea	= scant ½ oz.	= scant 14 g.
1 ,, China tea	= ¼ oz.	= 7 g.

NOTE: *To obtain smaller quantities, halve for dessertspoons and quarter for teaspoons.*

1 American cup butter	= 5 ozs.	= 140 g.
1 ,, ,, grated cheese	= 3½ ozs.	= 98 g.
1 ,, ,, icing sugar	= 4½ ozs.	= 126 g.
1 ,, ,, castor sugar	= 7 ozs.	= 196 g.
1 ,, ,, flour	= 4½ ozs.	= 126 g.

1	,,	,,	flaked fish	= 6 ozs.	= 168 g.
1	,,	,,	ground (minced, ENG) meat	= 5 ozs.	= 140 g.
1	American	teaspoon	solids	= 1 level teaspoon ENG.	
1	,,	dessertspoon	solids	= 1 level dessertspoon ENG	
1	,,	tablespoon	solids	= 1 level tablespoon ENG	
1	,,	pint = 2 American cups		= 16 fl. ozs. = 448 g.	
1	,,	cup fluid		= 8 ,, = 224 ml.	
$\frac{1}{3}$	,,	,, ,,		= 3 ,, = 84 ml.	
$\frac{1}{4}$	,,	,, ,,		= 2$\frac{1}{2}$,, = 70 ml.	

NOTE: *American cup measures are obtainable through the U.S. Trade Center 57, St. James's Street, London S.W.1. or Selfridge Ltd., Oxford Street, London, W.1*

BULK BUYING CONVERSION TABLE

1 stone	=	14 lbs.	=	6 kg. 272 g.
1 quarter	=	28 lbs.	=	12 kg. 544 g.
1 half cwt.	=	56 lbs.	=	25 kg. 88 g.
1 cwt.	=	112 lbs.	=	50 kg. 176 g.
$\frac{1}{2}$ gallon	=	4 pts.	=	2 l. 240 ml.
1 gallon	=	8 pts.	=	4 l. 480 ml.

COOKING TEMPERATURES CONVERSION
Oven

Gas Mark $\frac{1}{4}$ =	approximately	240° F. =	approximately	120° C.
,, ,, $\frac{1}{2}$ =	,,	265° F. =	,,	130° C.
,, ,, 1 =	,,	290° F. =	,,	145° C.
,, ,, 2 =	,,	310° F. =	,,	155° C.
,, ,, 3 =	,,	335° F. =	,,	170° C.
,, ,, 4 =	,,	355° F. =	,,	180° C.
,, ,, 5 =	,,	380° F. =	,,	195° C.
,, ,, 6 =	,,	400° F. =	,,	205° C.
,, ,, 7 =	,,	425° F. =	,,	220° C.
,, ,, 8 =	,,	445° F. =	,,	230° C.
,, ,, 9 =	,,	470° F. =	,,	245° C.

Oil Temperatures

Slightly smoking hot = 390°–400° F. = 200°–205° C.
Just below slightly smoking hot = 360°–385° F. = 180°–195° C.

Water, Milk etc.

Boiling = 212° F. = 100° C.
Blood heat approx. = 98° F. = 37° C.
Freezing = 32° F. = 0° C.

COOKS' PROPORTIONS CONVERSION TABLE
Gelatine

1 oz. gelatine = 28 g.	will stiffen 560 ml.	fluid or sweetened fruit juice
$\frac{1}{2}$ oz. ,, = 14 g.	,, ,, 560 ,,	mayonnaise or thick sauce
$\frac{4}{5}$ oz. ,, = 22 g.	,, ,, 560 ,,	thick (canned) fruit syrup
$\frac{1}{4}$ oz. ,, = 7 g.	,, ,, 420 ,,	stiffly whipped cream

Roux Based Sauces

THICK 1½ ozs. flour, 1½ ozs. butter, 15 fl. ozs. liquid
= 42 g. flour, 42 g. butter, 420 ml. liquid
MEDIUM 1½ ozs. flour, 1½ ozs. butter, 17½ fl. ozs. liquid
= 42 g. flour, 42 g. butter, 490 ml. liquid
THIN 1½ ozs. flour, 1½ ozs. butter, 20 fl. ozs. liquid
= 42 g. flour, 42 g. butter, 560 ml. liquid

Coffee

2 ozs. coffee to 1 pt. boiling water = 56 g. coffee to 560 ml. boiling water

CONVERSION TABLES—LINEAR

The manufacturers of pots, pans, and other kitchen utensils have been using centimetres to the nearest 1″/cm. for many years and the following is their standard conversion table.

For Straight-sided Pots and Pans

Diameter in Inches	Fluid Contents in Pints	Diameter in Centimetres
5	2	14
6	4	16
7	6	18
8	8	20
9	10	22
10	12	24

For Cake Tins

$4\frac{3}{4}''$ = 12 cms.	$10\frac{1}{2}''$ = 26 cms.
$5\frac{1}{2}''$ = 14 ,,	$11\frac{1}{4}''$ = 28 ,,
$6\frac{1}{2}''$ = 16 ,,	$12''$ = 30 ,,
$7\frac{1}{4}''$ = 18 ,,	$12\frac{3}{4}''$ = 32 ,,
$8''$ = 20 ,,	$13\frac{1}{2}''$ = 34 ,,
$8\frac{3}{4}''$ = 22 ,,	$14\frac{1}{4}''$ = 36 ,,
$9\frac{1}{2}''$ = 24 ,,	$15\frac{1}{2}''$ = 38 ,,

Thus a 14″ × 10″ × ¾″ Swiss roll tin would convert to approximately 35 cms. × 25 cms. × 2 cms.; an 8″ diameter Victoria sponge tin to 20 cms.; and a 16″ × 14″ rectangular baking sheet to 39 cms. × 35 cms.

CONSOLATION

It is impossible to convert lineal yardage into equivalent metric measures without the use of decimal points of centimetres. So, when it comes to cooks' cutting measurements, and if you adjust with difficulty to the complexities of decimal points, FORGET THEM. Home cooks can continue cutting 3″ sausage rolls instead of 7·692 centimetre ones. If it suits you better to go on cutting a 12″ diameter circle of puff paste instead of 30·768 cms. *no one will ever know*!

C.H.B.

C

six · TO THE LAST GRAIN OF SALT

We hope you will agree with us that it is fair to say that both the inexperienced young cook hostess and the slaphappy mature one get themselves into a tizzy over entertaining. The former just does not know and has got to find out, the latter has never taken the trouble to record her findings over the years and by temperament is rarely possessed of an accurate memory. For these two alone a book about cooking for guests must contain tried and tested information on quantities as far as possible down to the last grain of salt, if the types we have enumerated are not to be lumbered with post party panic as well. These we define above all as *Those Confounded Left-Overs*.

At very large parties it is almost impossible to be spot on in the amount that you provide and which will result in no left-overs at all, particularly at dance suppers. Some invited guests are also hostesses who give dinner parties before dances and, alas and alack, some of these will be very liberal while others may just veer slightly towards being parsimonious. In Fanny's young days there was one such powerful "entertainer" who gathered as many scalps together as possible for pre-ball dinners. They, when brought on, in her cars to the ball, were always referred to in the county as the gobble-de-gooks. Undernourished on arrival, rampant by the time supper was served, they made a Gadarene rush for the buffet tables and worked their way through whatever was available with the relentless thoroughness of a horde of locusts.

However, what we can do, is to supply you with estimate charts based upon our own personal findings over the years and cross-checked with those of quantitative experts in top-flight Continental catering establishments.

SOUPS   Caterers' cup: 5 fl. ozs.
        Small soup bowl: 6 fl. ozs.
        Beaker: 7 fl. ozs.
        Family soup bowl: 8 fl. ozs.
        Large cup particularly suitable for *Soupe à l'Oignon*:
        9 fl. ozs.
        Old-fashioned soup plate: 10 fl. ozs.

In considering the soup chart it is essential to remember that like all good rules there are exceptions. The speciality soups like regional *Bouillabaisse* are served in quantities which have no bearing to the above; but then nobody in their senses would serve this at a luncheon or dinner party!

Then there is the question of which container for what. We are as vehement in our detestation of soup plates for any hot soup, except perhaps *Bouillabaisse,* as we are of wine coolers for wine. Like English toastracks—defined in this family as draughts with wires round—the soup plate defeats the cook's purpose from the onset. Unless gulped at the double it is quite impossible for a normal serving of piping hot soup to remain so to the last spoonful if drunk with seemly leisure. Palate-wise the counsel for perfection is surely the lidded soup bowl and we appeal to you to set the example at your own table by picking up cup handle or little two handled soup bowl and drinking from it, say, the last quarter of the contents, a practice which is currently regarded as "rather vulgar". So is wiping round a plate with a piece of bread to mop up the last and best of a gorgeous sauce but why should it be when anybody who does so is automatically paying a compliment to the cook at the same time as giving themselves pleasure of delectable *bonnes bouches*?

Remember this is deliberately written as a chat book like its predecessors the Daily Telegraph Cook's Book and Daily Telegraph Sociable Cook's Book (*Fontana* 6/–) to try and bridge the gulf between the reader, and the authors, and achieve the same relationship between ourselves in print as we would have if we were sharing a new discovery with you in our own kitchen. Therefore we make no apologies for another digression.

It was unthinkable when we came out to comment upon the food or wine at a party—that convention was swept up happily during the second world war when cooks *Were Not* and when the most gently brought-up women were compelled to cook even though their education never included how to make a cup of tea or boil an egg. Food was talked openly at the table and food compliments showered upon the creator of any delicious dish.

Now we have just returned from a visit to that enchanting little country Luxembourg and are fired by the Luxembourgeois example. *They* send flowers to the hostess early in the afternoon of any dinner party. *We* send them afterwards, thus the situation frequently arises that the house is smothered in flowers when the party is over and the host and hostess away on some lawful occasion, having spent quite a lot of money in the case of urban entertainers on costly shop flowers. Join us in a campaign to put an end to this nonsense. From now onwards we shall send our flowers sufficiently long enough before for the busy modern woman to have time to arrange them. In the case of intimate friends we shall telephone them and say we are doing so and why, because this will stop them spending unnecessary time and money. In more formal circumstances we intend sending them the day before with a little covering note of explanation.

Now back to our soups . . . whenever possible either rinse the containers in boiling water before pouring in hot soups or chill them in the refrigerator alongside the soup bowl or jug until the moment of service. Just remember that any soup made with eggs cannot be allowed to reach boiling point or the eggs will curdle. *Fish* A 7–8 lb. whole salmon will lose approximately 2 lbs. to head, bone and skin. Therefore when estimating how much to allow per portion you first deduct all the trimmings (for the stock-pot) and thereafter allow 5 ozs. per serving.

When dealing with salmon steaks you can safely estimate three to the pound from middle cut for a fish course portion or two for a main course portion. The only way you *could* use salmon steaks for buffets is to cook half-pound ones, skin and bone each steak into two portions and dress them out individually under *chaud-froid* sauce, aspic or with top-garnishes of savoury whipped cream or mayonnaise.

Reckon on freshwater trout weighing $6\frac{1}{2}$–$7\frac{1}{2}$ ozs. for a fish course—say "*au bleu*" or "*aux noix*"; 9–10 ozs. for a main course dish, but certainly not more than 6 ozs. for a buffet. The same quantities apply to lake or rainbow trout, but salmon trout should be estimated in the same way as salmon or turbot. Deduct the head, tail, bones and skin from the weight and then allow 9 ozs. of the flesh for a main course and 5 ozs. for a fish course or buffet.

Neither mackerel nor whiting are other than family dishes. You want them between 10 and 12 ozs. per head for the hungry and between 8 and 9 ozs. for slightly smaller appetites. Haddock belongs inside the strictly family circle too (except at ball suppers) so when serving cooked in milk with poached eggs on top, buy 14 ozs. for a hungry man or boy and 9–10 ozs. for the less voracious.

You will very rarely encounter tiny turbot or halibut steaks, but these are such splendid cuts that you can always buy big ones and serve half per head. A good portion will weigh 14 ozs. of which half is enough per head sauced at a dinner or luncheon. If you want to dress out a dish of either for a buffet, it is far better to buy 1 lb. steaks and divide them into four portions after cooking than to buy smaller pieces with a higher ratio of bone.

The number of sole and plaice fillets you will need per head is impossible to estimate as it will entirely depend upon the size of the fish from which they are taken. One day a fishmonger has large fish, another day they are very small and in between he may well have only medium ones. Your guide therefore is weight. Four ounces makes a large portion of egged-and-breadcrumbed or batter-fried filleted plaice or sole, either as one big fillet or two small ones. You will only need 3 ozs. for a medium portion and 2½ ozs. for a portion cut into small strips for *Goujonnades* of sole or plaice. When cooking fillets in a sauce however, allow two 2 oz. fillets or one 4 oz. fillet because despite sauce and garnish the fish *contracts* during cooking, whereas it is increased in size by either batter or crumbs.

You all know that nine oysters is the ideal number at a dinner. Six is a bit mingy, twelve overdoing things unless there are only three courses; but you should take into consideration when ordering them whether they are small, medium or extra large. For the biggest six *is* (just) enough. For the two smaller grades, stick to nine.

We find that 1–1¼ lb. lobsters are the smallest we like to split in halves and serve as a hot fish course. The catering trade thinks differently and the official text book estimate is pretty mean. We reason that as lobster is so expensive anyway, it is better to do without it altogether than just have about enough to whet appetites. For a lobster, prawn or shrimp cocktail you will need only 3 ozs. of meat or 4 ozs. for a *timbale*.

The dreary business of dressing crab is just about as twitch-making as boning quail. We have done both—often—and we recommend neither! But be careful where you buy ready-prepared crab-meat by the pound or ready-dressed crabs. The reputable fishmongers will sell you unadulterated crab-meat; but there are more firms than you would think who put out crabs to "dressers" and then impose on you reconstituted dehydrated potato, blended with the brown and white meats and bunged into the rest. Of The Real Thing, estimate 4 ozs. per head for a fish course, 6 ozs. per head (with salads) for a main course and choose your own for "dressing" whenever possible because you want cocks not hens as with lobster.

We reckon on 1 pt. of mussels per head for *Moules Marinière*, or *Velouté de Saumon*† plus 1 pt. for the pot on every 6 pts. This is to cover the incidence of ones which gawp open before cooking—a sure sign they are lethal instead of edible. Served cold in a mayonnaise or cocktail sauce mixture, you will want 9–12 per head depending on their size. One dozen is the number for one portion stuffed in shell. The same applies to *palourdes* (Cockles) when you are fortunate enough, like one London restaurant of our acquaintance, to get your hooks on them. When starting a meal with prawns tucked into a rocky pyramid of ice, you must again be governed by size. Four is enough of the really huge ones, 6 of the big chaps and 8 of the rather mingy things sold by the pint.

When it comes to fishy items served as an *hors d'oeuvre*, the rule is 2 ozs. *caviare*, 3–4 ozs. smoked salmon, 3–4 ozs. smoked eel and 2½–3 ozs. prawns in shell. There should be a minimum of 6 snails per head. You should allow two skinned fillets of a medium smoked trout (i.e. one half of the fish) per head, or four if the fish are small ones. For the family, let them eat these fish—one each from the bone if small ones—half each if large, and when serving shrimps either brown or pink for that delectable *Pas de Calais* opening course dish *Crevettes Chaudes** reckon on at least 4 ozs. per head.

A composite dish of scallops, say, Scallops *Mornay* with a border of Duchess and each one served in a scallop shell, should be estimated on the basis of 2 small, 1½ medium or 1 large scallop per portion. Always use the very smallest for fried scallops weighed, of course, before turning in flour, egg and breadcrumb, with the minimum of 3 and a sprig of fried parsley if using as an opening dish or 4 as a fish course. 4 ozs. of whitebait is adequate for a fish course, 6 ozs. for a large plateful. Allow a 10 oz. red mullet per head or 7 ozs. of fillet—frankly we do not think the grey are worth bothering with, but we took quite a lot of trouble and got rather muddy dragging weed out of our river with a rake in order to find an adequate-sized freshwater crayfish in a hurry. The 3 oz. crayfish yield the right sized tails (four per person) for doing them *en brochette* with other ingredients; 3–4 ozs. is the average weight for chopping up and using the tails (which are really the bodies) in an *Omelette aux Ecrevisses*, allowing one extra whole crayfish per head for top garnish for each individual omelette, while *Ecrevisses à la Crème* need whole fish, minimum weight 4 ozs., allowing 6 per head for a table course, or up to a dozen per head for a crayfish feast.

Should you ever contemplate making *Quenelles de Brochet* from pike—we remind you this dish is among the jewels in the crown of French gastronomy—it is useful to know what is indeed true of all fish that the percentage of wastage when trimming or filletting is very high and indeed, at spawning time, is over fifty percent. As a general guide a 6 lb. pike would trim down to about 4 lbs. outside the spawning season; a 10 lb. turbot to around $5\frac{1}{2}$ lbs., or a large sole weighing $1\frac{3}{4}$ lbs. would fillet to a fraction over a pound, a medium one at just under 1 lb. would give you about $\frac{1}{2}$ lb. and a 6 oz. baby under $3\frac{1}{2}$ ozs.

With this basic information behind us it is time to turn our thoughts to those demanding occasions when we have really big parties on our hands—the wedding, the christening, the twenty-first birthday supper dance with possibly breakfast at dawn—and over the years we have come to the conclusion that one of the main wastage items is bread.

If you serve bought bread rolls to the older generation, one per head and half as much again as your total number will be sufficient. If the bread rolls are home-made, you will need to allow two per head and twenty-five per cent over and above. If you are cooking for teenagers, use the proportion given for home-made bread in bought bread and half as much again if home-made!

The above only applies when you are serving butter which, as any surplus is not wasted, you should always do. Although the connoisseurs will never eat butter with cheese, the proportion of these to average guests is extremely small and if the butter is *not* there, the cheese will be—when everyone has gone home! Reckon on three "curls" from a standard butter curler per head, i.e. $\frac{1}{2}$ oz.

None of the above applies if you are entertaining French people. They always eat masses of bread and whatever their age we allow three rolls or three wedges of French *flute* apiece as a minimum.

If you are estimating cheeses for a dinner party of from six to twelve people, you will need to allow 2 ozs. per head. For a small buffet of, say, 20 to 30 this would come down to $1\frac{1}{2}$ ozs. per head. Over 50 you can reduce it to 1 oz. per head; but at a cheese and wine party, whatever your numbers, you are more likely to need 3-4 ozs. per head as an overall minimum, but this is a dangerous area.

You will need to know something about your guests' palates in making your choice of cheeses. The Continentals will go straight for the Gruyère and probably leave the Emmenthal; polish off the ripe and slightly runny Brie; totally disdain the Camembert unless there is nothing else as it never tastes as good in England; become slightly emotional over a prime Blue Stilton; be very appreciative of a not too salty Gorgonzola or Roquefort; Blue Bresse will be a bit *comme çi, comme ça*; Tomme de Raisin will be popular and little triangles of lactic cheese wrapped up in silver paper are more likely to stay wrapped up, unless they are all ravenous after whatever else you have provided! Moreover, they will not touch any of them if the cheeses fail to make their appearance until after the pudding and they are most likely to ask for bread if you pursue the English custom of providing biscuits only.

Conversely, the average English guests, particularly the young, will eat the range of good English cheeses first, notably the ones that are not blue, whereas you can cozen the Continental with the more way-out English speciality cheeses such as Dorset Blue Vinney or sage cheese, but beware of Caerphilly which is not a Continental vote catcher.

Cheese is really only a temptation when someone has completed the main course and, to this point dined well, if there is a last splendid glass of red wine available to wine lovers, for they will know that the flavour of any cheese, even mousetrap, is wine's greatest partner. If they have not fed well, they will be thankful for any cheese to fill in the gaping cracks.

It is always helpful to have as many items as possible in portions, but not necessarily in separate containers. Individual portions of fish laid out on large dishes enable you to estimate your numerical requirements nicely, provided of course these are not crammed so closely together that one portion is squashed to pulp while the adjacent one is being lifted onto a plate. Meat, game, poultry, *gâteaux* and the huge area covered by the term puddings, plus mixtures either sweet or savoury used to fill into *canapés, brioches, tartelette* or *barquette* cases, all lend themselves to this form of presentation. When they are set out in this way, it is exceedingly easy to count portions in relation to the numbers expected.

A 9½″ diameter flan ring makes a container for sweet or savoury items which provides 8 good-sized portions for a course at a meal —say, a *Quiche* (hot or cold) or a *Tarte Française*—but the same sized container would cut into 12 portions on an assorted buffet. An 8″ diameter flan ring would provide 6 main meal portions or 8 small ones which are quite adequate on a buffet.

Potato, Russian or raw grated vegetable salads and similar items will vanish at the rate of 3½ ozs. per head.

Duchess potato shapes should be scaled off and weighed up in 2 oz. portions and you should allow at least two per head with a main course dish; 4 ozs. per head of *Pommes de Terre à la Crème*, 4½ ozs. of chips (if you must), 3 ozs. of *Pommes Pailles* or *Pommes Allumettes* and 2½ ozs. of one individual *Pommes Anna* (p. 182.). The classic *Pommes Anna** (made in a *soufflé* mould) serves four in a 5″ diameter mould, eight in an 8″ diameter mould and twelve in a 9½″ diameter mould.

The same type of moulds, if filled to within ½″ of the rim with cream pudding mixtures, hold enough for four in the 5½″ diameter size (with top garnish), eight in the 8½″ diameter and ten in the 9½″ diameter size. Oddly enough, if you pour these creamy pudding mixtures into little custard glasses, individual casseroles or *ramequins*, you get an extra one out of the smallest, two out of the medium and three out of the large *soufflé* mould.

Fruit salad—if the usual pond—must be estimated at 6 ozs. per head; if like ours, then 5 ozs. is quite sufficient provided you apportion the mixture beforehand; otherwise the assembly will stick with it until the bowl is emptied!

When dividing cakes or *gâteaux*, cut small, thick slices rather than long, thin ones. Cake is anathema when it tastes of the knife. The maximum for a layered *gâteau* made in a standard Victoria sponge tin is 12 and the good minimum is 8. The best buffet party shape is a long, narrow rectangular flan frame. Ours, measuring $4\frac{1}{2}'' \times 14''$, yields 14 slices for a meal, but if made up of several layers these can be halved for a buffet, thus making 28 portions. If this flan frame is used for pastry cases, these figures will vary. With a vegetable mixture as the filling to be served with a main course dish it would only yield 10 portions and indeed you should allow the same for a fruit or any other sweet flan or *torte*.

If you buy or make ice cream in bulk and use proper ball cutters (stockists p. 291.) dipped in boiling water after each scoop, you will get far more portions than you will ever do from elegant slices cut from an ice cream pudding at the table. Whether you use small or large cutters, only you can decide, but it may help your decision when you start calculating to know that you should estimate two balls (1 oz. each) from the small cutter and one large ball (scant 2 ozs.) from the large one.

At table you will need 1 lb. of hulled strawberries or raspberries, per 3 servings, but at afternoon garden parties or large buffets 4 ozs. per head is enough. Would you please try dredging and/or serving these with sifted icing sugar or soft brown pieces sugar and cream rather than castor sugar? Incidentally *Sauce Champagne**—though you may say it is gilding the lily—is our idea of perfection with either raspberries or strawberries or above all with tiny wood or mountain strawberries, *Fraises des Bois*, which can be grown easily from seed (stockists p. 291.) in this country. The sauce can be made two days in advance of using, if stored in mild refrigeration.

Johnnie and I were given this sauce in a garden restaurant on the outskirts of Brussels some years ago. On our return home we dumped our luggage and made a dash for the kitchen to see whether, while the sauce was green in our memories, what we had worked out was correct. We deduced that it had to be *Sabayon**, made with champagne instead of a sweet white wine, whipped twice; first until cold over ice and then with half its bulk of stiffly whipped cream. Happily we were right and it has proved one of our outstanding successes ever since. You want to allow 2 tablespoons per serving, at the rate of 1 oz. per tablespoon, but because of the aeration of this mixture we have found it to be nearer 1¾ ozs. Remember you can always check these things yourself if you lose the odd English inhibition that only dry goods can be popped on-to the scales!

When it comes to the sugar for strawberries allow 1 oz. sifted icing sugar for one serving at the rate of 3-to-the-pound and ¾ oz. to each 4-to-the-pound serving. With pieces sugar allow ¾ oz. to each 4-to-the-pound serving and a mean ounce to each 3-to-the-pound serving. You increase these quantities very slightly if serving loganberries or rasberries and redcurrants mixed as the acid content is much higher.

Estimates on standard loaf sugar for sweetening tea and coffee have to be worked out for large numbers on the basis of the rapidly increasing percentage who prefer a slimming sugar substi-tute in tablet form and those who of course do not take sugar at all. We have found that this therefore works out at the rate of a standard lump per head with an additional 10 on every 60 lumps, plus of course a cylinder of your chosen sweetener. For a medium teacup of coffee, one small lump of sugar per head and no extras for a small after-dinner coffee cup which only contains 3 fl. ozs. If you are serving cream with either you allow a scant dessertspoon for the 3 fl. oz. cup and a scant tablespoon for the 4 fl. oz. cup.

The estimates for *canapés* and *petits fours* can fairly be lumped together. They come under two headings. Those offered by all the big outside catering firms, in our experience, are either based on biscuits, little bits of damp flannel toast or little *croûtons* which have not been passed through egg and milk, consequently move slowly and the folk we know who have been persuaded to work on the basis of 4 per head, find this is more than enough. With really delicious home-made ones—again speaking from personal experience—we reckon on a minimum 8 per head and there are never any left. This is of course either at a drinks party or as part of the light fare at a wedding reception, as it is sheer madness for a hostess to stuff up her hungry guests in the drawing-room and take the sharp edge off their appetites before they come to the table.

Exactly the same kind of contrast persists between bought *petits fours* and home-made ones. You can reckon that you will be lucky to have 2 per head consumed of the former and less than 4 per head of the latter. Here again there is a proviso; if you are putting *petits fours* on the table and the women are staying for the port, after which you collect them and take them out of the dining room, there will simply not be enough time for them to go on nibbling the home-made ones, as they will do if you have them brought through to the drawing room to be handed again with coffee and liqueurs.

Items like chocolates based on our *canache*, liqueur-flavoured creams, or grapes, strawberries, the segments of orange or tangerine dipped in sugar disappear at an alarming rate; the more you put out, the more will be eaten. Of course, if you are going to cope among your own close friends with comments like, "May I take one home for Willie?" you need to have a few little bags in the kitchen and you fill them up at speed from your reserve. At least, you do if you are like us and your only reward will be some exceedingly wibbly and mis-spelt letters which we are sure you will agree are adequate compensation!

Finally, when making coffee here is a simple table for you:

$$1 \text{ heaped tablespoon} = \tfrac{1}{2} \text{ oz.}$$

2 heaped tablespoons to 1 pt. freshly boiled water makes a good brew of coffee and this is considerably enhanced for after-dinner coffee by infusing it with a vanilla pod. One coffee cup of coffee holds 3 fl. ozs.; one small teacup 4 fl. ozs.; both leaving room for the cream. If you are working in bulk you can safely estimate that allowing for splashing and other small dramas you will get 100 coffee cups of coffee from $\tfrac{1}{2}$ lb. freshly ground coffee beans.

MEAT AND OFFAL

ENTRECÔTE $6\tfrac{1}{2}$ ozs., 5 ozs. minimum.

FILET MIGNON 4 ozs.

FILLET STEAK $6\tfrac{1}{2}$ ozs. large, 4 ozs. minimum.

MINCED RAW STEAK (STEAK TARTARE) 5 ozs.

PORTERHOUSE STEAK $2\tfrac{1}{2}$ lbs. (should serve 2).

ROAST BEEF 8 ozs. with bones, 6 ozs. without.

SILVERSIDE 8 ozs. boneless.

TOURNEDOS 4–5 ozs.

WHOLE FILLET OF BEEF for 10 people: $3\tfrac{1}{4}$ lbs.

BEST END NECK 7 ozs. with bone; 6 ozs. without.

LAMB CHOP 5 ozs.

LAMB CUTLETS grilled or crumbed: two weighing 3 ozs. apiece.

LEG OF LAMB 5½–6 ozs. with bone.

NECK AND BREAST OF MUTTON for Irish stew: 8 ozs. mixed.

FILLET OF PORK 6 ozs.

PORK CUTLET 6½ ozs. with bone.

PORK CUTLET breadcrumbed: 6 ozs.

FILLET OF VEAL 4–5 ozs.

MEDAILLONS OF VEAL two weighing 2 ozs., minimum one 3 oz.

ROAST VEAL 6 ozs. with bone; 5 ozs. without.

VEAL CUTLET 5–6 ozs.

VEAL ESCALOPE *panée* 4–5 ozs., *nature* 4–5 ozs.

CASSEROLING MEAT off the bone: 5 ozs. per head.

CALVES' BRAINS 5 ozs.

CALVES' LIVER 4 ozs. with bacon; 4½–5 ozs. without.

SWEETBREADS 3 portions to the pound allowing for wastage of skinning and clearing the superfluous appendages.

POULTRY AND GAME

CHICKEN 2–2¾ lbs. (serves 4); 3–5 lbs. (5–8 portions if properly carved).

POUSSIN 12–15 ozs. (½ bird per portion).

SPRING CHICKEN 1–2¼ lbs. (serves 3).

SUPRÊMES OF CHICKENS' BREAST for main course for a dinner party: 2 from each bird weighing 3¼ lbs. when plucked, drawn and dressed.

DUCKLING 4 portions.

DUCK (large) 5 portions.

GOOSE 10–12 portions.

TURKEY 10–11 ozs. overall.

GROUSE 1 bird.

HARE 10 ozs. per head overall.

HAZELHEN 1 bird.

PARTRIDGE 1 bird.

PHEASANT, cock: 4 good portions.

PHEASANT, hen: 3–4 portions.

PIGEON (small) whole bird; (large) half bird.

QUAIL 2 birds.

RABBIT 10 ozs. per head overall.

SNIPE 1 bird.

WOODCOCK 1 bird.

VEGETABLES

ASPARAGUS giant forced 4–5 stems, medium real 6–8, sprue for the connoisseur 4–6 ozs.

ASPARAGUS PEAS 6–8 pods per head.

BEANS, BROAD 3½–4 ozs. young small, 4–5 ozs. large skinned.

BEANS, BUTTER 2 ozs. per head prior to soaking.

BEANS, FRENCH, sliced: 2½–3 ozs.

BEANS, RUNNER 2½–3 ozs.

BEETROOT served separately on buffet 2–2½ ozs. per head; round whole sauced at table 2 very small, 1 small to medium.

BROCCOLI SPEARS 2 large, 3 medium, 4 mini.

BRUSSELS SPROUTS 8 proper ones meaning miniature, 6 medium. At all times abstain from serving overblown miniature cabbages. Proportion of chestnuts to sprouts: ½ lb. cooked skinned chestnuts to 1 lb. trimmed sprouts.

CABBAGE 3–4 ozs.

CARROTS 4 ozs. per head.

CAULIFLOWER 1 small to medium yields, when carefully trimmed and the base of core removed, 4 portions for a main course accompaniment.

CHICORY 1 small head per portion.

CELERY use, as a main course accompaniment, a small trimmed cooked heart, or one whole medium-sized or one large-sized split in half.

COURGETTES 3½–4″ in length, 2 per head, whole or sliced poached in butter.

CUCUMBER as salad 2 ozs. per head, in salad ¾ to maximum ounce per head.

MANGE TOUT 6–8 pods per head.

ONIONS as crisp fried main course accompaniment 1½ ozs. maximum per head.

PARSNIPS 5 ozs. per head.

PEAS 4–4½ ozs. shelled weight.

PIMENTOES as salad 1½ ozs.; in salad ¾ oz.

SPINACH as accompaniment to main course 6 ozs.

TOMATO sliced as salad 2 ozs. per head; sliced in salad ¾ to maximum 1 oz. per head; whole stuffed to accompany main course dish 2 small, 1 medium.

Smoked Eel · Beurre blanc · Liver Pâté Cream · Tchina
Farce aux Fruits de Mer · Beignets de Fromage
Escargots Feuilletés · Miniature Anchovy Croissants
Savoury Almond Paste · Cherry and Grape Canapés
Tartelettes au Fromage · Tartelettes aux Crevettes
Tartelettes aux Laitances aux Harengs ou Maquereaux
Rouleaux au Saumon fumé, aux Pointes d'Asperges,
aux Anchois ou aux Anguilles
Potted Beef · Salatmarinade · Gorgona Sauce · Meat Balls
Mustard Cream Sauce · Pork Rolls

In the preceding chapter we referred to the consumption rate of home-made *canapés* versus the bought ones and this chapter is about the kind that could in fact spoil a good dinner if they were offered too lavishly. Conversely, they are the making of a drinks party, the success of which, remember, really depends in retrospect on guests not going away feeling stale and edgy after perhaps too many drinks and not enough to keep them company.

The partners are as important in this field of entertaining as the wines *vis-à-vis* food partners are at the table. We have found for some years now that if we offer dry sherry, dry Madeira and dry white port, the highest consumption is the Madeira, the next highest is the port and the sherry has become the also-ran.

Oddly enough this happens with certain foodstuffs too. At one time any *canapés* made with smoked salmon went first unless there was *caviare*. Smoked eel has now moved well out in front in our experience. At the time of writing this is good news because it is far less expensive, besides being very filling. We of course never know what additional increases there will be in the case of foodstuffs but while smoked salmon is costing us at least 24/- a lb., in the last few days we paid 16/- per lb. for a whole, unskinned fat eel weighing 1½ lbs. We stress fat eel, not those nasty, thin, mean fillets sold by the pound, of very little flavour and far less value for money. Remember smoked salmon must be very thin indeed; eel is only worth eating when it is fat. To prepare smoked eel remove the head and tail and then peel the skin away—it is thick, strong and very easy to do. Then behave as if you were eating a sole on the bone at the table, run your knife down the centre of the saddle and remove the four fillets.

· Smoked Eel ·

For *canapés* each fillet needs to be divided lengthwise and then cut into 2¼″ strips. Place each one on a finger of savoury short paste*, puff paste or bread passed through the standard egg and milk mixture and fried to a crisp golden brown. The classic service is with lemon. The simplest way to do this so that people keep their fingers clean, is to cut small lemons in halves, remove the pips and stick a small fork into each separate half. Then the fork can be held in one hand, the lemon squeezed in the other and neither fingers nor gloves are defaced.

· Beurre blanc ·

We recently experimented with a new sauce based on a simple *Beurre blanc*. This most elementary sauce can carry innumerable variations of flavouring. For a small quantity place 4 ozs. of butter in a roomy bowl and for the simplest kind of labour use a hand electric mixer. These are so inexpensive and so efficient that in our very large kitchen we have several. They can be taken to pot or pan, the best ones have three speeds and they get far harder use today than any of the table models. Have ready a small pan of bubbling water and a teaspoon. Whip with one hand until the butter is loose, add a teaspoonsful of boiling water and whip again. Continue this adding of teaspoonsful of hot water and whipping until the mixture is light, white and fluffy. Then whip in lemon juice for smoked eel. Use a few drops of anchovy *purée* for small fillets of mackerel (topped, tailed, boned and grilled gently on one side only until firm and then split into neat finger fillets). Last week—as gooseberries were in season—we liquidised and then sieved a few unsweetened, cooked ones and blended them into the *Beurre blanc* instead for piping over our mackerel fillets. They vanished at speed. Alternatively if you have fresh fennel, chop this extremely finely and work it into the otherwise completed *Beurre blanc*. Remember that, like dill, this herb is at its best with fish.

· Liver Pâté Cream ·

Now let us deal with some fillings for the enormously versatile bread *bouchée* cases which are explained on p. 278. in our garnish chapter. Our *Caviare* Cream† is an all-time winner and so is a simple Liver *Pâté* Cream for which of course, if you are feeling very *luxe*, you can use the real *pâté de foie gras truffé*. Otherwise cream down the contents of a 4 oz. tin of the Swiss variety *Le Parfait*, add a dessertspoonful of sherry, a teaspoonful of brandy

anchovy fillet coil or a caper, or sprinkle the top all over with poppy seed. Arrange on small d'oyley covered plates or salvers just like sweet *petits fours*.

· Cherry and Grape Canapés ·

During the cherry season bring black or white cherries together with cream cheese, but let us warn you straight away that the cherries must lose their stones and still remain on the stalks—otherwise they will be messy, so do not try this idea if you are in a great hurry. When the stones are out, stuff the cherries with cream cheese, dip the little bulges of white into milled nuts or freshly milled parsley and pile up on a d'oyley covered dish. For the grape version of this *canapé*, you will need wooden cock-tail sticks as each grape must be peeled, de-pipped and then given the cream cheese and parsley or milled nut treatment. Both should be kept in mild refrigeration until the moment of service. They are at their best when very cold.

A very pretty effect can be obtained quite easily by turning small skinless slices of very thinly cut *charcuterie* into baby cornets. Each one must be placed on a small *croûton* or finger of baked puff pastry for eating with ease. Choose your filling, say, Liver Pâté Cream and invest in one cornet (stockist p. 291.) which is all you need. Wrap, say, a slice of salami around the tip, hold the overlap in position with the thumb and first two fingers of one hand and slide off the cornet shape. Then, still holding firmly, pick up an icing bag filled with the liver cream, pipe a tiny dab under the overlap to hold it securely and squeeze into the little cornet until this is filled. Decorate the tip with herbs, paprika powder or nuts. Set on its chosen base and move onto something else.

· Tartelettes au Fromage ·

An enormous number of variations will be at your disposal if you invest in the special tin made for miniature pie/tartlets. They are quite deep for their size. You can bake a dozen in each tin and the diameter you ask for is $1\frac{3}{4}''$ (stockists p. 292.). Line these with savoury short paste* and start your *canapés* trays with a dozen *Tartelettes au Fromage*. They are really minute; a good tea-spoonful fills each one so the mixture proportions are exceedingly small. Put 3 generous tablespoons of thick white sauce into a bowl. Dice a rasher of back bacon small and fry dry until crisp.

Add it to the sauce with 1 heaped tablespoon of minutely diced Gruyère and 1 rounded dessertspoonful of grated Parmesan. Mix well together. Season with pepper anyway but the addition of salt will of course depend upon the bacon. Spoon into the lined-out tartlet cases. Wet the top of the paste lining with a tiny brush dipped in cold water, affix baby "lids" stamped out from remaining paste and bake one shelf above centre at Gas Mark 6 until these lids are a pale golden brown which we find takes about 11 minutes. Serve hot or cold.

· Tartelettes aux Crevettes ·

Transform this filling by omitting the cheeses but hang onto the bacon and when that is fried, add minute pink shrimps—about 2–3 ozs. If they are not tiny, chop them before adding. Finish with a heaped dessertspoon of freshly milled parsley heads, season with pepper but again taste before adding salt lest the shrimps are salty. Then proceed as explained and thus achieve *Tartelettes aux Crevettes* which can also be served either hot or cold. By this time you will have realised that innumerable little bits of left-overs can be tiddled up to make other fillings along the same lines and bring added variation to your *canapé* collection.

· Tartelettes aux Laitances aux Harengs ou Maquereaux ·

If you merely use this miniature pie/tartlet tin to bake little open cases, you can achieve a very different filling with either herring or mackerel roes. We never cease to be astonished at how few people use the latter. When they clean mackerel, they throw the best—the roes—away. Call these little canapés *Tartelettes aux Laitances aux Harengs ou Maquereaux*. Put a dozen soft herring roes, or two dozen mackerel roes, into a small thick pan, cover with 7½ fl. ozs. dry white cooking wine and 5 fl. ozs. strongly reduced fish stock made from fish heads, tails and spine bones. Simmer for a few moments until "set". Rub through a sieve, work in a pinch of salt, of cayenne pepper and of ground nutmeg. Now in a separate pan dissolve 1 oz. butter, add a rounded dessertspoonful flour, cook over a moderate heat until a firm thick paste and add the *purée* gradually, cooking and stirring until all is thick and creamy. Chill. Finish with a tablespoonful of thickly whipped cream and fill into baked tartlet cases.

· Rouleaux au Saumon fumé, aux Pointes d'Asperges, aux Anchois ou aux Anguilles ·

When we serve *Tchina* (p. 51.) we usually serve minute Swiss roll shapes of transparently thin crustless brown bread and butter. Let us be frank here and admit that developing the theme of these *rouleaux* recently has been caused by the fact that we are now the possessors of quite a small lightweight bread cutter with a wide range of adjustable thicknesses. This is called a Graef (stockist p. 291.) and with the exception of flat items like smoked salmon, we slice everything from bread to beef in it with such speed and ease we wonder however we managed before. Hence the prevalence of speedily made *Rouleaux au Saumon fumé.* Slice the bread, cut off the crusts, spread with softened butter, cover with a transparently thin slice of smoked salmon, roll up, dab a scrap of butter at each end and dip the ends in milled parsley. Or make *Rouleaux aux Pointes d'Asperges . . .* just roll an asparagus tip in the buttered crustless bread and finish as explained. You can use anchovy fillets for *Rouleaux aux Anchois*, very narrow strips of smoked eel for *Rouleaux aux Anguilles* or such simple things as sardines, topped, tailed, boned and emulsified with a little mayonnaise or cream and the merest flick of anchovy *purée.*

We had to take some up to Television Centre for a programme recently. Being the fools that we are, we insist that everything shown on The Box is in prime condition for being eaten up by the studio personnel afterwards because we maintain that this is the only way in which they can tell whether the food is good or not. They are thus standing proxy for our viewers. We had to leave at the crack of dawn, so perforce the *rouleaux* were made the night before. We layered them with waxed paper in a long rectangular plastic box with a well fitting lid and are happy to report they were perfectly moist when presented and eaten some twenty hours later.

One point about presentation . . . try to dish them on a d'oyley covered narrow oval "flat" whether metal, silver, china or earthenware. Lay a long line down the centre and continue piling one row above the other in diminishing quantities until you end with one on the top. This is one way to make them look most inviting for your guests.

· Potted Beef ·

If the occasion is informal and you are intending to supply spreads rather than individual mouthsful, you might serve a dish of brown bread and butter *rouleaux* to accompany a jar of *Potted Beef*. Put it up in a terrine or a straight-sided jar which will do very well if you remember to wrap it in a snowy napkin for the table.

You will need about ½ lb. of slightly underdone cold roast beef, 4 ozs. butter, ½ lb. tongue, ¼ lb. of ham trimmings, a rounded tablespoonful of mixed herbs (thyme, parsley and bay leaf), 1 grated shallot or small onion, 1 mean flat saltspoon of pepper, the same of salt, 2 ozs. mushrooms (or stalks only), 1 standard egg, 5 fl. ozs. good meat stock, 2½ fl. ozs. claret type cooking wine and 2 or 3 drops of carmine colouring. Mince the meat. Add all remaining ingredients and ideally liquidise, failing which you will have to sieve it! Then press into the chosen lightly buttered container, stand in a meat baking tin, run hot water into the tin until it is nearly filled, cover the top of the container with kitchen foil and a saucer and carry carefully to the oven to put on the middle shelf. Cook for 30 minutes at Gas Mark 4. Remove from the baking tin, uncover and run a ¼" thick depth of melted (or for perfection clarified) butter over the top. We need scarcely add that any left-overs can be eaten up by the family over a period of 4–5 days provided it is refrigerated. Perhaps it might be as well to remind you that for them that likes it, the addition of 1 or more crushed garlic cloves can only be a good thing!

In the form of a *post scriptum* we want to give you a short *aide memoire* of recipes which come under an American heading with which we really must dissociate ourselves! The terrible omnibus word dip-'n'-dunk is simply not for us and we are pretty confident that it is not for you either. So for this little horror may we ask you to read drinks party items and the accompanying cold sauces into which they can be dipped. Moreover, we trust you will also agree that when a large quantity of these items is assembled for the young, none of us will subscribe to those obscene little flowerlet or chubby "childlet" notelets which are sometimes misguidedly despatched in lieu of invitations.

The basic essential component is a large vegetable and salad platter. The contents to be laid out upon it are dependent upon the season. In early summer you can have fingers of raw, scraped carrot, matching chip-wide strips of cucumber, trimmed spring onions and radishes, heart of cos lettuce leaves, cold cooked asparagus and heart of cabbage lettuce leaves spread with savoury mixtures and rolled up into tight little sausages. These are then speared onto wooden cocktail sticks.

· Salatmarinade ·

Experience has taught us, apart from *Bagna Cauda*† and classic *Vinaigrette**, Viennese *Salatmarinade* and Mrs. Marshall's *Gorgona Sauce* are the two most popular sauces. For *Salatmarinade* assemble 1 rounded teaspoon castor sugar, 1 rounded teaspoon paprika, ½ rounded teaspoonful each of salt, dry mustard and crushed celery seed, 1 flat eggspoon milled black peppercorns, 2 fl. ozs. tarragon wine vinegar and 5 fl. ozs. olive oil. Put all the ingredients, except the oil and vinegar, into a wooden bowl. Add the vinegar, a few drops at a time, and work away vigorously with the back of a wooden spoon until you have achieved a very smooth paste. Then, still working away with the wooden spoon, add the oil very gradually. When the whole mixture is completely homogenous, pour into a bottle, cork down and, like cough mixture only nicer, shake very thoroughly before using.

· Gorgona Sauce ·

As the name gives no clue to its contents we will explain before you bother to read the recipe that *Gorgona* is a tomato and anchovy sauce for which you chop 6 drained, dried anchovies finely and put into a wooden bowl with 1 equally finely chopped medium shallot and 2 medium gherkins. Add a raw egg yolk, work it in with a wooden spoon, then work in 2 tablespoons of olive oil very gradually always keeping the wooden spoon moving. Add a rounded teaspoon of chopped parsley and follow with 1 generous dessertspoon of tarragon vinegar. Finally work in the sieved pulp of 2 ripe, skinned tomatoes.

· Meat Balls ·

The little meat balls—also impaled on cocktail sticks—which we find most successful are made with ½ lb. of finely minced or scraped raw beef, 1 very finely grated medium shallot or onion, 1 optional crushed garlic clove, a pinch of both salt and pepper, a flat teaspoonful of dry, unmade English mustard and a standard egg. Work the whole lot up together to a nice stiff dough. Roll into little balls—slightly smaller than ping pong balls if you please—then roll them in flour and deep fry them in oil which has only been brought up to slightly below faint smoking haze temperature. Marry these with curried *coulis* for which you merely add to the classic *Coulis** 1 rounded teaspoonful of real curry paste.

· Mustard Cream Sauce ·

High on our popularity list is cocktail-stick-skewered chickens' livers in bacon. You simply cut up the livers into small neat pieces, fry them briskly in a shallow pan with melted butter, then soft grill No. 4 cut back bacon and roll up each little piece of liver in a scrap of the bacon. Pair these off with *Mustard Cream Sauce*. Start with 1 oz. melted butter, 1 oz. sifted flour and 1 heaped dessertspoon dry English mustard worked up to a soft ball or *roux* in a thick pan. *When the taste of the flour has been cooked out*, which takes about $1-1\frac{1}{2}$ minutes, add a pint of boiling water very gradually, cooking and beating well after each addition and lastly beat in salt to taste. Remove from the heat and beat in 3 egg yolks singly while the mixture is still very hot. Beat in $2\frac{1}{2}$ fl. ozs. double cream and then the strained juice of $\frac{1}{4}$ lemon. Last of all whip in $2\frac{1}{2}$ extra ozs. of softened butter. This does not mean oiled, please remember, and finish the sauce with a generous pinch of black pepper and a dozen pressed finely chopped capers.

There is one more point to remember concerning this type of sauce which can be got out of the way a couple of days before your entertainment. You must cover the levelled-off surface of each one with a fitted circle of greaseproof paper wetted thoroughly under a cold tap. Then when you peel the paper off, the sauce will not be disfigured by a nasty top crust, which is either beaten in to the ruination of the overall texture or thrown away, which is positively sinful!

· Pork Rolls ·

If you happen to have the remains of a joint of roast pork with crackling, seize the opportunity to make little *Pork Rolls*, which can either be dipped into Mustard Cream Sauce or sharp apple *purée* which, being translated, is nothing more than tart, peeled, cored, thinly sliced apple poached in the absolute minimum amount of dry cider which will stop the fruit burning while being stirred until cooked sufficiently to rub through a sieve. Incidentally, this has a flat and despondent appearance which is immediately offset if you add a few drops of carmine colouring to give it a little lift. For the pork part cut very thin small slices of the lean meat, trim into rectangles and cut up $2\frac{1}{2}''$ strips of crackling, roll the pork over the crackling, secure with cocktail sticks and add to your collection.

Soufflés aux Artichauts · Fond d'Artichauts Mornay
Fonds d'Artichauts Forestière · Croûtons d'Artichauts
Fonds d'Artichauts aux Foies de Volaille
Oeufs Mollets aux Fonds d'Artichauts Chaudfroid
Gâteaux de Foies de Volaille · Pâté de Saumon
Pâté Maison · Pâté Familial · Potted Crab and Halibut
Preserved Chickens' Livers · Pâté de Canard
Pâté de Canard en Croûte · Soufflé au Pâté de Foie
Pêches farcies · Beignets de Pêches · Savoury Apricot Cups
Beignets d'Artichauts · Avocado Cream · Cheat Aspic
Crème aux Avocats · Oeufs Mollets aux Tomates
Our Deep Quiche · Provençale Cabbage Roll
Stuffed Vine Leaves · Baby Coulibiac
Toasts des Gourmets · Mushrooms in Sour Cream
Italian Mushroom Salad · Pomidoro col Tonno
Insalata di Patate col Tonno · Oignons Monte Carlo

eight · **SHALL WE GO IN?**

Hors d'oeuvres are really rather like the schoolboy's definition of Caesar's wife, "All things to all men" (and women). They fall into two categories: hot and cold. They have been severally named, including the Rabelaisian *"amuse-gueules"* and indeed in earlier times *"entrées volantes"* or *"petites entrées"*. By definition they are considered in France, the centre of the gastronomic world, to belong *"en dehors du menu"*. Consequently, when they are preceding a large menu, they must be small and delicate, just to perform the function of stimulating the taste buds!

Conversely, we have, in summer, several vast hors d'oeuvre spreads which run such a gamut of fish, meat, salad and vegetables, *luxe* and very inexpensive items. They become a meal in themselves, supported solely by breads and butter and followed only by puddings, *tartes*, *gâteaux* or fruits.

In modern France they constitute the first course at luncheon on almost all catering levels; they are available for dinner in restaurants, except on *à la carte* menus and almost never in a private house, the exceptions generally being oysters or *Assiette des Fruits de Mer*. There are other European countries where *hors d'oeuvres* are served at the beginning of a luncheon in such vast quantities that it is agony to go on and eat several courses afterwards, as in Scandinavia where the *smörgasbord* or *smørrenbrød* is such a pitfall to the uninformed.

We can still recall an excellent instance of this on the island of Ibiza, in Saint Eulalia, the village Elliot Paul used in his book "Death of a Village". There we confronted a great pile of transparently thin smoked ham looking for all the world like a dish of autumn leaves; sardines in rather pungent oil and those gorgeous Spanish prawns called *gambas*, flanked on one side by minute octopus in tomato *coulis** and on the other by Russian salad *reeking* of garlic. These were ranged alongside little scraps of brains dipped in fritter batter and deep fried, fried whole mushrooms with the stalks left on, red and green pimentoes cut into strips and turned in oil, green and black olives, slices of cold cooked kidneys in a piquant sauce, hunks of goats' cheese and innumerable bowls of raw grated vegetables.

France would accept all these things but would merely add in slices or a wedge of *pâté*, beetroot salad—the beetroot of course cut like chips and dressed with oil and top garnished with rings of raw onion; side dishes of spring onions and trimmed radishes, a plate of assorted *charcuterie*, a bowl of real French potato salad, jars of cocktail onions and gherkins. In the south there would also be cheese straws and minutely chopped anchovies and black olives treated in the same fashion. This is the region where cold *ratatouille* crops up in the same *mélange*. Under the heading used by Madame Baudoin at La Bonne Auberge, *"La Caravane des Hors d'Oeuvre"*, this would mean a great roll of minced seasoned meat in cabbage leaves, a wedge of the cold green omelette called either *Omelette Verte** or *Torta di Bleia** which looks like a cheese and cuts like a cake; stuffed vine lea frolls (p. 78.), *Pissaladière** and in this procession or *caravane*, sardines, tuna, anchovies and Scandinavian preserved herrings would appear on napkin-covered plates *in their tins*. Alternatively you can turn yours into wooden bowls.

The inevitable English egg mayonnaise makes infrequent appearances. You are more likely to get something like *Tchina* (p. 51.). Whatever the gargantuan assembly, if you are wise, wash everything down with a *vin rosé* and consume yards of French bread and butter. When we are having large numbers, we keep butter by taking a round earthenware dish measuring 10½" by 2" deep. Onto this we slap two ½ lb. packs of butter, with four more ½ lbs., one above the other, on top. Then, with a small table knife, we rough the whole thing up into a crude iceberg while the butter is still fairly soft and refrigerate it till the moment of service when we run ice cubes around our iceberg and decorate with a few sprigs of parsley.

Now let us utter a tiny word of warning. Once upon a time there was an Englishwoman who was reproved by a Frenchman from the Lozère for eating globe artichokes after they had been cooked. Having sung the praises of the raw artichokes to our friend, he departed and she returned to England and at her next dinner party presented the ones she had brought home from the

Laon as *Artichauts à la Croque-au-sel* with an accompanying *vinaigrette**. Being very young they ate well but by the end of the meal it was perceived that her guests were suddenly wearing black teeth! Our sole experiment in this field visited a similar affliction on us which lasted for three days so let us limit our discussions on this versatile *hors d'oeuvre* item to some of the cooked variants.

Cut off the stalk level with the base, clip the top pointed leaves to make a little flat surface, plunge into slightly salted fast-boiling water, cover and simmer steadily until a single base leaf pulls away easily. The counsel for perfection of course is to cage them with fine string so that the water does not make the leaves soggy, but this is laborious and we have given up the whole thing in favour of steaming our artichokes which is much easier and equally successful.

· Soufflés aux Artichauts ·

If the occasion arises when you wish to be an outrageous show-off, prepare them for service* when they are cold and remove the majority of the inner leaves, leaving just enough to make a strong outer wall or ring with the artichoke bottom or *fond* clearly visible inside. Then for 6 people make half the quantity of standard *Soufflé au Parmesan** and before folding in the egg whites, add a *purée* made from 6 extra artichoke bottoms. Provided you have trimmed these clear of all stringy bits of base stem, they can be emulsified with a little bit of the sauce and returned to the pan for re-heating. Then add your egg whites, pile high and roughly into the artichoke "cases", put on a baking sheet and bake one shelf above centre at Gas Mark 7½ for between 8 and 9 minutes, or until well risen and a rich golden brown on top. These *Soufflés aux Artichauts* are impressive.

· Fonds d'Artichauts Mornay ·

We all know perfectly well that the easiest way to obtain *fonds d'artichauts* is from a tin and the flavour is extremely good, so let us work on the basis that when you can obtain the fresh, you will and give you recipes for which you can use either. A good old standby of course is *Fonds d'Artichauts Mornay*. These are vastly improved if on each base and under each sauce coating you put a thick *purée aux epinards*. Pick the stalks from 2 lbs. spinach, wash it very thoroughly indeed, shake in a *saladier* or cloth and tip as it is into a small pan. Add nothing, set it over a moderate heat and stir with a wooden spoon until the juices begin to run and the spinach collapses. The overall cooking time is a maximum 7 minutes. Then express the juices, sieve the spinach, reduce the juices by simmering to a mere tablespoonful, beat this fluid back into the spinach with a rounded tablespoonful of grated mixed Parmesan and Gruyère cheese. Season with salt, pepper and nutmeg to taste. Mound little domes of the mixture into each artichoke bottom, coat them with cool *Sauce Mornay* and use little scraps of crisp-fried rindless bacon to prod like tiny flags into the top of each mound. These are for serving cold but obviously the same thing can be done hot if you add the bacon at the last.

To make *Sauce Mornay*, stir 3 ozs. finely grated Parmesan cheese into 1 pt. *Béchamel** which has been heated in the top of a double saucepan. Add ½ oz. butter in small flakes beating well, between each addition taste and correct seasoning.

· Fonds d'Artichauts Forestière ·

Another delectable little dish is *Fonds d'Artichauts Forestière* that can in fact not only appear as an *hors d'oeuvre* but make a splendid accompaniment to little lamb cutlets which have been very neatly trimmed and cooked until they are just a delicate pink in the middle. Chop up 4 ozs. mushrooms finely, put them in a small thick pan with a tablespoonful of thick cream, another of dry white wine, a teaspoonful of raw grated onion juice, and a mere walnut of butter. Simmer gently until the mushrooms collapse and the mixture is loose and cooked—a maximum of 5 minutes completes this job. Then add fine soft brown breadcrumbs until you can mould this mixture up into 9 artichoke bottoms. Arrange on a bed of cress or picked watercress sprigs. Coat with *Sauce Mornay* (above) and trellis the top with fine strips of drained, wiped anchovy fillets.

· Croûtons d'Artichauts ·

A third and much simpler method is to slice 9–10 artichoke bottoms into quarters, toss them in a shallow pan containing just enough hot melted butter to skin the base and add a crushed garlic clove and a small teacup of matchsticks cut from cold cooked chicken. Turn this in the mixture until thoroughly heated and pile onto classic *croûtons** stamped from rounds of new bread cut with a plain or fluted 3″ diameter pastry cutter. Sprinkle liberally with milled parsley and serve piping hot. *Croûtons d'Artichauts* are compulsive eating and you should not let people have more than one each if there is a good deal to follow.

· Fonds d'Artichauts aux Foies de Volaille ·

If you want to be very *recherché* you can ring the changes still further on this one by adding to the given mixture for *Fonds d'Artichauts Forestière* an equal quantity of small pieces of chickens' liver fried in butter and deleting the chicken matchsticks in which case the title becomes *Fonds d'Artichauts aux Foies de Volaille.*

· Oeufs Mollets aux Fond d'Artichauts Chaudfroid ·

Finally there is the slightly tricky marriage between two of the suggestions we have already made which produces *Oeufs Mollets aux Fonds d'Artichauts Chaudfroid.* You can spread the interior of each artichoke bottom with either the spinach or the mushroom mixture. Then soft boil an egg for each one for 4 minutes precisely, peel it gently under a thin stream of cold water to ensure you do not break it, remembering that you need to be very light fingered in order to achieve success, and then press the fat end of each egg gently onto the chosen paste. Coat with *chaudfroid*—real or imitation—and put a tiny collar of milled parsley or chopped chives around the rim where the egg sits.

· Gâteaux de Foies de Volaille ·

Talking of chickens' livers reminds us of a treasured old recipe for *Gâteaux de Foies de Volaille* which will do your reputation no harm. Assemble 4 chickens' livers, 1 very small shallot and a tablespoonful of milled parsley. Chop up the chickens' livers and shallot and mix in the parsley. Add 2 generous tablespoons of *Béchamel* sauce* and the crumb of a 1″ thick crustless slice of stale bread cut from a standard loaf. Before you make this addition, pass the bread through top-of-the-milk until it collapses and then beat it in. Beat in 2 egg yolks, season to taste with salt and pepper and add the 2 very stiffly whipped whites. Turn into little buttered dariole moulds, set these in a baking tray and run a ¼″ of hot water round them when they are settled in the pan. Make a canopy of kitchen foil overall tucking the edges securely into the rim of the baking tin and cook at Gas Mark 4 for 20 minutes middle shelf. These *can* be served hot but we prefer to serve them cold and hand piping hot toast from our box.

You will need approximately $\frac{3}{8}$ yard of 36" wide material; a plastic, lidded, rectangular box, ideally 9" × 5$\frac{1}{2}$" × 3$\frac{1}{4}$" in depth; approximately 1$\frac{3}{8}$ yards $\frac{1}{4}$" braid, galon or edging to finish exterior of box; approximately $\frac{3}{8}$ yard 36" wide thinnest felt and a tube of Uhu. Cover the exterior of box and lid with chosen material affixing with adhesive. Affix edging to top and bottom and felt to interior base, sides and inside of lid. Cut a felt inner "lid" $\frac{1}{4}$" smaller all round than the box's lid. Stick one long side of this to corresponding side of box $\frac{1}{8}$" below closed lid line. The box will hold at least a dozen diagonally halved, crustless toast slices cut from a standard sandwich loaf.

· Pâté de Saumon ·

Now we are encroaching on the realms of *pâtés* or terrines. So let us give you our *Pâté de Saumon* and recommend you to serve toast in a box for this one too. You will need a pound of frozen Pacific salmon which is quite good enough for turning into *pâté*, one standard batch of basic water *choux* paste*, 4 ozs. plaice, 2$\frac{1}{2}$ fl. ozs. double cream, 2$\frac{1}{2}$ fl. ozs. white wine, a sprig of fennel, a leaf of lemon peel, 2 peppercorns and 2$\frac{1}{2}$ fl. ozs. water. Put the plaice, white wine, water, peel and peppercorns with the fennel into a pan in which the liquor covers the fish. Poach until plaice is tender, remove it, pound or emulsify with the cream while the liquor simmers down to a tablespoonful, remove the peppercorns, bay leaf and fennel and beat into the cold *choux* paste. Butter a small (5–5$\frac{1}{2}$" diameter) classic *soufflé* mould liberally. Skin and bone the salmon raw and cut the flesh into neat fingers, coat the sides and base of the mould with some of the choux paste mixture hereinafter called a *panade*. Lay in salmon fingers and when they are all used up, cover with the remaining *panade*. Smooth off the top surface carefully, cover the whole with kitchen foil, stand in a meat baking tin half filled with hot water and cook at Gas Mark 3$\frac{1}{2}$, middle shelf, for about 40 minutes. Chill and serve.

· Pâté Maison ·

From here it is a natural progression into simple *Pâté Maison*. This is a modest one to which we are particularly attached but we feel it really should be defined as a winter *pâté* because your prime need is for ½ lb. saddle of hare meat and ½ lb. of raw rabbit meat. To this you add 2 garlic cloves, a medium shallot or small Spanish onion, a ¼ lb. lean pork and ¾ lb. raw unsalted pork fat cut from the rind. Mince all these items except the garlic together. Mix them thoroughly in a bowl. Add the garlic and then stir in 1 small sherry glass of cooking sherry, 1 domed teaspoon of salt, 1 generous grate of milled black peppercorns and ideally 2 table-spoons of brandy. Treat it exactly like the preceding cooking method for *Pâté de Saumon* but check it after 45 minutes at Gas Mark 3½, centre shelf, by driving a skewer or steel knitting needle through the centre. If the bubble comes up bright pink, continue cooking for 15 more minutes but if the bubble comes out beige, remove it from the oven and press it. The best way to do this we have found is to use the sliding base of a 5–5½″ diameter cake tin, to remove the foil from the terrine or *soufflé* mould, to cover the surface with a buttered paper, to put in the cake base and put the heaviest possible weights on top before refrigerating it until the following day. At this point we must remind you that the induc-tion of a small handful of shelled pistachio nuts after the mixture is assembled and before it is put in the *soufflé* mould, raises the status of this *pâté* very considerably. In our opinion there is no substitute for this rather costly nut in this context but you must choose.

· Pâté Familial ·

You can do the same with an even humbler *Pâté Familial* for which you can substitute 1 lb. pig's liver for the chickens' liver and otherwise follow the recipe exactly. Pass 1 lb. pig's liver, 10 ozs. pork fat and a 1″ thick slice of crustless stale brown bread through the mincer with 2 crushed garlic cloves and a little shallot. When you have done this, it is entirely up to you whether you add the remaining ingredients and cook or whether you rub the minced mixture through a sieve which makes it much more delicate. Either way beat in a flat teaspoon of milled black pepper-corns, a heaped teaspoon of salt, ½ eggspoon ground nutmeg and a tablespoonful of brandy. Treat it exactly as for the other two *pâtés* but allow 1–1¼ hours cooking time according to the depth of the *pâté* container. When you remove it from the oven, you should have enough dissolved pork fat to hand to run a ¼″ thick "lid".

You do not press this *pâté*. What we suggest therefore is that you dice up 4 ozs. raw unsalted pork fat very finely, place in a small heat-resistant container and put in the oven on the very bottom shelf so that the pork fat dissolves while the *pâté* is cooking and then all comes together as merry as a marriage bell and you do not have to hang about waiting.

· Potted Crab and Halibut ·

If you are a *pâté* addict, it need scarcely be explained that either of the two foregoing meat and wild game *pâtés* can be cooked *en croûte*. For newcomers this, it should be understood, is just a raised pie paste† which is rolled out fairly thinly, lined into the chosen container, the trimmings rolled up and rolled out again to make a "lid" and a few decorative leaves to cluster round the $\frac{1}{4}$″ diameter hole which you leave in the centre.

If you turn to the Sociable Cook's Book you will find the really *recherché pâtés* which will serve you on grander occasions, but do you, we wonder, know that really enchanting mixture of *Potted Crab and Halibut*? It is hard work and time-consuming but the result is gorgeous. Pick all the flesh, brown and white, from $1\frac{1}{4}$ lbs. cock crab. Place in a mortar. Steam 1 lb. halibut, remove skin and bone and add to the crab meat. Think of someone you loathe, take up the pestle and bash away like mad until the fishy mixture becomes a smooth paste. Pound in 2 ozs. of butter and then work in black pepper, salt, coriander and powdered dried fennel to taste. Pack into an attractive terrine and if you really want to waste more time, cover with clarified butter. Otherwise just melt good unsalted butter down. We like to serve this with hot *flutes* (long sticks) of French bread which we wrap in foil and heat through in the oven at Gas Mark 1 for 10–12 minutes.

· Preserved Chickens' Livers ·

It is very good to have a jar of *Preserved Chickens' Livers* in your refrigerator where it will last for at least three weeks. It is very simple to do and only calls for $\frac{1}{2}$ lb. of chicken fat or goose fat which has been rendered down and 2 lbs. of chickens' livers, pepper and salt to season and a teacupful of dry sherry or Madeira —the one called Sercial in this case. Just be perfectly sure when examining the livers, you remove those nasty little yellow-green bags with meticulous care; they are the gall bladders, when burst they will stain the livers and from them is derived the phrase "as bitter as gall". Put a quarter of the chosen fat in the bottom of a stone jar or steep-sided casserole, lay in one third of the chickens' livers, sprinkle with salt and pepper, moisten with a third of the chosen wine, repeat twice more and finish with the remaining quarter of the chosen fat. Stand in a meat baking tin with a 1″ depth of hot water run all the way round it, cover securely with lid or kitchen foil and cook slowly on middle shelf at Gas Mark 3 for 1 hour. Remove from oven and take off covering or lid. Now cover, right on top of the contents, with a plate, saucer or cake tin base which fits, cover with weights, refrigerate and tie down under several layers of foil for refrigerator storage until needed. This is another item which should be served with our piping hot toast in a box.

· Pâté de Canard ·

Both are fairly humble *pâtés*, so now let us take you through our best luxury one *Pâté de Canard*. This is neither cheap nor quick to make; but, we think, the results justify the expenditure of both time and money. You will need one large duck, 8 ozs. diced, de-rinded streaky bacon and 6 ozs. of the same just rough-cut, 8 ozs. diced, raw, unsalted pork fat and 10 ozs. of the same just rough-cut; 2 small eggs, 8 tablespoons brandy, salt, pepper and 3 ozs. shelled, whole pistachio nuts. Remove all the duck fat, reduce, strain and set aside to use as the fat in raised pie paste.† Cut off the legs and thighs. Set these aside for the moment. Cut away and dice up the rest of the duck flesh. Put it in a bowl with the brandy, diced bacon and diced pork fat. Rough cut the meat from the legs and mince with the rough-cut bacon and pork fat. Beat the brandy and the eggs into this mixture. Blend with the mixture of diced items. Season with salt and pepper. Fold in the pistachio nuts. Turn into a shallow terrine, cover with foil, stand in an outer pan of hot water and cook at Gas Mark 3 middle shelf for 40–45 minutes depending on depth of container.

If you want a "shorter" mixture, with a lower content of pork fat, add 14 ozs. lean veal to the items which you mince. When either are cooked—and the one with the extra meat will take 5 minutes longer—remove from the oven, cover with a fitting cake base or plate, put heavy weights on top and, when cold, refrigerate for a minimum 24 hours.

· Pâté de Canard en Croûte ·

Bear in mind that all these given *pâté* mixtures freeze well
and if you take them out when frozen, dip the containers immediately into hot, not boiling, water to loosen, you can turn the
rock-hard *pâtés* onto foil, wrap them up, label them and put them
back until you need them, thereby winning back your containers
into current useage. Incidentally, the aforementioned duck fat
Raised Pie Paste is precisely what you need, as a base and sides
"lining" to your terrine and as a "lid" if you should want to turn
your *Pâté de Canard* into *Pâté de Canard en Croûte*. In this case, forget
our *pâté* cooking instructions. When you affix the final paste lid
make a hole in the centre so that after cooking on the middle
shelf Gas Mark 3 until paste is a good biscuit colour, you can pour
in aspic jelly at the syrupy stage.

· Soufflé au Pâté de Foie ·

Still on the *pâté* theme and by no means as extravagant as it
may seem at first glance is a *Soufflé au Pâté de Foie* because it can be
made with that admirable bought *pâté* called *Le Parfait*. Of course
it goes without saying that if you can run to the real thing, so very
much the better. The remainder is constant. Begin by making the
usual *roux* with 1½ ozs. butter and 1½ ozs. flour, then thin it down
gradually in the usual way with small additions of dry white wine
until you have persuaded it to absorb ½ pt. Then beat in ¼ pt. top-
of-the-milk or single cream. Add 5 ozs. of real *foie gras* or its
substitute and beat this in until the whole mixture is smooth. Now
take off the heat and beat in 3 egg yolks singly. Finally finish the
mixture with 8 large or 9 standard separated egg whites which
have been fairly stiffly beaten but not stiffly enough to remain in
the bowl when it is tipped upside down, so please test this slowly!
Turn the entire mixture into a buttered 7½" diameter *soufflé*
mould, level off the top completely flatly, being careful to push the
mixture against the sides of the mould to ensure a hundred per
cent success and an even "rise" and push onto one shelf above
centre speedily at Gas Mark 7½ to bake for 15½ to a maximum
16 minutes, when the top will be a rich golden brown. Although
you may wonder at the quantities, we have not made a mistake
in recommending the small proportion of egg yolks which appear
in this recipe. There are exceptions to every rule and this is one

of the *soufflé* ones. When it is done, do remember about carrying it carefully to table without rushing madly about in case it collapses.

· Pêches farcies ·

If you can bear it, there are just two more we must give you for either real or substitute *foie gras*. The first is called *Pêches farcies* and for it you will need small, ripe but firm peaches. You must allow one whole one per person. Skin them and here the boiling water/iced water process is the best because the skin, unlike that of tomatoes, is really too delicate for the much swifter process eminently successful with a tomato, when you simply impale the tomato on a fork, turn it over a modest flame until the skin blisters and cracks and peel off the skin in a trice. Halve your peeled peaches. Turn to p. 50. for Liver Pâté Cream and replace the removed stone by piping in this mixture, then pair them off once again by pressing them closely together and serve them icily chilled on a bed of delicate, picked sprigs of watercress or meticulously washed cress.

· Beignets de Pêches ·

This is the simpler way of serving this delicious *hors d'oeuvre* but if you want to go on and turn your *foie gras* stuffed peaches into *Beignets de Pêches*, dip each one into fritter batter* and fry briskly until richly puffed and brown in slightly smoking hot oil.

· Savoury Apricot Cups ·

You can of course do the same thing with apricots which are far less expensive, but we tell you frankly we would rather leave the recipe alone than give it an inferior taste. Far better we suggest, to take unskinned but stoned, halved apricots and steep them overnight in a marinade of strong *vinaigrée**. Then fill them with real or substitute liver *pâte* cream, dome up inside the drained cups and arrange them on a bed of lettuce leaves.

· Beignets d'Artichauts ·

If you happen to share our enthusiasm for artichokes and especially their *fonds*, you will not be surprised at our passion for serving them in as many different ways as possible. One of the most delicate, *Beignets d'Artichauts*, is done in moments with the drained contents of one or more tins of this favourite of ours. Just dip them in a fine, carefully made fritter batter* and fry them very fast indeed to only a pale golden brown. Pile them onto a napkin-covered dish, sprinkle them with powdered paprika and hand a separate little jugful of boiling hot double cream lightly seasoned with salt and pepper.

· Avocado Cream ·

Another family obsession is for avocados which we have been reproved for ever calling "avocado pears", so permit us to air our new-found knowledge. We may as well confess that the recipe we are going to give you for our *Avocado Cream* took quite a time to get absolutely right so do not run away with the idea that it is just a little thing we have tossed off in a hurry. Let us take it very seriously and assemble the ingredients before we start: 3 ripe avocados; 2½ fl. ozs. dry white wine; 1 oz. butter; 1 oz. flour; 2 separated egg yolks; salt and pepper to season; ½ pt. milk; 2½ fl. ozs. top-of-the-milk or single cream; 2½ fl. ozs. double cream; 4 tablespoons water; ½ oz. powdered gelatine. Dissolve butter in a medium thick pan, stir in the flour, cook and stir until the mixture forms a soft ball leaving the sides and base of the pan clean. Dilute with gradual additions of wine, beating well between each addition. Start adding milk gradually with further beatings between each addition until all milk is absorbed. Remove from heat, beat in egg yolks and when mixture is again smooth and cool, beat in skinned, stoned, emulsified avocados gradually. Dissolve gelatine in water over low heat and until clear and syrupy. Beat into mixture and finally beat in blended creams. Taste, correct seasoning, pour into an oiled ornamental mould or a 6–6½" diameter *soufflé* mould. Refrigerate until set, turn out for service and border with any chosen salad items. This mixture is not thickly set and if a tall mould is to be used, add a further rounded dessertspoon of gelatine when dissolving the given quantity. Just remember it tastes better when only lightly set!

We then extended our experiments with dariole moulds. When having a number of people to a buffet, service is so much tidier on the part of one's guests when things are in individual con-tainers and the dishes have a sporting chance of going on looking reasonable after the first wave of attack has ended! This amount of mixture will fill twelve so begin by brushing the interior of the moulds very vigorously with olive oil. Your successful unmoulding of these items will depend on how well you do the job.

· Cheat Aspic ·

Then rinse each mould out with real or phoney aspic, by which we do not mean bought packet aspic which is too phoney altogether for us, but the home-made quickie which really does not taste at all bad. Empty out the contents of a tin of consommé. Dissolve ¼ oz. gelatine in 4 tablespoons cold water in a small pan and over a low heat. While it dissolves, add the strained juice of ½ lemon, 3 fl. ozs. of tap water and 2 tablespoons of dry sherry to the consommé; then stir in the gelatine and stir over ice until it becomes really syrupy. One more word of warning here to the impatient. It must be syrupy so do not try to short-circuit this performance; otherwise when you turn either the real or the phoney aspic around the sides of the mould it will absolutely refuse to cling and you will be driven wild with frustration.

Put each dariole mould into fairly fierce refrigeration as soon as you have swilled the aspic around. Once it has set repeat the performance to get a really good wall. Then pour in the avocado mixture. If you so wish, freeze until the night before you need them and leave in refrigeration until the morning to give them time to get their breath back after being frozen. Unmould onto your chosen dish, surround with cress and serve with understandable vanity.

· Crème aux Avocats ·

We are just the tiniest bit complacent about having found this mixture because there is so much you can do with it. If you omit the gelatine and dilute carefully with numerous tastings and top-of-the-milk or single cream, you have only to hand a bowl of chives separately and you have a splendid iced soup *Crème aux Avocats* which does not belong here at all but it seems such a pity not to follow this theme right through once we have embarked upon it!

· Oeufs Mollets aux Tomates ·

For *Oeufs Mollets aux Tomates* put a dab of mayonnaise on the base of each tomato water lily (p. 273) and then slip in a 4-minute-

boiled, meticulously shelled egg, pointed end uppermost. Stiffen
$\frac{1}{4}$ pt. of mayonnaise* with a teaspoonful of gelatine dissolved in
the usual way†. Whip over ice until it reaches piping consistency,
fill into an icing bag with a small ornamental pipe affixed, pipe a
necklace to secure the *Oeuf Mollet* at the base, thus pushing out
still further the petals of the tomato flower, and then stick one
cucumber slice just like the spokes of the wheel in between each
petal. Place a tiny "hat" on the top of each egg. You make these
by halving and hollowing out really small tomatoes, leave the
skin on, smear the interior with mayonnaise and slap it on the top.

· Our Deep Quiche ·

Just after the war we were motoring with friends from the
northern coast to Provence and, belting down, we noticed, near
enough to justify an overnight stay on the way back, a very
charming little place called the Hostellerie des Remparts. We
immediately resolved to break our journey there for the last night
before taking the *via dolorosa* back to England. It turned out to be
memorable because amongst other excellent dishes they gave us
what was undoubtedly the best *quiche* we have ever tasted. We
promptly wrote about it in the Daily Telegraph, then as is not
usual with us, we forgot all about it and only a few weeks ago
asked each other the rhetorical question, "Why on earth don't
we try to do a total recall and see if we can recapture it?" [Its
great virtue apart from flavour was the fact that it was really deep,
like a steep display Madeira cake.] Finally, we achieved what we
wanted and put it out on a buffet for a number of guests to see
whether in fact they reacted as we hoped and, as they did, we want
to share it with you. Butter and flour the sides of a $6\frac{1}{2}''$ diameter
sliding based cake tin. Cover the base with a fitting circle of
buttered and floured greaseproof paper. Then line out base and
sides with savoury short paste*. Butter and flour the outside and
the base of a $5\frac{1}{2}''$ solid based cake tin. Place a fitted circle of
buttered-on-both-sides greaseproof paper over the base of the raw
paste in the larger tin. Slide in the smaller tin so that it acts as a
support for the paste while it is being baked, as otherwise the
whole contraption would collapse. Bake at Gas Mark 6, middle
shelf, for 25 minutes until it is a pale biscuit colour. Withdraw
inner cake tin and paper. Flatten the inner base if it shows any
inclination to be puffy. Pour in the *quiche* mixture and return to the

oven Gas Mark 5, one shelf above centre, for 5 minutes and then reduce the heat to Gas Mark 2 for 1 hour 15 minutes.

For the filling assemble 7 standard eggs, 12 fl. ozs. single cream, 12 fl. ozs. top-of-the-milk, salt and pepper to season, 3 ozs. grated Parmesan cheese, approximately 2 ozs. chopped No. 4 cut raw back bacon and enough Gruyère "leaves" to cover the top of the mixture. Blend cream and top-of-the-milk and whip into the eggs. Add the Parmesan and salt and pepper to season. Put the bacon on the base of the pastry case and pour in the mixture. Arrange Gruyère leaves on top and bake as instructed. Do not get into a panic over the extravagance of eggs in this recipe. Like our Cheese Cake (p. 236) a little goes a very long way indeed and therefore justifies the outlay.

· Provençal Cabbage Roll ·

Since we worked it out we have been through a rare English heatwave during which we served slices of our *Quiche* as a first course at a garden dinner. Apart from the conventional records which we keep in our menu book, we are prone to graphic little jottings like, "They found it very rich—serve smaller portions," or "Make more—everyone came back for seconds." In this instance the note read, "Use again—very successful." In much the same way *Provençal Cabbage Roll* can be made to do double duty as part of an *hors d'oeuvre caravane* and as a main course item to be served with a good assortment of salads.

You begin with a tight white cabbage which is placed in a deep container so that a kettle of boiling water can be poured over the top. While the outer leaves are softening, lay a clean tea cloth on your working surface and cover the centre of it with overlapping butter papers to make a wide rectangle. Then you start heaving up the cabbage and pulling off the outer leaves, from which you must cut narrow Vees from the stem end in order to remove the hard unwanted stalk. Overlap these over the butter papers to make a base. Return the cabbage to the hot water and keep doing this until you have detached all except the tight white heart. Grate this coarsely and toss into a roomy bowl. Grate a large Spanish onion coarsely and place in the same bowl as the grated cabbage. Add 1¼ lbs. of minced lean veal (or beef for the family), a generous teaspoon of Worcestershire sauce, a flat dessertspoonful of powdered paprika, a generous pinch of mixed spice, 2

crushed garlic cloves, a generous pinch of thyme or lemon thyme,
1 large egg, 1 heaped teaspoon of concentrated tomato *purée* and
4 ozs. soft white or brown breadcrumbs. Work up to a paste and
gradually pack over the cabbage leaves, shaping as you go until all
the mixture is used up and you have a huge salami-sized sausage
sitting on the leaves and measuring approximately 20″ long.

Brush all over the top and sides with a little melted butter, press
more stalk-denuded cabbage leaves over the entire exposed surface and bring up the side leaves until you have completely
obscured the giant sausage by these. Then bring up the butter
papers, wrap in the cloth and give a firm outer wrapping of
kitchen foil. Tie down the length in four or five equi-distant
places, sink into a large pan with sufficient stock to cover the
"parcel" very generously, bring to a steady simmer and maintain
for 1½ hours. Drain, chill, refrigerate overnight, then "undress",
cut away strings and set on a platter or narrow strip of wood for
slicing and service.

· Stuffed Vine Leaves ·

You all know—at least we suspect you do—that small tins
of vine leaves can be bought from Continental delicatessens. The
vast majority of you will also know that in this country the vine
leaf stuffing in-ratio, vine to seasoned savoury mixture in fillings, is
mostly in that immortal Fifty-Fifty, one chicken (savoury filling),
one horse (rice), so, *en passant*, we remind you that stealing a little
bit of the filling from Provençal Cabbage Roll, shaping it into
small sausages and rolling vine leaves over these gives you a far
better finished product and is not nearly so fattening.

· Baby Coulibiac ·

While on the subject of rolls do you know *Baby Coulibiac*?
The single big one has many versions in Russia, of which the most
famous is made with Royal Sturgeon *not* salmon. Down the centre
of the filling you lay *vesiga* (stockists p. 292). This is sold dry in
England. It looks rather like rock-hard, beige angelica. It is
extremely costly so pray do not over-shop for it as a couple of
ounces soaked overnight in water until it becomes white and soft
is all you need for a very big *Coulibiac*. *Vesiga* is the spine bone of
the sturgeon. It is completely soluble after the pre-treatment we
have explained and it does impart a special flavour to the dish; but

we are not proposing that you use it for the miniatures. Before we give you the recipe we feel bound to remind you that there is also a very humble version used by the poor Russian peasants of the past. Like you we are, of course, given to understand there are no poor in Russia today. In this version the quantity of rice is vastly increased and cabbage takes the place of sturgeon.

For the *hors d'oeuvre Baby Coulibiac* you assemble bought or home-made puff paste, cold cooked rice, chopped hard-boiled eggs, milled fresh parsley, melted butter, salt and pepper and salmon, not sturgeon. It is too rare in England, a circumstance which is readily understandable as the few that are caught must be offered to the Queen before they are sold to the likes of us. We use frozen Pacific salmon because we think this is quite good enough and are averse to mixing good Scottish, Wye or Severn salmon with a great many odds and bobs!

Roll out the puff paste very thinly and cut into 5″ squares, remembering that when you start the filling assembly, to control it so that the finished mound is contained within a 2½″ area, leaving enough space exposed for it to be rolled up completely and the lengthwise edges pinched together. Start with a small base spreading of cooked rice, cover with a thinner spreading of chopped hard-boiled egg, sprinkle with parsley, moisten with melted butter, trellis with matchsticks of raw skinned, boned salmon, season with salt and pepper and repeat. Moisten overall with a little more melted butter, brush the exposed paste edges with raw beaten egg, roll up the edges and tuck in the ends. Brush top and sides with egg, arrange on a wetted baking sheet and bake to a rich golden brown one shelf above centre at Gas Mark 6. Again you can serve these as individual portions for a fish course but if you want to be very grand, you not only hand a separate sauce-boat of melted butter but also top each roll with a transparently thin small slice of smoked salmon.

· Toasts des Gourmets ·

Let us now share with you Curnonsky's epicurean *"Toasts des Gourmets"*. This is an exact translation from the original as dictated by the author just before he died. He was an absolutely splendid old man known throughout France for most of his life as *Le Prince Elu de Gastronomes*. Mix together in a bowl 7 ozs. of chopped button mushrooms, stalks and all, with the same amount

of chopped, lean, cooked ham trimmings. Add 8 fl. ozs. of thick
classic *Sauce Béchamel** with 3½ fl. ozs. double cream and for pity's
sake do not let the mixture become floppy, which it will do if you
do not make the basic *Béchamel* thick enough. Melt enough
butter in a shallow pan to fry 8 small crustless squares of white
bread cut from a narrow sandwich loaf. Drain these, shake a few
drops of Kirsch over each and divide the ham and mushroom
mixture equally between them, smoothing off the tops evenly and
carefully. Sprinkle the tops fairly thickly with grated Parmesan
cheese and brown briskly under a strong grill.

· Mushrooms in Sour Cream ·

Always when we are writing for you we think in a sort of
cook's daisy chain, one recollection being sparked off by the
preceding recipe. In this context the association of ideas is mushrooms because whenever we put raw mushrooms in sour cream
in an *hors d'oeuvre* selection and however much we make, there
are never any left over. You do not have to use button mushrooms however—flat, field or tree mushrooms will all do very
well. Just follow the standard routine. Sling ¾ lb. into a colander,
pour a kettle of boiling water over them to free them of any
bacteria, dry in a clean cloth and slice fairly thinly. Mix with a ¼ pt.
carton of dairy soured cream, spread into a shallow dish and
sprinkle the top with paprika.

· Italian Mushroom Salad ·

There is another version of this simple but little known
salad, at which the Italians excel. They use fairly large button
mushrooms, slice them very thinly, moisten them with olive oil,
season them with pepper to taste, add a very small crushed garlic
clove and mix all together with the strained juice of a small lemon.
You will meet this all over Italy but the Genoese improve on
their standard method by trellising the top of each shallow dishful
with well drained, wiped, lengthwise-divided anchovy fillets.

· Pomidoro col Tonno ·

They also contribute to a good *hors d'oeuvre* table the
tomato stuffed with tuna which they call *Pomidoro col Tonno*.
For this cut "lids" from medium to small tomatoes, hollow out
completely and fill with a mixture of stiff red mayonnaise blended

with as much slightly oily, pounded tuna fish from a tin as will
make the mayonnaise a good piping consistency.

· Insalata di Patate col Tonno ·

This reminds us, you must also have *Insalata di Patate col
Tonno*. Take 6 small to medium new potatoes and steam them in
their skins. Peel and slice them as for *sauté* potatoes while still
warm, spread them out, and sprinkle lightly with salt and pepper.
Slice a large onion transparently thinly, separate the rings, blend
well in with the potatoes and put the mixture in a serving dish.
Swill with a small teacupful of olive oil and a tablespoonful of
red wine vinegar. Refrigerate until just before serving, fold in
about $\frac{1}{4}$ lb. of diced tuna and scatter capers overall. The incidence
of onion is high but not too high if you cut them very thinly;
otherwise it will be horrid.

· Oignons Monte Carlo ·

Indeed the French version of *Oignons Monte Carlo* is based
entirely upon onions as you might imagine. Place 1 lb. of the
smallest golden Spanish onions or French shallots in a thick pan.
Add 8 fl. ozs. of wine vinegar, 6 tablespoons of olive oil, 3 ozs.
soft brown sugar (pieces) and finish up by tossing in 2 sprigs of
thyme, 2 torn bay leaves and 6 ozs. seeded raisins or sultanas.
Bring to a whispering simmer and maintain, turning occasionally
with a wooden spoon for $1\frac{1}{2}$ hours over a mere thread of heat.
Pour into an earthenware pot and serve well chilled. Incidentally,
before serving, taste the liquor and if you think salt and pepper
would enhance the flavour add them; otherwise abstain. We say
this with great emphasis because in the final account the only
thing that really matters to a cook is that people will eat whatever
he or she has made with the maximum pleasure and appreciation.

Therefore follow the golden rule and go easy with the salt and
pepper in your cooking. It can always be added even though the
counsel for perfection is that you need never put salt and pepper
on the table, but better to ignore this than run the risk of overdoing something which cannot be undone. Unless you know
somebody extremely well, you need to be a clairvoyant to ascertain
their tastes down to the last grain of anything, which is another
very good reason for annotating your menu book with things
like, "Henry very craftily concealed his *fonds d'artichauts* under the
last lettuce leaf—remember not to give them to him again!"

Velouté Dame-Blanche · Velouté aux Concombres
Velouté aux Petits Pois Frais · Crème de Cresson
Crème aux Fruits de Mer · Purée de Laitue au Bacon
Crème aux Pistaches · Emergency Celery Soup
Crème d'Ecrevisses · Potage Familial · Potage de Noces
Soupe de Vendanges · Potage aux Haricots Verts
Soup Garnishes · Potage purée de Tomates
Crème de Marrons · Crème aux Laitances d'Harengs

nine · SOUP IT UP

It is all very well for Lewis Carroll to wax lyrical over "Soup of the evening, beautiful soup", but not always very well for the cook hostess to cherish the illusion that soup is always a good idea. Economically, it takes the edge off appetites, as a time-saver it is a gem because even soups with eggs in, like the great *Germiny**, can be advance-made and pre-heated without any fears of curdling, provided of course they are submitted to indirect re-heating over a pan of boiling water. We are soup addicts and regard an evening meal as incomplete without a family brew but it can be a very great mistake.

You will remember perhaps that in the preceding chapter we referred to the way in which Avocado Cream adapts superbly to service as an iced Avocado Cream Soup. The laugh was on us when we offered this at the onset of a garden buffet luncheon recently with the barometer stuck not at wet and windy, as is its custom in this island, but at set fair and a mere 82 degrees in the shade. Not a scrap was left but almost everything else was, because the soup was too rich and too filling for such a very hot day. In fact in its own classically correct way it was just as much a disaster as it would have been if we had brought out little steaming bowls of *Soupe à l'Oignon** instead!

The standard of home cooking today is so much higher that there are very few housewives left in blissful ignorance of the very basic menu-making rule that a rich soup must be followed by a simple and therefore contrasting second course, that two cream-laced items must not be allowed to pursue each other and that the essence of a well balanced meal is a complete change of gastro-nomic tempo for each succeeding course; but there is more to it than that. The best *Vichyssoise* in the world, whether served hot or cold, is basically a starchy item, so always look forward to the rest of your meal before making your final soup decisions, lest you follow such a soup with a pastry item—starch on starch in fact!—

or on a hot summer's night might follow Spanish *Gazpacho*†
(which is really a salad which floats) with a fish salad, or the completely obvious clanger of serving a *bisque* before a fish course, or a
game soup and then going on to a pheasant, a partridge or a
grouse. Not for nothing did Escoffier wail about the "difficulties
attending the arrangement of menus". He said, "Very few people
know what an arduous task the composing of a perfect menu
represents," and he also said, "The setting up of a presentable
menu is rarely accomplished without lengthy labour and much
thought, and for all that the result is not always to my satisfaction."

So now let us examine what one can safely assume he regarded
as "rare accomplishments" by his standards since they are
published in one of his own books. He follows a *consommé* with
caviare, trout and devilled whitebait; a *velouté* of *petits pois* with
Suprêmes de Poulet au beurre noisette: a *bisque* of crayfish with a
timbale of quail. He precedes *Homard Américaine* with a clear turtle
soup and *Sole Newburg* with *Bortsch*. *Crème de Concombres* is served
before *Saumon Véronique*, a cold *Consommé en gelée* is permitted to
come before a *mousseline* of sole and *Poule au Pot Henri IV* paves
the way for a saddle of venison in a cream sauce. The lovely
Velouté Dame-Blanche comprises the overture to a capon cooked *à
la Périgord* with *foie gras* and truffles.

· Velouté Dame-Blanche ·

The very thought of this last soup sets us drooling so here is
a very slightly modified version for, we hope, your pleasure.
Soften 1½ ozs. butter and work 1½ ozs. of carefully sifted flour
into it over a low heat. Moisten this paste little by little with 1½ pts.
of clear chicken stock. Pound 12 sweet almonds in a mortar with a
pestle with just over 3 fl. ozs. of fresh water and then rub through
a clean cloth, twisting the cloth to accelerate this laborious procedure. Add the result to the *velouté*. Finish the soup just before
service with softened butter rubbed through the fingers until the
mixture takes on a delicate sheen. Taste, correct the seasoning and
scatter each serving with minutely chopped chickens' breast.
Simple enough, it just needs care and proper stock, not little
bouillon cubes or you and your friends will be the ones to suffer.

· Velouté aux Concombres ·

Escoffier also made a beautiful *Velouté aux Concombres* which you would do well to copy, particularly if you intend serving that much nicer presentation of lamb than ever a Crown Roast can hope to be—Guard of Honour. Steam 1 lb. unskinned cucumber for 10 minutes. Mince and then put in a frying pan with 3 ozs. good butter and simmer very gently for 5 minutes. Scrape the mixture into a roomy saucepan, add 1 pt. basic *velouté**, sieve and dilute to the required consistency with white stock. Then add Escoffier's famous liaison garnish with small bread *croûtons* and if thought desirable, stir in a little cream to taste. The great man's liaison simply consists of taking, to the proportions we have given you, 2 ozs. of the relevant vegetable—in this case cucumber—but this time weigh after skinning, grate finely and put in a saucepan with its own juice from the grating. Dry it out until just before it burns on the bottom of the pan by shaking the pan over a low heat, controlling this so that the cucumber is really tender in the liaison when it is added to the soup. Then add as much butter as it will hold without throwing a receding greasy fringe and stir into the soup.

· Velouté aux Petits Pois Frais ·

If you substitute 1½ lbs. shelled *petits pois* for the cucumber, you will achieve *Velouté aux Petits Pois Frais* which can safely precede *Poulet Normande* (p. 149), or if you want to make a four-course menu, insert *Truite aux Amandes** between the soup and the chicken dish.

· Crème de Cresson ·

We have a bank where the wild thyme grows because we jolly well planted it there, but we also have watercress for which we can take no credit. For a long time we eyed it with considerable suspicion and left it severely alone. Then it became so luxuriant that we rang up the local authorities and found out that by the side of our fairly fast flowing millstream, it is safe to pick and turn into that lovely and delicate soup, *Crème de Cresson*. Please read that sentence carefully and see that you run no risks by foolhardy experiments with watercress which can be dangerous unless you have found out the facts about it from whoever is authorised to give them to you in your vicinity; otherwise ignore the plants and use bought watercress which, as one of our logical friends is in the habit of saying, will be subtly but delectably different.

Whatever cress you are using, wash the equivalent to six shop bunches *with great thoroughness* in lashings of running cold water, pick the small sprigs away from the main stems, discard those and simmer the rest in slightly salted water for 15 minutes—not too much slightly salted water please, just enough to make a sort of pond. Emulsify the lot. Make the usual *roux* with 1¼ ozs. of flour and the same of butter. Add the water cress *purée*, gradually, beating as usual between each addition. You will find the result is much too thick to be drunk—it would have to be sucked up which would be a bore. So this is where you exert your own choice between diluting with milk or with a white stock. Just see to it if you choose the latter, that it is made with either veal or poultry bones, trimmings and what a much loved old family cook referred to as "hoffal". When the stock is made and cleared, reduce it by simmering it down to half quantity before adding it to the soup. This done and the soup now made slightly too thin, achieve a final equilibrium by blending together 2 egg yolks and 2½ fl. ozs. of the best available cream. Draw the soup pan to the side of a low heat, beat this mixture in fast, taste, correct seasoning and reheat for service over hot water *lest the egg yolks curdle*.

You can do a lot worse than follow this soup on a three course menu with *Tournedos Tivoli* (p. 123), *Sauce Béarnaise**, or if four courses are wanted, try *Brochettes de Crevettes flambées* (p. 106).

· Crème aux Fruits de Mer ·

It is no use pretending that *Crème aux Fruits de Mer* in its splendid original is an economical soup that you can toss up in a few minutes. Nothing can be economical which is made with lobster unless you happen to live in the Bay of Paleocastritsa on the Greek island of Corfu. Paradoxically the best guide book of this island bemoans the cost as being inordinately high which of course it is, if you consider thirty shillings a head for half a kilo of lobster plus all the trimmings for a three course meal other than a raging bargain.

As we are not writing a cookery book for Paleocastritsians, we are going to give you a much humbler version which for 6 portions calls for 6 ozs. mixed brown and white crabmeat, 1 lb. white fish trimmings for the stockpot, ¼ pt. dry white wine, 4 ozs. shrimps, 2 pts. cold water, ideally a sprig of fennel but if not 2 parsley stalks, a bay leaf, a leaf of lemon peel, top-of-the-milk or cream, 2 peppercorns (no salt, the shrimps will supply what is needed) and a mere teaspoonful of that splendid old Swiss cheese Sbrinz, only recently available in England (if not, use Parmesan). Put the trimmings into a roomy pan with the water, the peppercorns, the bay leaf, the fennel or parsley stalks and lemon peel. Heat moderately to reach a slow rolling boil and maintain for at least 30 minutes which gives you nice time to shell the shrimps and add the shells to the stock before this is completed. Then strain the stock which should yield 1½ pts. after simmering. Add the wine, stir in the crabmeat and three-quarters of the shrimps. Then add top-of-the-milk, single or whipping cream to taste. Fill into boiling-water-rinsed soup bowls when serving hot, or icily chilled ones when serving cold. In both cases scatter the remaining shelled shrimps over the surface of the bowls of soup. Clearly you would never serve a fish course after this but you could serve an egg one, so *Oeufs pochés au vin rouge*† will do very well and a little *Gigot d'Agneau feuilleté** thereafter.

Of course we made rather a sweeping statement when we said that you could not follow a fish soup with a fish course; we should have added at a formal luncheon or dinner, but if you were having a fish meal—which is something we adore—you could precede the soup with that gourmet's delight *Assiette des Fruits de Mer**, follow it with a *Paupiette de Turbot* (p. 101) and finish with a Cheese Ice Cream (p. 206) with hot cheese sauce.

· Purée de Laitue au Bacon ·

The simple statement that there is always too much or too little is one that needs no explanation to country people with kitchen gardens. You have either six pyramidal, lousy-looking, bolted lettuces on what was once a proud row or else you wonder what in heaven's name you can do to use up a vast surplus in prime condition. One of the answers is to make *Purée de Laitue au Bacon* and by giving it this name, pray do not accuse us of dropping a clanger because there is no French word in the entire language for bacon and as far back as the thirteenth century the phrase "*le grand bacon*" occurs. Wash, pick and drain exceedingly thoroughly 2 large cos lettuces. Tear them up as if in a rage. Soften 2 ozs.

salted butter in a pan, toss in the lettuce and let it poach gently to a
pap. Rub through a sieve, return to the pan, add 1½ pts. milk and
at least 8 strips of rind cut from good sized rashers of bacon. Add
1 oz. very finely chopped onion and let the mixture simmer over a
mere thread of heat until the onion is tender and the liquid tastes
of the bacon. Withdraw the rind. Correct the seasoning and pour
piping hot into heated soup bowls. Whip up 3 fl. ozs. double
cream stiffly, add a generous heaped tablespoonful of finely
scissored chives and, when blended, drop a small blob into the
centre of each serving. Hand *croûtons* separately.

   This is a good but simple soup which could pave the way for
Devilled Whitebait (p. 109) or a boned eel wrapped in puff pastry
and baked to a rich golden brown for serving with *Sauce à
l'Estragon**. It could also precede *Rognons de Veau* and if you skip
the eel, you could serve *Rognons de Porc entiers en feuilleté* with
Sauce Madère.

· Crème aux Pistaches ·

   Having offered a sop to Cerberus in the shape of a modest
lettuce soup, let us give you Voisin's *Crème aux Pistaches*, one of
the great soups of *haute cuisine Française* which the passionate cook
may possibly appreciate just for reading, if it is beyond her purse
for actual making. The last time we bought pistachio nuts was in
Greece, where they are relatively cheap, at a splendid little
Athenian shop owned, believe it or not, by Mr. Pericles Aescula-
pius, but in England they are a murderous price. Nevertheless for
this soup you will need ½ lb. You will also need 2 pts. of super-
latively clear, sticky *Consommé au Volaille*, ½ pt. double cream and
4 egg yolks. Just shell the pistachio nuts, pound them in a mortar
with a pestle, put them in a pan with the *Consommé* and simmer
them until they are absolutely collapsed and tender. Put them into
a thick strong piece of linen of rectangular shape, get some unfortunate member of the family to hold the two corners at one
end, while you hold the two opposing corners gathered up in one
hand and with the other, work away doggedly with the back of a
wooden spoon until there are only scraps of rough residue in the
linen and the *purée* has escaped into the bowl below. Scrape any
purée which clings to the back of your pre-historic *tamis* or
cloth. Beat the cream and egg yolks lightly with a fork in a bowl.
Place the *purée* in the top of the double saucepan over hot water,

add the egg yolk and cream mixture, stir until blended and piping hot, taste—only once is necessary, the rest is pure greed!—correct the seasoning with salt and pepper and serve.

We turned up our menu books after a heated discussion on what should follow this epicurean brew. One school of thought maintained it could precede a *Filet de Boeuf feuilleté**, another said this was far too coarse and maintained that the perfect main course was woodcock spit-roasted and served with pieces of bread put in the drip tray under the spit so that the trails of blood dripped over them during the cooking time. Our menu books confirmed the latter and also that at a small, rather special post-theatre supper party this soup was followed by little boned quail in aspic, while at a dinner party the soup preceded spit-roasted grouse, with never a trace of breadcrumb which is an English trick none of us can comprehend.

· Emergency Celery Soup ·

After such a flight of fancy let us revert to our muttons, rather than our milk-fed lamb, and give you a simple *Emergency Celery Soup* which can be whipped up when you are faced with the problem of producing a reasonable little meal in an unreasonably short time. Empty the contents of a large tin of celery into an emulsifier and after emulsifying, rub through a sieve; otherwise you are likely to excavate little shreds from your teeth which is inelegant! Stir in $1\frac{1}{2}$ pts. milk and 2 ozs. grated Parmesan. Bring to the boil, add a spoonful or two of cream or top-of-the-milk, if possible, taste and correct seasoning. Pour into soup bowls and scatter finely scissored chives over the top of each portion.

If you happen to have a first rate stock-pot on the go which really tastes of something more than a dissolved *bouillon* cube and tap water, replace the milk with stock, use more top-of-the-milk or cream to finish and we are prepared to gamble a full 99 per cent of the guests will think that you have made a fresh celery soup. This is an interesting one because it is a marvellous opener when you happen to be serving jugged hare or indeed any strong brown sauced casserole or *salmi* like a *Salmi de Perdreaux* made with last season's old birds, or a *Salmi de Pigeons aux Raisins*, which is quite exceptional if only the breasts are used and the rest is put in a stock pot for a family brew.

· Crème d'Ecrevisses ·

Since we have moved to our new home, we have become acutely conscious of the marvellous qualities of English freshwater crayfish. We are fortunate in having a river, which is up till now free from polution, running through our garden. By having a regular Friday delivery during the crayfish season of cods' heads, we ensure Saturday feasts of *Crème d'Ecrevisses* and a family brew for the following night from *les restes*. That probably reads like the outer edge of lunacy even for us, so let us explain.

Tie a cod's head securely to the base of an ordinary plastic or wire hanging flower basket. Tie a length of string to the rim from which these baskets are normally hung and lower the contraption into the river. Go back an hour later with a bucket two-thirds filled with clear cold water, haul up the basket and pick off the crayfish into the bucket of water. They will be found clinging to the basket and trapped inside gorging the cod's head like leeches on an explorer hacking his way through a swampy bit of jungle. Return to the river any which are less than 3".

Clean the rest with extreme thoroughness in masses of cold running water and place the fish in a large pot. For 12 people allow 4 crayfish per head. Cover with a bottle of inexpensive dry white wine, re-fill the bottle with cold water, add that with a torn bay leaf, a large sprig of fennel, 4–5 peppercorns and a transparently thin peeled rind of a lemon. Clap on the lid and bring to a fast boil over a fierce flame. Reduce heat till liquor simmers and simmers until fish are a brilliant pink colour, approximately 12–15 minutes overall cooking time. Strain and return liquor to clean pan. As soon as the fish are cool enough to handle, pull the bodies from the heads and claws—they come away like silk—shell them, cut each into three and return to the liquor. Add ½ pt. single or coffee cream, bring to the boil, taste, correct the seasoning with salt and stir in 2 generous heaped tablespoonsful of finely milled fresh parsley. Provide plenty of hot crusty French bread and very cold butter.

Smash down the residue of heads and claws for the family leftover soup, put in a pot with the shells from the bodies and tails and add a quart of fish stock obtained by simmering for 20 minutes 1½ lbs. sole or plaice trimmings scrounged from the fishmonger. Strain and thicken by stirring in little balls of *beurre manié*, work flour into butter until it forms a malleable paste; roll between the palms of the hand into ¼ oz. balls. Serve in bowls with small squares of toasted crustless bread on top of each serving. Sprinkle these floating squares with grated Parmesan or Sbrinz, brown fast under the grill and fill the family up very satisfactorily with that lot.

· Potage Familial ·

Incidentally, this reminds us that we have never yet given a party of any size without finding ourselves surrounded by food the night before but with absolutely nothing to feed the working team, because everything belongs to the party. For this reason we now include a big brew of *Potage Familial* with which to fill ourselves up, accompanied by little bits of savoury left-overs heaped on to hot buttered toast or fried bread *croûtons*. Strain and clean 2 quarts of bone stock. Add to this 1 lb. rough chopped onions, 4 parsley stalks, 1 lb. rough chopped carrots, the white and green of 2 coarsely chopped leeks, 1 *bouquet garni**, 2 large or 4 small tomatoes and 2 crushed garlic cloves. Let this mixture simmer until everything is very tender, fish out the *bouquet garni* and emulsify or sieve. Correct the seasoning with salt and pepper. Put a rounded tablespoonful of grated stale cheese into each bowl. Pour the soup on top and that is that.

· Potage de Noces ·

While being at our most eccentric let us share a passing reference to honeymoons and soups. There is a renowned one which a not very young couple made in a very elegant flat in a very elegant block. No odour emerged from their culinary rites; the vast quantity of garlic in fact kills its own pong and pungent flavour, but the resultant brew was appreciated both during drinking it and . . . er . . . afterwards. The name in the French region of its origin—Périgord—is *Potage de Noces* and the method for achieving this is . . . take 2¼ pints of veal stock and place in a pan with 12 large peeled whole garlic cloves. Add a *bouquet garni* comprising 1 sprig sago, 1 small bay leaf and 1 sprig thyme. Bring all to the boil, simmer for 15 minutes, remove *bouquet garni* and sieve. Stir 2 egg yolks together with a tablespoonful of oil and pour the sieved hot purée on to this, back and forth, to and from the pan two or three times. Taste, season with salt and pepper and, according to the Périgord *grandmère* who whispered this last bit to us many years ago, add a teaspoon of brandy and a teaspoon of curaçao to each serving. Please do not ask us what to serve afterwards because the answer is simply more brandy and more curaçao! Traditionally, it was served by peasant families to the bride and groom after they had been put to bed.

· Soupe de Vendanges ·

Let us stay in this Périgord neck of the woods for the harvest soup or *Soupe de Vendanges* served during the season of grape harvesting. To make a big jorum put 4 ozs. of clean chicken, duck, goose or clarified pork fat into a pan and stir in 4 ozs. flour. Pack down into a pint jug enough cooked vegetables from a *Pot-au-feu*† to fill it. Sieve them while the *roux* is cooking out its remaining taste of flour and then add to the *roux* gradually, beating well between each addition. Work in 1½ lbs. peeled rough-cut tomatoes and dilute, when the tomatoes are pulped, with about 3 pts. of *pot-au-feu* liquid, or use as much more as you need to achieve the desired consistency. This is the kind of brew which is much appreciated by a crowd of youngsters when they come back ravenous from an evening expedition.

· Potage aux Haricots verts ·

One of the reasons why we have taken to steaming and sieving vast quantities of either French or runner beans for freezing in waxed cartons is the soup which we are going to give you now—*Potage aux Haricots verts*. For it you need 1½ lbs. bean *purée*, 1 crushed garlic clove, 1½ ozs. finely grated Parmesan or Sbrinz, 1½ pts. milk, 2 tablespoons chopped fresh chives, salt and pepper to season, ½ pt. stock and 1 finely grated raw shallot or onion. Then all is done very quickly. Bring beans, onion and garlic to a slow rolling boil with the milk and stock. Season with salt and pepper, stir in the cheese and either serve piping hot with chives scattered over each portion or chill and serve icily cold. Apply this recipe to spinach, tomato, broad beans, cauliflower or Brussels sprouts *en purée*, and whether the *purées* have been freshly made or taken from the freezer, you have a good range of speedily made family soups. Turn them into *crèmes* instead by replacing half the given quantity of stock with wine and a quarter of the given milk with single or coffee cream.

· Soup Garnishes ·

You can draw on a whole raft of accompanying "garnishes" which can be passed separately, or a few of each can be arranged on the side of the plate holding each soup bowl. One which is so easy that it is like a little bit of kitchen magic is made with small triangles of leaf-thin bought puff paste (stockists p. 292). Just toss them singly into smoking hot oil where they will blow up like little *Blériot* balloons and turn a rich golden brown. Spread them out and season them just with salt and pepper, or else with powdered paprika, or with celery salt instead of salt and then the pepper as before. Take a 6″ × 12″ strip of the same paste rolled very thinly, brush the exposed surface all over with raw beaten egg, scatter thickly with a mixture of Parmesan or Sbrinz and Gruyère or Emmenthal. Roll up tightly, lop off into ¼″ slices, brush the tops of these with raw beaten egg and bake one shelf above centre at Gas Mark 7 until lightly browned and puffy. They will only take 7–8 minutes at most. Then there is the Caribbean accompaniment—one of the very few things that we found were worth eating—green banana or even slightly under-ripe ordinary banana chips. Slice up the chosen fruit in the ordinary way, toss into slightly smoking hot fat, drain on kitchen paper and serve as explained.

· Potage Purée de Tomates ·

As doubtless you have found out so often yourselves, some of the best soups are the most simply made, *provided* the base fluids are of high quality. A typical example of this is Ali-Bab's *Potage purée de Tomates*, for which you need to stir 8 ozs. of fresh or frozen tomato *purée* into 3½ pts. of *consommé*. Taste and correct the seasoning and that is all. However, the author comments that it should be served with diced *croûtons*, or with a dessert-spoonful of perfectly cooked grained rice in each bowl. He further notes that by throwing in fresh cream or cream soured with juice of a lemon you achieve *Potage crème de Tomates*. For Ali-Bab's given quantities, you will need 1 carton of single cream and the strained juice of a small lemon, just stir the two together very gently, pour the soup on top in a thin stream from the pan, repeat back into the pan and serve.

Now let us pause for a moment and reflect on our own omission, for you will become astigmatised before you can find any explanation from us covering the all important point that whoever replaces the given quantity of good stock required so often throughout these pages with *consommé*, will by its addition be raising whatever the soup is into a higher culinary echelon. If you turn to Simple Aspic and Standard Classic Aspic in the Sociable Cook's Book, the second in this trilogy, and follow exactly what we have written there *merely omitting the gelatine*, you will have the *consommé* that you need.

· Crème de Marrons ·

For example you will want it for *Crème de Marrons*. Nick 1 lb. chestnuts with a pair of scissors or a small sharp knife and put in a steamer until you can pull away both the inner and outer skins. Then crumble them roughly, put them in a pan with 2 pts. of *consommé*, simmer for 10 minutes, emulsify and, for perfection, then put through a *tamis*, the cone-shaped professional metal sieve which gives you a far finer *purée* than ever you can achieve with an ordinary round domestic one. At this stage you keep your *purée* for finishing at the last moment, having remembered to measure off everything so this does not turn itself into the last three-quarters-of-an-hour and "now I'm late for everything!" Blend a breakfastcupful of single cream with 2 separate egg yolks, stir this into your *purée* in the top of a double saucepan over hot water, dilute if you consider it too thick with more *consommé*, taste, correct the seasoning with salt, pepper and a generous pinch of celery salt and at the last stir in a tablespoonful of onion juice. You obtain this by grating a large onion coarsely and pushing the pulp through a little tea strainer to express the mixture.

· Crème aux Laitances d'Harengs ·

If you want to be a little way out without spending too much money, try one of our own very specials *Crème aux Laitances d'Harengs*. Steam 1 lb. of soft herring roes in the top of a steamer, which you have lined out with kitchen foil and dabbed about on at random with a skewer to make a few small holes. Make the usual *roux* with 2 ozs. butter and 2 ozs. flour. Dilute this with 5 fl. ozs. of dry white wine and sieve into it the cooked roes with their own moisture. Add 1 pt. milk gradually, beating well between each addition. Season with a little salt and rather more pepper and finish it off with single cream to taste. Float a tiny ball of butter rolled thickly in fresh milled parsley over the top of each serving.

Finally you, most busy and hard-pressed cook hostesses, we want to have the pleasure of assuring you that the *consommé*, stock or any of the basic soups which we have given you up to the point where they are finished with cream, egg yolks or anything else, can be frozen in waxed cartons to save you basic labours at party times. In recent years it has become a matter of routine here to have a couple of *consommé* days and thereafter a couple of stock days twice annually, in early autumn and in the spring. This enables us to serve soups, above which otherwise the dinner table candlelight would seldom flicker.

Homard Mélanie · Fish Fumet · Filets de Sole à la crème
Filets de Sole Forestière · Sole Véronique
Filets de Sole Hollandaise · Filets de Sole ou Turbot Hongroise
Paupiettes de Turbot · Sauce Champagne · Truite au Vin blanc
Truite en papillote Forestière · Truite en gelée au Fenouil
Crêpes aux Moules · Crêpes Farcies aux Crevettes
Crêpes au Crabe · Crêpes Villervillaise
Omelette aux Moules, ou Crabe ou Villervillaise
Brochettes de Crevettes Flambées
Brochettes de Moules
Coquilles de Fruits de Mer, de Crabe et Normande
Feuilleté de Fruits de Mer, de Crabe ou de Moules
Devilled Whitebait · Brandade de Morue
Casserolettes de Sole · Rissoles

As we explained to you in the first of this trilogy, there is no necessity to give either yourself or the lobster the discomfort of being boiled alive, so do not let the title mislead you. But do accept that fish cookery is essentially a delicate and subtle art which begins at all times with absolutely fresh fish, since anything else is an abomination.

A hard core of the very foolish indeed, in this country, still persist in clinging to the fundamental misconception that sauces are used to disguise poor or even whiffy materials. A sauce is unworthy of a name unless it fulfils the essential function of developing and flattering the basic natural flavour of the item with which it is served. Nowhere is this more so than in fish cookery and this is our only reason for flinching a little at the use of red wine with fish—it eclipses! Of course it is perfectly classic. *Sole Bourguignonne* is a prime example but, honestly, there is not much taste of sole by the time it has been infused with burgundy, so use dry light wine, *flambé* with brandy very sparingly and aim to have as light a hand with fish's own herbs, dill and fennel, as the Americans have with the vermouth in a dry martini.

· Homard Mélanie ·

This is probably why we rate the great Madame Mélanie's *Homard Mélanie* as the finest hot lobster dish of all. The method of cookery, the whole final combination in fact which *brings out the fullest flavour of the lobster* and is incapable of sublimation or distortion.

You will need to allow half a 1¼ lb. hen lobster per head. Happily for the squeamish you can buy these cooked, provided they are really freshly cooked, not dry inside and shrinking away from their shells. Discard the pouch and the head, remove large and all small claws and take all the flesh from the shell. Dice this small and mix with every possible scrap of claw meat and the coral until each of these three are evenly distributed throughout. Then pack the flesh back into the shells and put as many as you require head to tail in well-buttered meat baking tins. Assemble a small bowl of mixed, grated Parmesan and Gruyère (1 part Gruyère to 2 parts Parmesan)—no others will do, a bowl of fine, soft, white breadcrumbs, a bottle of cream, a bottle of light, dry white wine, some milled black peppercorns and a bowl of milled parsley. Half-an-hour before serving pour enough dry white wine into each prepared half lobster shell for it to come within $\frac{1}{4}''$ of the rim. Pour a thin stream of the cream on top until the mixture of the wine and cream runs over into the baking tin. It should do this sufficiently liberally to cover the bottom for $\frac{1}{4}''$. Now scatter the mixed Parmesan and Gruyère lightly over the meat in the shell and over the cream/wine in the base of the tin. Do the same with the parsley and the breadcrumbs with which you must be a little more heavy handed. Sprinkle the entire surface area lightly with the pepper and then dot minute flakes of butter over the brimming shells. Cover with foil and place in the oven at Gas Mark 4 one shelf above centre. Twenty minutes later, take them out, put each half lobster serving into a good (in this context) old-fashioned soup plate and divide the pan mixture equally so that each portion in its shell sits in a delicious little pond. Serve plenty of French bread.

Accompany this dish with a bottle of Montrachet or a Pouilly-Fumé and only go into a silent seethe of fury *if everyone does not take a piece of crust to sop up the last vestige of self-made sauce from their plates.* When we had finished with the two huge half lobster servings given to us by Mélanie's great friend Mado Poncellet, to whom she entrusted her recipe before she died, Madame bustled towards us, paused for an instant, patted us approvingly on the shoulders and commented, *"Très bien mangées, mes enfants."*

· Fish Fumet ·

Now let us talk for a moment about that essential basic, *fish fumet*, which Escoffier defines as a kind of essence extracted from fish, etc. The extraction is done by simmering fish, fish trimmings and all the shells and claws of shellfish as for a basic fish stock†. Give it about 45 minutes to a maximum hour of gentle simmering, then strain it and simmer again until—you must be sick of the phrase by now—what was a lot of very lightly flavoured fluid becomes a very small quantity of very strongly flavoured fluid which is sticky on the lips.

· Filets de Sole a la Crème ·

Try one very simple exercise with 6 medium fillets of sole which have been skinned completely. Butter a shallow heat-resistant dish, lay in the 6 fillets, sprinkle them lightly with salt and pepper, swill them with enough dry white cooking wine to half-cover them and put a piece of kitchen foil overall so that they will half-steam, half-poach on the middle shelf of your oven at Gas Mark 4 for about 8–10 minutes—no more. Drain the liquor away, lay the fish on their serving dish and slip them back in the oven low down at lowest setting, with the same piece of foil over them so that they do not dry out this time. Strain the buttery sole-flavoured wine into a small pan. Add a dessertspoonful of fish *fumet*. Boil up. Add about 3 fl. ozs. double cream. Bubble this fiercely until it reduces sufficiently to thicken. Pour lovingly over the fish and pipe a delicate border of Duchess potato* as a small wall around the edge and you have in less than half-an-hour a beautiful dish of *Filets de Sole à la crème*.

· Filets de Sole Forestière ·

Develop the theme a little. Remove the stalks from ¼ lb. mushrooms, slice without skinning and toss into the strained simmering wine liquor with the *fumet*. Add the cream and do your reduction. Take a wooden spoon, scoop up enough of the mushrooms to make a little mound down each of the fillets, then finish as already explained and you have got yourself a dish of *Filets de Sole Forestière*.

· Sole Véronique ·

Now this time do exactly the same thing but omit the cream altogether. Just simmer the *fumet* and wine fluid together gently and when it has reached the syrupy stage run 1½ ozs. of good softened butter through your fingers on to the sauce. Pour over the sole on the serving dish which must be a heat-resistant one. Make sure that at this point you have ready a small teacupful of peeled, preferably but not arbitrarily, Muscatel grapes. When the top is glazed to a nice golden brown under a gentle grill, either arrange the grapes in a little pile in the centre or put small piles

strategically between the sole fillets. Serve at once and this time
you have got yourselves *Sole Véronique*.

· Filets de Sole Hollandaise ·

Once again follow the same formula to the point where you
have strained off the fish-flavoured wine liquor. Add the *fumet*
as before with 5 fl. ozs. of double cream and 2 ozs. skinned tomato
flesh which has been rubbed through a sieve and is devoid of pips.
Let this mixture simmer until it is very thick indeed and then
removing from the heat, beat in 1 heaped tablespoon of lukewarm
Hollandaise† but on no account re-heat or it will curdle. Pour
this quickly over the fish, surround the edge with little crescents
of baked puff paste and eat at once. It is Lucullan and is called
quite simply *Filets de Sole Hollandaise*.

Go on and do exactly the same thing from the very beginning
through all these suggestions using skinned fillets of turbot
instead of sole, change the word "sole" to "turbot" each time and
you have all you need for your menu. You will just need to allow
about 1–1½ minutes more in the oven to balance the slightly
thicker fillets that you will be working with on these occasions.

· Filets de Sole ou Turbot Hongroise ·

One of the most rewarding of classic dishes is *Filets de Sole ou
Turbot Hongroise*, and it belongs right here because, again, it calls
for some *fumet*. Put 1 oz. of butter into a small pan, add a small
tablespoonful of very finely chopped shallot or *faute de mieux*
onion and a flat coffeespoon of paprika powder. Cook very slowly
so that the onion becomes tender but completely uncoloured.
Then add 3 tablespoonsful of a light dry white wine and 3½ fl. ozs.
of fish *fumet*. Set it over a thread of heat to start simmering. Take
2 tomatoes, peel, remove all pips, chop coarsely and add to the
pan mixture. Butter a heat-resistant dish. Fold over 6 smallish
skinned fillets so that tapering and blunt ends meet. Arrange in a
circle on the dish, go on simmering the liquor until it is really too
thick and then thin it back to a good coating consistency with
very lightly whipped cream. Heavily whipped cream coarsens a
sauce of this kind and should be avoided like the plague. Finish
the sauce with a drop at a time of lemon juice using a total of 1
teaspoonful. Taste, correct seasoning with salt and pepper, coat
the fillets: you have a dish of which you never need be ashamed.

The only thing we have found when sharing these recipes with friends is that almost everyone tends at first to be afraid of the strong reduction. They will stop short so that the sauce is not a sauce but a pond, so be bold and resolute. Remember that it is far better to have just sufficient sauce of the right consistency than a lot of pond fluid. Frankly, as we say to the kids when we are teaching them, not only is sauce-making the greatest and most subtle of all the culinary arts but reduction or *la réduction* is the key to all the most perfect hot compound sauces.

· Paupiettes de Turbot ·

Now we come to *Paupiettes de Turbot, Sauce Champagne*. This is one of the most delicate and exciting cold buffet luncheon or dinner items but it *must* be made carefully. *If* the turbot is over-cooked the whole thing fails; *if* the Hollandaise† is added to the cream mixture and the juices *over-heat*, it *will* separate; and *if* the *Hollandaise* is made overnight (which it can be quite easily except in heat-waves) and then *refrigerated*, it will become useless. So although the type in this book is uniform throughout and we cannot say, "Please read the small print carefully!" we do plead for all these instructions to be read carefully because the ingredients are costly, the occasion will have to be a special one and we are not anxious to receive cross letters claiming failure.

Take a large, shallow heat-resistant dish for 12 fillets, i.e. 12 people. We used one measuring 16½″ × 10″ (inside measurement) by 2″ in depth. Butter the base and sides with 2 ozs. of butter. Trim the fillets—this means cut away the little frilly edge bits lay fillet flat side downwards on your working surface and put half-a-dozen small shelled shrimps over the tail of each. Add a teaspoon of stiffly whipped double cream to each, season very lightly with salt and pepper and roll up. Repeat this with all 12 fillets. While you are doing this, cover all the turbot trimmings (which of course you have insisted on being given with your fish) and the frilly bits liberally with cold water; add 4 parsley stalks, 1 bay leaf, the thinly peeled leaf of lemon peel and 2 peppercorns. Bring to the boil, skim and simmer steadily for 30–40 minutes. Strain liquor into a clean pan, reduce by simmering to 6 fl. ozs. and chill.

· Sauce Champagne ·

Place the prepared fillets in lines of three down the prepared dish. Swill with the cold reduced stock, then with a quarter bottle of champagne. Dry white wine may be substituted, but do not forget to change the name if writing a menu. Season lightly over-all with salt and pepper, cover the top lightly with wide foil and bake one shelf above centre at Gas Mark 4 for 15 minutes and no longer! Lift out the *Paupiettes* carefully, allowing each one to drain before laying it on either an oval or a rectangular metal dish. Place the liquor in a small saucepan, cover and refrigerate over-night if pre-preparing the dish. Make the *Hollandaise* and keep at room temperature with a slightly damp tea towel over the top. Stamp out and bake 24 crescents of bought or home-made puff paste, cut these with a 3½" diameter fluted circular cutter, arrange them on a wetted baking sheet, brush the tops with raw beaten egg and bake briskly one shelf above centre at Gas mark 6 until rich golden brown. Store in an airtight container overnight. On the day of service bring ½ pt. double cream to the boil, reduce to a gentle simmer and continue cooking for 10 minutes. Add the strained liquor in which you cooked the fish and continue simmering until the cream is a light beige colour and very thick. Remove from heat, beat down for a few moments to cool it slightly and then beat in the *Hollandaise* spoonful by spoonful. Spoon it carefully over the *paupiettes*, encircle the dish with the puff pastry crescents and serve when cold.

· Truite au Vin Blanc ·

Say you have a man in the family who brings you home a creel of trout and lays them out with loving care upon the lawn. Freshly caught they are of course incomparable cooked as *Truite au bleu**, but have you ever tried giving them the cream and wine treatment—not in the oven, oh! dear, no—just in a roomy, thick iron skillet over the gas. Time and again now that we have our own trout stream, some wretch comes in with a skeinful just as we fondly imagine we have cooked the evening meal. It is a sin to keep them waiting and quite impossible when the fiend is a guest, so you pull out the pan, turn on the heat, regulate it fairly low, toss in a generous nut of butter, a couple of tablespoonsful of perfect olive oil and when these are thoroughly hot and blended lay in the fish till the pan is well filled. Count ten slowly while the skin sizzles on the underside and turn them over gently without splitting. We keep two pairs of lifting tongs expressly for this sort of job. Grab them just below the precious head which contains those two *gourmet* titbits, the pearls. Simultaneously grab just above the tail and with one quick flip of the wrists, the fish is over in one piece. Count ten again, by which time the oil and butter will have been practically absorbed, but there is a remnant of grease remaining and of course this must go. One short dollop from the cooking brandy bottle, one quick turn of the tap to bring the flame up to full and tip the rim of the pan to it so that the brandy ignites. Then just shake like mad for the 30 seconds it needs to burn out the grease with this flaming brandy. Down with the heat to moderate again, pour in about 4 fl. ozs. of dry light white wine, let that bubble up, pour in enough cream to raise the liquor level to just cover the fish, but really so that only the bubbling of the ebullition makes the covering and if you withdrew the pan from the heat, the upper sides of the fish would show again. Now simmer for just long enough to cook the trout through—another 4 minutes should do easily. Lift them out, drain them and set them on a long narrow dish. Squeeze a thread of lemon juice onto your sauce, leaving it bubbling furiously, taste it, bring out the flavour with salt and pepper and when it is thick and beige, pour it lovingly over the *Truite au Vin blanc*.

Properly speaking there are only two accompaniments which make this dish an experience—leaf-thin brown bread and butter and a bottle of thoroughly chilled Pouilly Fuissé—that confounded bread and butter is the rub. It takes too long to butter and then slice bread transparently thin even with the sharpest French knife, which is why we never cease to bless that cook's darling, our most recent acquisition, the Graef (stockists p. 291) slicer. This will sail through anything at speed, whether a sandwich loaf or a rolled boned silverside of cold salt beef.

· Truite en papillote Forestière ·

If you cannot face all that, butter some 18″ × 10″ rectangles of kitchen foil on the dull side, lay the whole cleaned trout down the centre, cover the top with finely chopped mushrooms, season with pepper, moisten with melted butter and fold up loosely but lock in the ends securely. Put on a flat baking sheet, bake for

about 15 minutes at Gas Mark 4 on the middle shelf, and that is all
you need do for *Truite en papillote Forestière*.

· Truite en gelée au Fenouil ·

For our next treasure you will need larger trout which either
you or your fishmonger must fillet very neatly indeed. Be sure that
you have two fillets for each person to be served. Begin by making
the *farce*. We allow 2 ozs. shelled shrimps per person, so for six
portions 1 lb. 12 ozs. shelled shrimps in a mortar with a pestle,
adding to them one 1″ thick crustless slice of white bread, 2
chopped hard-boiled eggs, a pinch or two of freshly milled black
peppercorns, a couple of dessertspoonsful of double cream, only
lightly whipped please, and enough dry white wine to pound into
a good thick spreading paste. Divide equally between six fillets,
pat out smoothly, cover with the remaining fillets, wrap in
buttered foil, bake at Gas Mark 4 middle shelf for a maximum
14 minutes, withdraw, unwrap and chill. Arrange them fairly
wide apart on a 2½–3″ deep earthenware or glass dish and cover
them with aspic. When set, divide with a hot wet knife and then
trim each little overcoated trout neatly. Set on 6 heart of cos
lettuce leaves and if feeling very fancy, garnish with tiny stamped
out petals of red pimento to make miniature flowers. Border each
with some of the residue aspic foamed up with a fork, scatter
minutely chopped fresh fennel very sparingly overall and send to
table as *Truite en gelée au Fenouil*.

Have you ever thought what a godsend to the cook/hostess it is
that you can make and keep transparently thin pancakes for use in
both sweet and savoury dishes? You can do the most wonderful
things with them with fish and they have the added virtue of
making a little expensive shellfish go a very long way. If serving
as a main course you need to allow 2 rolled stuffed pancakes per
head but only one as a fish *entrée*. Once again we have a constant
basic method for them and a pre-prepare one at that. Make your
chosen filling, spread it inside your pancakes, roll them up into
cylinders, lay them down a shallow buttered heat-resistant dish,
moisten—no more please—with little flicks of dry white wine,
cover with a good basic *Béchamel* sauce* by just spooning carefully overall, scatter the surface lightly with grated Parmesan,
then equally lightly with fine breadcrumbs, moisten with more
drips from the single cream bottle and refrigerate until 20

minutes before service. Then pop a sheet of foil over the top, slip into the oven Gas Mark 4, one shelf above centre, for 15 minutes, whip off the foil, slide under the grill for 1 minute, turn around to bubble the other side for 1 minute and take to table.

· Crêpes farcies aux Moules ·

You can achieve a beauty with *Crêpes farcies aux Moules.* Scrub, beard and steam the mussels as usual*. Remove them from the open shells and for, say, 30 which is enough for 6 *crêpes,* turn them into the following mixture: 2 heaped tablespoons of mayonnaise*, 2 scant tablespoons of unbeaten cream, 1 heaped tablespoon of freshly milled parsley, a generous squeeze of lemon juice and a flat teaspoon of anchovy *purée,* blended well together.

· Crêpes farcies aux Crevettes ou aux Crabes ou Villervillaise ·

Use the above mixture with ¼ pint minute whole shrimps or chopped up prawns instead of mussels and you achieve *Crêpes farcies aux Crevettes ou aux Ecrevisses* or with ¼ lb. flaked crabmeat (50 per cent brown and 50 per cent white) *Crêpes au Crabe.* One day when you are feeling lavish, be a devil and make the *Crêpes Villervillaise,* a creation of the late Monsieur Mahu who was a *Chevalier de la Courtoise* many years before Johnnie managed to win himself the same distinction. Here of course the sauce is the thing. Soft fry a small chopped shallot and a tiny crushed clove of garlic in ½ oz. of butter and a dessertspoonful of oil. Then burn out the grease with 2 generous tablespoons of cooking brandy as previously described in this chapter. Add 3 fl. ozs. of dry white wine, 3 fl. ozs. of fish *fumet,* 2 tablespoonsful of fresh tomato *purée,* a teaspoonful of chopped fresh parsley and a pinch of cayenne. Take a very small hen lobster (not more than ¾ lb.) and while this mixture is bubbling in the pan, toss in the chopped coral, work it down with the back of a wooden spoon, withdraw the pan from the heat and gradually work in 1½ ozs. softened butter. This is the point where you add the chopped flesh of your little lobster, a dozen cooked shelled mussels and a dozen whole shelled shrimps. Finally lace the sauce heavily with cream as thick and as rich as you can manage. Scoop up the mixed fish without much liquor and use it to spread over your pancakes before rolling them up. Set them on the usual buttered dish, pour the pan contents on top, cover lightly with foil and cook fast, one shelf above centre, Gas Mark 7 for about as many minutes or just until piping hot.

· Omelette aux Moules ou Crabe ou Villervillaise ·

Now use these four fillings all over again for a range of omelettes made of course *à la Mère Poularde**.

If you are serving 6 people, it is far, far better to use half your filling in each of two omelettes for 3 than to make a whacking great omelette for six. As soon as the omelette is set underneath in its pan and still wet on top, turn the heat right down, spoon out the mussels from their sauce and spread them over the omelette's wet surface. Flip over, make the second fold in turning out and swill with the remainder of the sauce. This will give you *Omelette aux Moules*. To do the job really properly, we reckon you need 14 standard eggs for 6 people. Anyway, that is what we use and never less. Follow the same routine with the crab mixture for *Omelette au Crabe* and with *fruits de mer* for *Omelette Mahu* or *Villervillaise*. This last has far more liquid than the others, so for very special occasions, turn out the other three omelettes while they are still very wet, swill them with cream, scatter them with cheese, dot them with flakes of butter, brown fast under the grill and then send to table.

· Brochettes de Crevettes flambées ·

We really cannot forsake shellfish for a little while longer. You must have our two favourite *brochette* recipes and we will start with *Brochettes de Crevettes flambées* for which you will need rice. For six people take an ordinary $9\frac{1}{4}'' \times 5\frac{1}{4}'' \times 2\frac{3}{4}''$ bun tin and oil it thoroughly. Cook $\frac{1}{2}$ lb. rice until it is *al dente* and grain separate. Strain it, turn it into a bowl and mix in very thoroughly $1\frac{1}{2}$ ozs. butter, a heaped tablespoon of milled fresh parsley and the finely grated rind of 1 very small lemon. Press down into the prepared bun tin with all your strength, put it on a flat, oval heated serving dish upside down, hold the bottom (which is now the top) firmly at each end of the dish, give it a violent shake and the rice will come out in a mould. Tent it in the extra thick foil which is now obtainable and keep warm at Gas Mark $\frac{1}{2}$, low shelf.

Allow 6 ordinary prawns on each of six skewers, or 4 of what the average fishmonger sells frozen today and euphemistically calls scampi, which we feel sure you know are not true scampi unless they are from the Adriatic! These, remember, are raw. Then impale these on your six skewers, alternating them with the de-rinded rolled up "eyes" of six No. 4 cut rashers of back bacon. Brush them with melted butter and put the skewers on a grill rack in the "low" position. Grill them slowly, brushing these raw chaps at least once more with the melted butter as the shells begin to darken so that they do not get like charcoal. Turn and repeat on the opposite side. Remove the skewer loads, put the grill pan in the "high" position, replace them, drip a little brandy from the bottle overall and return to the fierce grill so that the brandy ignites and burns its flavour in furiously in a few seconds. Lay in a row on the top of the rice mould and serve. With cooked prawns you will need to change the method a little. Prepare and soft cook your bacon pieces under the grill, then roll them up and alternate them on the skewer with the cooked prawns. Then just allow them to heat through on both sides at low, brush with melted butter, then give them the brandy treatment and all will be well.

· Brochettes de Moules ·

The *Brochettes de Moules* are also served in the same way with rice, or of course you can skip the moulding bit and put a neat, little flat-topped mound on each plate and lay the finished *brochettes* on top. If you want something lighter and more *luxe*, allow 2 skewerloads of mussels per head and 8 mussels to each skewer, steam these in the ordinary way until the shells are open, turn each mussel in melted butter, then in fine soft white bread-crumbs and skewer. Grill gently just until the crumbs are golden brown all round, omit the *flambé* altogether and serve as already explained.

· Coquilles de Fruits de Mer, de Crabe et Normande ·

There are still two more ways in which, like professional chefs, you can ring the changes on the shellfish mixtures recorded for *Crêpes aux Moules*, *au Crabe* and *Villervillaise*. Remember that the *Villervillaise* has a lot of its own sauce, as given for the *crêpes*, but the mussels and crab mixtures have their top additions of cream, etc. So when you have made up these two filling mix-tures you add *Béchamel** in small quantities until you get a floppy blending. Turn these into *coquilles* by using deep scallop shells, one per person, with a good fat border of Duchess potato* piped right around the edge of each shell. Then fill in the mixture, coat lightly with single cream, scatter lightly with Sbrinz or Parmesan and finish with a top sprinkling of soft white breadcrumbs and a few flakes of butter. These are baked in the oven just before service at Gas Mark, 5 one shelf above centre, for 10–12 minutes, or until lightly browned and bubbling on top. This is how you achieve *Coquilles de Fruits de Mer*, with the *Villervillaise* mixture, *Coquilles au Crabe* and *Coquilles Normande*, with the mussels.

· Feuilleté de Fruits de Mer, de Crabe ou de Moules ·

The last way of using them is with bought or home made puff paste. Cut a 4″ square for each in ¼″ thick rolled out puff paste. Then ½″ in from the edge drive a small pointed knife almost to the bottom and draw a smaller inner square, i.e. 3½″. Brush the tops carefully with raw beaten strained egg, making sure that the egg mixture does not come over the incised inner line. Bake at Gas Mark 7 one shelf above centre until the paste has risen steeply and turned golden brown. Take from the oven, run a small pointed knife round the inner squares to loosen them, lift them off and turn them upside down on your baking sheets beside the square cases. Remove any gooey paste from the cases, dry off for 5 minutes with the lids, on the bottom shelf Gas Mark 3. These are super for pre-preparation because you bake your cases as explained and when cooled on a rack, pack them tightly together on an ordinary baking sheet, tent them with foil and put them away in the refrigerator or alternatively you can put them into a plastic "burper" box and store them on a dry goods shelf. The day before your party, make up whichever you choose of the same old trio, crab, mussels and *fruits de mer*, as explained in our previous set of recipes for the *coquilles* and 40 minutes before they are needed—meaning you do them after you are dressed and ten minutes before your guests come in—fill the chosen mixture into the pastry cases, clap on the lids and put them in the oven middle shelf, Gas Mark 1, if you are serving them as a second fish course or Gas Mark 2 if you are serving them as "starters" exactly 30 minutes later. When writing menu cards entitle them *Feuilleté de Fruits de Mer, Feuilleté de Crabe* or *Feuilleté de Moules*.

Before we really say goodbye to shellfish let us remind you that you will find in the egg chapter a number of suggestions for making *soufflés* including those with shellfish.

· Devilled Whitebait ·

When whitebait are in season, but not when they are sold all slimy from the deep freeze, try a dish of *Devilled Whitebait*. Wash, drain and pat dry in a cloth the requisite amount of whitebait which means at a dinner a maximum of 3 ozs. per head. Mix together in a bowl 5 ozs. flour, 1 heaped dessertspoonful of curry powder, 1 rounded dessertspoonful of paprika powder, 1 rounded teaspoon of dry English mustard and 1 level dessertspoonful of salt. Pray note that this will be the only instance when we are compelled to give you curry powder instead of true Masala paste and we do it simply because this turning mixture for the little fish *must* be dry. The secret of completely separating crisp, little deep-fried whitebait is not what you could call complicated! You just turn a small handful of whitebait each time in the flour mixture, throw them into a sieve and shake off the surplus flour over the bowl. Then you scatter them over the frying basket and plunge the basket into the slightly smoking hot oil. You see they can only come out crisp and separate if they go in in this way. If you plonked your handful in together, that is how they would come out. They take 30 seconds to fry and you turn them on to kitchen paper to drain. Unless the oil is a low temperature pond, there will only be a fraction of grease anyway. Then you pile them into a pyramid on a napkin-covered salver, decorate them with fried parsley, hand pieces of lemon separately and accompany them with transparently thin slices of buttered brown bread.

One word about the lemon and we can move on. It is charming to serve lemon baskets. They look so pretty with a dab of parsley in the middle. The described presentation is considerably enhanced if you flute your lemon and then cut it into little turreted slices for halving and arranging as a continuous decorative border round the rim of the salver, but to put it bluntly, these are a damned nuisance at the table. It is so much cleaner to halve small lemons, remove the pips and drive a small silver fork into each one, so that you and your guests can squeeze the peel of the lemon, exerting a slight pressure from the fork in the other hand and so moisten the fish without moistening the hands to the wrists.

· Brandade de Morue ·

Not long ago we had a cooking session with six highly intelligent women, all of whom thought that the legendary classic *Brandade de Morue* was far too difficult for them to tackle and anyway that cod could not be the basis of a party dish. They all made it with ease and at speed; they all freely confessed they were converts to it. But of course we are never satisfied, so we want you to be converts too.

You will need 2¼ lbs. cod, 14 ozs. steamed, sieved, very dry potato, 7 fl. ozs. hot olive oil, 10½ fl. ozs. hot top-of-the-milk or single cream, salt and pepper to season, 1–2 crushed garlic cloves. Soak the cod overnight in cold water. Then cook, skin, bone and flake the fish. Emulsify with the garlic and potato. Turn into a thick pan, stand over a very low heat and very gradually—ideally using a hand electric mixer—whip in the oil first, then the milk or cream. Season to taste. Either turn the mixture into a baked, bought or home-made puff paste *croustade* and affix "lid" or heap on to *croûtons*.

· Casserolettes de Sole ·

We make no apologies for the inclusion of *Casserolettes de Sole* in this chapter. We must, however, render unto Caesar . . . ! We made these for the British Broadcasting Corporation in our 1969 series, "How to Give a Dinner Party" and the recipe was published in what we rather complacently think was the very elegant booklet which we wrote and the BBC published in support of this series. So here it is baldly stated because we think it needs no chat. The ingredients are 1 lb. savoury short paste*, 6 ozs. skinned fillet of sole, ¼ pt. milk or top-of-the-milk, 2½ fl. ozs. single or unwhipped whipping cream, 1 egg, 1 extra separated yolk, 1 oz. finely grated Parmesan or substitute very hard cheese, salt and pepper to season, 12 transparently thin "leaves" of Emmenthal, ¼ pt. (unshelled weight) brown or pink shrimps. Roll out the prepared paste fairly thinly. Line into 12 plain 4¼" diameter, ½" deep patty tins, previously lightly dusted with flour. Trim off the edges neatly. Cut the sole into matchsticks and use to cover the bases of all cases. Whip together milk, cream, egg, extra yolk, grated cheese and generous pinches of salt and pepper. Shell shrimps and arrange equally over sole matchsticks. Spoon in whipped mixture within $\frac{1}{8}$" of pastry rims. Lay a leaf of cheese on top of each. Set all on a metal baking sheet and bake at Gas Mark 6, one shelf above centre, for 5 minutes. Reduce heat to Gas Mark 2 and bake for approximately 20 minutes or until pastry is browned at edges and mixture browned and domed centrally. Remove carefully to chosen serving dish.

· Rissoles ·

Now we do need some chat because we want to answer the somewhat startling rhetorical question: *what about rissoles?* This term has been so degraded by English cooks that it gives people the shudders, yet properly made rissoles can be made fit for any dinner party. We are quite happy to confess that for one of our own very special dinners entitled Tovarich for reasons which we explained in our first memoirs *Something's Burning,* rissoles were very amiably received. The nasty connotation implied by the name "fishcakes" stems from the wrong ingredients being used. There is no potato, reconstituted instant or grown in the soil. There is no incidence of crumbled bread being used to eke out decrepit old left-overs of cooked fish.

It all begins with a very thick *velouté* sauce* and it brings us back with fish *fumet* (please turn back to p. 98). Put 2 ozs. of sifted flour on to $1\frac{1}{2}$ ozs. melted butter in a small pan, work to a very stiff paste and then work in 2 dessertspoonsful of fish fumet. When this has been beaten thoroughly, add $\frac{1}{4}$ pt. of dry white cooking wine in small additions, beating well between each one. Add 8 ozs. of flaked salmon, white crabmeat or mixed white and brown, or roughly pounded hen lobster flesh with the coral, or shelled shrimps or prawns. When you have worked this in, you will find it extremely difficult to get it blended because it is so stiff. Therefore, still working over a very moderate heat, bring down the mixture with mean, gradual additions of top-of-the-milk or single cream until it will fall off your wooden spoon when this is lifted up and shaken. Add a teaspoonful of lemon juice, taste and correct the seasoning with plenty of pepper and only a fraction of salt, if any. Remove from the heat and as fast as possible, beat in 2 raw separated egg yolks. Turn on to an oiled surface, ideally a bit of marble, spread out with a metal spatula until smooth on top and about $\frac{1}{2}$" thick. Chill very thoroughly indeed by either refrigerating or if you think your refrigerator is

not cold enough, by slipping into the freezer for just long enough
for the mixture to become firm enough for you to stamp it out
into plain rounds (for ordinary service) or for special occasions
stamp with a cutlet-shaped cutter. Always remember to dip the
cutter each time you use it into a little dish of boiling water. Pass
the chosen shapes through raw beaten egg, coat thickly with fine
soft breadcrumbs and re-refrigerate until the moment of frying.
Then heat equal quantities of oil and butter together in a shallow
pan over a fairly strong heat. Then put in the fishcakes and fry
them briskly to a good golden brown. Drain on kitchen paper and
arrange on a shallow dish.

When we did our lobster ones for the Tovarich dinner we used
the cutlet cutter so that when they were fried and drained, we were
able to arrange them in line astern down a long narrow dish with
a little cutlet frill on the tapering end of each. They are good
enough to serve on their own or they will take—if they have been
properly fried—a little clarified butter well laced with fresh,
scissored chives and milled fresh parsley heads in equal proportions; or you can recourse to that most beautiful fish sauce *à
l'estragon** which you hand separately in a sauceboat like the butter.
Clarification scarcely needs any! You just melt the butter over
sufficient heat to make it seethe as it dissolves and then with
care and patience skim off all the frothy foam till the clear shiny
butter liquid is completely exposed underneath. Just remember
if you are re-heating this to do it over a little hot water. Real fishcakes do not like black butter and once clarified, it burns in a
trice.

Gigot d'Agneau farci en croûte · Guard of Honour
Noisettes d'Agneau en Couronne
Carré de Porc aux Marrons · Carré d'Agneau aux Marrons
Carré d'Agneau, ou de Porc, à la Soubise
Filets de Porc, ou Boeuf, aux Champignons à la crème
Filet de Boeuf aux Cèpes · Filet Casanova
Tournedos Tivoli · Tournedos Clamart · Tournedos Roumanille
Sauté de Veau Marengo (1) · Sauté de Veau Marengo (2)
Rouleau de Veau · Paupiettes de Veau · Sauce Espagnole
Paupiettes de Veau à l'Italienne
Escalopes de Veau en papillote Dvořák
Escalopes de Veau en papillote Ardennoise
Escalopes de Veau en papillote au Vermouth
Jambon au four Brillat Savarin
Langue Oporto · Cold Tongue with Piquant Sauce

The day meat rationing ended our distinguished Fleet Street colleague Miss Sheila Hutchins had a marvellous English Experience which she subsequently shared with us. She was then writing for the now defunct "News Chronicle". Her Editor requested her to celebrate the end of meat rationing with a special article so she settled to her typewriter, typed the title, "Meat For Carnivores" and in due course completed her piece. During the war and immediately afterwards, the cry of "boy" was replaced with the feminine gender and the girl to whom Sheila gave her copy instructing her to get it set up as quickly as possible and bring back the "pull", was absent for an unconscionable time.

Sheila became irritated. She went in search of the girl and ran her to earth doubled up with laughter leaning against the wall of a corridor and holding the pull. "Where have you been?" Sheila demanded wrathfully. "I'm ever so sorry, Miss Hutchins," said the child between giggles, "but I've been reading it, it's ever so funny." "And what," Sheila asked icily, "is funny about Meat for Carnivores?" "Well," said the girl, "you see my mum won't let my dad have meat. She says it brings out the beast in him."

There is a moral to this little tale. The women of Britain are cooking better and better every year. They are only hampered now that shortages, except financial ones, are ended by the mulish attitude of Englishmen, who still dig their toes in over "fancy messed-up dishes" and clamour for good, plain, wholesome dishes like Mother made. They overlook the plain fact that the only possible solution for the appalling present cost of meat is to spend time in the kitchen either in the very slow and painstaking cooking which all cheap meat requires or by "fancying up" the costly cuts to make them go further.

As for the sexual implication in our story, well, we have long awaited an opportunity of publicising our considered opinions on this subject. We have both got foreign blood; therefore in a

sense we can look at the English, in part anyway, from the side-
lines and we honestly believe that there is nothing wrong with the
very high percentage of frigids in this country which a little
knowledge of food and wine would not cure.

Think for a moment in an entirely different context. Assume
that for some reason or other you wish to be in a very spiritual
and aesthetic frame of mind. Try to achieve this after putting
down a "trad" Sunday "dinner" of mulligatawny soup, roast beef,
lashings of Yorkshire pudding and masses of oven-roast potatoes, washed down with beer, followed by a steamed treacle
pudding served with lashings of Devonshire cream, and with a
nice strong cup of tea afterwards. Comatose is what you will be
after that lot!

Now consider either a Charentais melon *nature* or *Assiette de
Fruits de Mer* with lemon, very thin brown bread and butter and a
glass of well chilled Chablis, followed by a small veal *escalope
nature* or a portion of *Rognons de Veau flambe's* piled onto a bread
croûton passed through egg and milk and fried. Marry this with a
glass of Burgundy, a mouthful of Stilton or peach and you will
feel as if you could take off. Of course, if your inclination should
be romantic rather than spiritual, drink your cup of strong black
coffee with a liqueur glass of mixed brandy and Curaçao.

As a great many people dislike innards, although others, like
ourselves, prefer them to hunks of meat, we have separated the
two and in this chapter will deal exclusively with what one of
our children inelegantly summarises as "flesh, not guts".

Lamb can be cook's darling whereas Fanny's father maintained
cold mutton is grounds for divorce; but to get the best end
product, the lamb from which the cut is taken must be both young
and small. Like women in trousers the dimensions must be
restricted, so let us assume you have a dear little prime leg of lamb,
and consider how best you may treat it when you are entertaining.

· Gigot d'Agneau farci en croûte ·

On p. 127-8 we deal with the vexed question of boning
and stuffing, so let us just assume now that you (or your butcher)
have boned out the leg and pick up the culinary threads when
this phase has been completed. Take a little rindless No. 3 cut
rashers of back bacon and roll them over skinned, halved, raw
lambs' kidneys. Slip as many inside as you can persuade to stay

there without popping out. Sew up the lamb and par-roast it one shelf above centre at Gas Mark 6 until, when you prod the flesh with a skewer, the bubble of juice pops out looking a very bright pink. Chill completely. Remove the tying threads. Roll out bought or home-made puff paste very thinly and spread the upperside with *pâté* or *pâté de foie gras* to the thickness of liberally buttered bread. Place the par-cooked meat in the centre. Then have a little rehearsal by drawing up the paste experimentally to discover just how much you will need to overlap a good inch *without stretching the paste at all.* This is where you need to exert care, for if you do stretch the paste, it will inevitably split during the contractions which will occur during baking. If you secure it loosely it will not split. Rehearse the amount of paste you will need to enclose the meat completely and trim off the surplus paste. Then wrap up the meat in the paste and turn over on its baking sheet so that the joins are underneath. Prepare an *Anglais**. Refrigerate this and the *Gigot d'Agneau farci en croûte* until just before dining. Then brush the paste all over with the *Anglais* and put directly into a pre-heated oven at Gas Mark 6 one shelf above centre. Thirty minutes later it will be a rich, golden brown and ready to slice up as easily as a cake.

· Guard of Honour ·

Say you want to use best end necks and like us consider a Crown Roast—a very good visual but a brute to carve speedily. Forget the Crown Roast and substitute the far easier to make and carve version known as a *Guard of Honour*. Working on the basis of from 7 to a maximum 9 bones to each best end neck, estimate your required number *in pairs*, because unlike a Crown Roast which can be made with two, three or more best end necks, a Guard of Honour can only be made with two, four or six if your oven could contain such a vast one. We will assume two are sufficient. They must both have the same number of cutlet bones. They must first be skinned and chined—the butcher can always do that. Then you will cut away all the bits of skin and flesh *between* the bones by cutting down from bone tip to a minimum depth of $2\frac{1}{2}''$. Turn the knife point at base, cut across parallel with the base of the joint, and cut up the other side. Then scrape off any little scraps which might be left so that bones stand away cleanly.

Now stand the pair of best end necks on your working surface face to face with the fatty sides outwards, pointed bone tips uppermost and gradually push the two pieces as near to each other as possible and so that each trimmed bone slips between its opposite number. Check if this sounds obscure. Put your elbows on the table. Then lock your extended fingers so that the first finger of the right hand is nearest to you and pointing left which the first finger of the left hand crosses, pointing right on the far side of the right hand finger, and so on down the line. Like this your fingers will be forming a "Guard of Honour", won't they? So now do the same with the meat bones. Cover the bone tips lightly with a piece of kitchen foil to stop them blackening in the oven and bake at Gas Mark, 5 centre shelf, for a deliberately unspecified time because only you can determine at what stage the meat will be cooked sufficiently for your tastes: blue or *à la Française*, pink or *à point* or beige thoughout, dry and ruined. Lift the Guard onto a serving dish. Press a cutlet frill over the tip of each bone and tuck well washed, picked, seasoned sprigs of fresh watercress in at each end.

· Noisettes d'Agneau en Couronne ·

We have just come up with a new dish which we gave at a reunion dinner in this house to the members of our Daily Telegraph Kitchen Committee—*Noisettes d'Agneau en Couronne*. By the only means we have ever employed to learn anything—doing it experimentally—we found that it is very easy to pare away the eye meat from best end necks in a long continuous strip. By slicing each one up into 1¼″ lengths we obtained a number of minute *tournedos* shapes which are known technically as *noisettes*. We allowed 3 per person. We marinaded 30 of them overnight in a bottle of white Beaujolais, so little known and so good, with 4 sprigs of thyme, 4 green peppercorns, a chopped heart of celery and a dozen de-stemmed, roughly torn sorrel leaves (we suppose you could use young spinach instead). We stamped out ten 5″ diameter circles of bread from slices cut across the base of a large cottage loaf and stamped these into ½″ rings by using a round 4½″ diameter cutter to remove the centres. In due course these were passed through raw beaten egg and milk mixture and slipped quickly into slightly smoking hot oil to turn rich golden brown. We then piled them into kitchen foil, bunched this up lightly and let them wait our pleasure on the floor of the oven at very low heat.

Into a pan lightly skimmed with hot butter and oil went the 30 baby bits of lamb to be sealed fast, turned over and sealed similarly on the underside before turning up the heat to fullest to flambé. We only used 3 fl. ozs. of Armagnac for this large quantity and went through the procedure exactly as explained*. Once the flames had subsided, in went the marinade mixture which was allowed to simmer gently until the *noisettes* were very bright pink inside. This is not because we like them so, but because the dish has to wait a little and you have to allow for it. We then took the *noisettes* out and kept them warm with the little rings or crowns of bread on the floor of the oven. Into the pan liquor went ½ pt. of double cream which was left to its own devices to bubble, bubble away over a pretty fierce flame until it was unctuously thick and creamy. This is when we tasted and corrected the seasoning for there was only one more thing to add—30 little round balls of skinless cucumber cut with an ordinary round Parisian cutter. These were merely dropped in, given just long enough to heat through and then out went the light. Out came the cucumber balls to join the *noisettes* and we strained the sauce into a heat-resistant bowl and consigned that to the oven as well. For service a "crown" *croûton* was laid on each heated plate, 3 little *noisettes* popped into the centre, 3 little balls of cucumber piled on top and the sauce poured overall. We served absolutely nothing with this main course dish.

One of the things the Cook-Hostess will do well to remember when tackling main-course dishes is that a number of recipes can be adapted to suit different meats. For example, *Carré de Porc à la Soubise* can become a *Carré d'Agneau à la Soubise* by merely switching the meat in exactly the same way as *Sauté de Veau Marengo* can become *Sauté de Porc Marengo*. Similarly, *Côtelettes de veau braisées* can become *Côtelettes d'Agneau braisées*, or *Côte de Veau aux Artichauts* be mix-switched for *Côte de Porc aux Artichauts*. Thus, as one dish is mastered, two become immediately available, constituting the easiest possible way for a home cook to widen her repertoire.

None of these examples are beyond the scope of any careful cook and none call for any spectacular *tour de main* or for the kind of culinary skill which requires much practice.

Carré, as you doubtless know, is the French name for a best end neck—one of the less expensive cuts which becomes progressively cheaper according to how much of the actual butchery you can do for yourself. Unless you are very practised, get the butcher to chine your best end necks for you. If you fail to have this done or to do it yourself, you will have a fine old wrestling match when you start carving; for the chine bone is the one which runs the length of the piece holding the eyes of the continuous line of cutlets together. Divested of this bone the cutlets are easily detached without empurpled struggles.

· Carré de Porc aux Marrons ·

For *Carré de Porc aux Marrons* peel off the skin from the fatty upper part of each best end neck and then trim away some of the surplus fat so that you only leave about a generous ⅛″. Place in a thick frying pan which has been well-heated over a low flame. Impact the fatty side on the hot iron and let it sizzle for 3 or 4 minutes until a little of the fat runs freely. Set it in a meat baking tin, swill it with about half a tumbler full of stock and the same of a cooking type red wine, such as a Rioja "claret". Roast at Gas Mark 4, middle shelf, fatty side uppermost until really well cooked because under-cooked pork is an abomination. Lift the joint onto its heated serving dish. Pour off the pan juices into a very small saucepan, lift off the grease with a few scraps of kitchen paper and reduce the remaining liquor to a mere tablespoonful. Use a small tin of *unsweetened* chestnut *purée* (stockists p. 292) to every neck of 7 to 9 bones and make sure that it is *unsweetened*, as both are imported from France. Empty the contents into a bowl. Add the reduced pan juice, 2 tablespoonsful dry Madeira and 2 tablespoonsful of double cream. Beat well together and stir over a brisk heat in a small thick pan until just below boiling point. Now add ground almonds spoonful by spoonful and continue simmering and stirring until there is a sufficiency of almonds in the mixture to make it of a firm piping consistency. Place in a nylon icing bag with a No. 7 crown pipe affixed and pipe into a decorative border all round the pork *inside* the rim of the dish. Pipe an extra border of Duchess potato* around the outer rim which you have left clear and slip into the oven at Gas Mark ¼ to await service.

We have already reminded you that a *carré* of lamb may be used in the same manner, but remember that it will want far less cooking time even at Gas Mark 5 which is what it needs, as lamb is not worth eating unless the flesh is still faintly pink. Incidentally, if your hands protest at manipulating a nylon icing bag filled with piping hot chestnut or any other *purée* you can avoid martyrdom by wrapping the filled bag in a folded cloth.

· Carré d'Agneau ou de Porc à la Soubise ·

An excellent dish, *Carré d'Agneau à la Soubise*, can be achieved with the same cut. We have given you the *Soubise* in the Cook's Book and we have explained how you roast the lamb in the preceding paragraph, so it is only the finishing touches that we need tie up together now. After roasting the meat and before adding the cream to the *Soubise* sauce, add the spoonful of reduced fat-free liquor. Then put in the cream. Surround the lamb with this sauce and border with little crescents of baked puff paste or little triangles of bread dipped in egg and milk and deep-fried to a rich golden brown. As we have now established, you can go on and do the same thing with a best end neck of pork for *Carré de Porc à la Soubise*.

· Filets de Porc, ou Boeuf aux Champignons à la crème ·

The same double act can be performed with fillet of pork or beef. So as not to muddle you, let us start off with the *Filets de Porc aux Champignons à la crème*. These are small, generally, about 1½″ in thickness and 7–9″ in tapering length. Begin by slicing up the fillets in about ⅓″ thick slices with your knife held at an angle so that the cuts slope as they do when you cut up a loaf of French bread. If the fillets are 9″ long × 1½″ diameter, you will only need 3 for four persons, or 6 for eight. If they are nearer to 7″, you should allow one per person.

Dissolve 1½ ozs. butter and 1½ fl. ozs. oil in a thick shallow pan. When both are piping hot, add the pork and turn briskly over a strong heat until the meat is sealed or "stiffened". Add 6 ozs. of fairly thickly sliced, unpeeled mushrooms. Give them a couple of brisk turns in the pan with the meat. Step up the heat to fullest, tip the pan to the flame, pour on 1½ fl. ozs. brandy and when it ignites, keep shaking the pan vigorously to encourage flames. Thus they will burn out the grease and burn in the flavour of the alcohol.

Reduce the heat to low/medium. Add a tumblerful of dry white wine and 2 fl. ozs. of good strong white meat stock. Simmer gently until the meat is tender. Remove the meat, add ¼ pt. of thick cream to the pan residue and step up the heat so that the mixture bubbles strongly. Taste, correct seasoning, let it simmer until it reaches a good sauce consistency, return the meat to the pan, blend it in well and stop cooking. Turn pan contents on to a large shallow dish and inside a border of grain separate freshly cooked rice, scatter parsley overall and if you like the idea, serve with cut lemon. Otherwise omit. Follow this recipe through absolutely faithfully using 1½ lbs. of fillet steak cut into chip-size pieces to achieve *Filet de Boeuf aux Champignons à la crème*.

· Filet de Boeuf aux Cèpes ·

There is, however, an extremely good alternative in *Filet de Boeuf aux Cèpes*. The original dish was made with a whole fillet, but there is a very agreeable modest alternative made with individual fillet steaks—at least it is agreeable if you have small, very thick fillets and rather like blotting paper if you have large thin ones. Prepare everything in advance except the frying of the *croûtons* and the grilling of the steaks. These can be left sitting on the grill rack and we know that you will not put them under your grill until it has been lit for at least 5 minutes and is viciously hot.

The incidence of fresh *cèpes* is so rare in this country that we are expecting you to use tinned ones (stockists p. 291), so empty the contents of a ¼ kilo tin into a strainer and wash them thoroughly under running cold water. Skim the bottom of a thick frying pan fairly generously with oil and add to it a sprig of thyme, a crushed garlic clove, and the *cèpes* cut into neat, convenient pieces if over-large. Set over moderate heat, shake the *cèpes* in the pan so that they are thoroughly coated in the oil, reduce the heat drastically, cover the pan and allow the *cèpes* to cook very slowly indeed until a scrap fished out and nibbled thoughtfully, is *really tender* to your palate. By this time the oil should have become almost completely absorbed by the fungi. Step up the heat and *sauté* them vigorously for about 5 minutes. Drain them, season with salt and pepper, scatter liberally with milled, fresh parsley and keep warm while you grill those steaks.

Remember to check on whether your guests want their steaks

rare, medium or ruined, which is always the synonym for "well-done". Grill close on each side for 1 minute to seal. Then lower the pan or the rack in the pan and allow 3 more minutes on each side for *rare*, 4 minutes for *medium* and 5 minutes or anything over it for "ruined".

While the steaks are slow-finishing, pass your *croûtons* through egg and milk, deep fry, drain and set on a serving dish. Place each steak on a *croûton*, heap liberally with the *sautéed cèpes*, surround with any surplus, place a bunch of well-washed and carefully picked watercress at each end, and remember to season this with salt and pepper and take to table. Footnote: Should you have any difficulty in obtaining this size tin, settle for dried *cèpes*. Soak them overnight and remember to use only a fifth to a quarter of the amount you would of tinned *cèpes*, as their weight multiplies in this ratio after soaking.

· Filet Casanova ·

Another excellent sturdy dish with fillet steak is *Filet Casanova*. Take 6 small thick fillets, 1½ fl. ozs. oil, 1½ ozs. butter, 4 fl. ozs. brandy, 4 fl. ozs. Marsala, salt, milled black pepper and 4 ozs. of the best *pâté* you can afford, right up to and including *pâté de foie gras truffé*. Rub the steaks with salt and with black pepper. Then turn them in a shallow container with the oil, leave them for 2 hours. Grill the steaks fiercely on each side for 1 minute to seal them and let them wait while you dissolve the butter in a thick, large, shallow pan. Add your *pâté* and let it simmer gently while working it a little with a wooden spoon. When it becomes a thick *purée*, work in the Marsala, simmer for about 1 to 1½ minutes, slide in the sealed steaks and allow them to cook for 2½ minutes on each side. Leave them in the pan, step up the heat underneath to fullest, pour in the brandy, tip the pan to ignite it and shake away vigorously to keep the flame burning for ideally 1 minute. Lift them out, arrange them on a warmed dish, pour the sauce overall and serve at speed. Either of these two steak dishes should satisfy an Englishman's passion for this particular cut of beef.

· Tournedos Tivoli ·

Far more suited to dinner parties are *tournedos*. A good butcher will cut them for you. They are simply the eyes of fillet of beef, cut up into 1½" deep pieces. Each piece is then wrapped around the sides with a very thin strip of raw unsalted pork fat. For the one we want to start with, *Tournedos Tivoli*, you will need one small grilled mushroom per *tournedos* and one half tomato, skinned and de-pipped, brushed with melted butter and grilled gently for a moment or two. You will also need a little round *croûton* of the same diameter as the *tournedos* and a batch of *Sauce Béarnaise** to hand separately. Then just prior to service and having kept the mushrooms and tomatoes warm and having the *tournedos* sitting beside a pan skimmed with a little butter and oil, heat these two through and butter-fry the *tournedos* on both sides until just pink in the middle. Then cut the strings, dispose of the pork fat, set each *tournedos* on its *croûton*, each half tomato, cup uppermost, on the top and tuck a mushroom inside of these. This is a plain and simple presentation which is not over rich.

· Tournedos Clamart ·

The same may be said of *Tournedos Clamart*, for which you do precisely as we have already explained. Put the prepared cooked *tournedos* on its *croûton*, then put a pre-prepared artichoke bottom filled with *petits pois* on top of the *tournedos* and just moisten it with a few drops of the remaining oil and butter in which the *tournedos* were fried.

· Tournedos Roumanille ·

The procedure for the *tournedos* is constant in *Tournedos Roumanille* but you must cut them a little smaller this time, season them and when they have been fried in the butter and oil, set each one on a grilled half of a medium firm tomato and arrange in a circle on your dish. Coat the *tournedos* with liberal spoonsful of *Sauce Mornay* (p. 66), flick the surface of the sauce with a few drops of melted butter, slip under the grill to glaze very fast indeed and on removing them, put a large stuffed olive on the top centre of each *tournedos* and encircle it with a little ring made from half a lengthwise-cut anchovy fillet. Into the centre of the dish pile crisp slices of *Beignets d'Aubergines** and be very careful to give these last a little seasoning of salt and pepper before sending to table. This is one of Escoffier's and although you may blink a little at the mixture of ingredients, we can assure you that the master was incapable of creating anything horrid!

It is a funny quirk maybe, but when we are talking to you like this, we get dried up if we go on too long on any one theme. Suddenly, the taste buds of our minds are sick of steak so let us rest beef altogether for a while and tackle some veal recipes instead.

· Sauté de Veau Marengo (1) ·

This is above all other meats the easiest, as well as the most popular, "party" meat. It is also the most expensive so let us embark cautiously with *Sauté de Veau Marengo*. This is so beautifully written by Escoffier that we give you the straight translation. He says: "Heat 1 pt. of oil in a *sauté* pan until it smokes. Put therein 2 lbs. of veal shoulder cut into 2 oz. pieces and fry briskly until well set. Drain away the oil tilting the *sauté* pan with its lid on for the purpose. Add a chopped half onion and a crushed half clove of garlic. Shake, fry and turn. Then moisten with ¼ pt. of white wine. Reduce (by simmering) to 2½ fl. ozs. and then add a quart of thin *Espagnole* Sauce, 1½ lbs. tomatoes (de-seeded and rough cut) and a faggot of herbs. When boiling place in oven, and cook gently for 1½ hours." Escoffier did not disclose what approximate temperature he used with his coal oven but with all respects to him we use one shelf below centre at Gas Mark 3. Then transfer the veal pieces one by one, not as he did to another saucepan but into a heatproof dish in which it can be presented. Add 15 small cooked onions and 5 ozs. raw unskinned mushrooms. Reduce the sauce to half quantity, strain over the veal, add 1 rounded teaspoon finely chopped parsley and return to the oven Gas Mark 4, middle shelf, for 15 minutes. Then serve surrounded "with small heart-shaped *croûtons* of bread crumb fried in oil."

There are endless variations on this *Sauté de Veau* with inexpensive breast or shoulder and if made with care, the flesh is always tender and delicate and quite good enough to serve on a simple occasion. Of course you can do a far more *recherché* version. Escoffier scorned it, he refused to have any *truc* with the legends from the battle of Marengo so you will become astigmatised looking in his work for any reference to *crevettes*.

· Sauté de Veau Marengo (2) ·

M. Raymond Oliver of the Grand Véfour in Paris is clearly less of a purist but his recipe for *Sauté de Veau Marengo* (2) is interesting enough to merit being brought to your attention. He asks you to heat 5 soupspoonsful of olive oil in a *cocotte*, throw in a clove of garlic, a generous pinch of salt, pepper and/or cayenne, and about 2 lbs. of breast of veal cut in "pieces". Stick to Escoffier's 2". He sticks to the sealing method in the seasoned oil and says when the veal is seasoned, you dust lightly with flour and make a form of rough *roux*, but his pinch of flour would not do much for anything, so use a flat dessertspoonful. Shake it over the meat pieces, turn well to work it about a bit to blend in the flour and then add ½ pt. of dry white wine, the *bouquet garni**, 2 shallots, 10 little onions (make it 12 shallots!) and 4 "beautiful" tomatoes (it will probably help you more if we interpret that as 4 large tomatoes which you treat as Escoffier instructed). Then stay with M. Oliver for his instructions to cover the *cocotte* and allow to cook over a gentle heat until the meat is becoming tender. Then throw in 6 ozs. peeled French olives and remove the *bouquet garni*. Cook 3 eggs in a little butter in a shallow pan and in a third pan cook 12 freshwater crayfish. Turn the contents of the *cocotte* onto a hot plate, border with the crayfish and the fried eggs and serve piping hot.

This is so similar in treatment to the famous chicken dish, *Poulet Marengo*, that it is really nothing more than a variation on the original theme. The story runs that this was created for Napoleon the night before the Battle of Marengo.

· Sauté de Veau aux Aubergines ·

You can also use a shoulder of veal for a variant which is classically known as *Sauté de Veau aux Aubergines*. Cut the meat from a very small shoulder into the usual 2" pieces but this time *sauté* them in a thick frying pan with about 2 ozs. each of butter and oil. As soon as the meat begins to stiffen on the second side, toss in 5 ozs. of finely chopped onion and reduce the heat so that all cooks gently for 5 minutes. Toss a dessertspoonful of flour over the top, turn and work it in and then add 8 fl. ozs. of dry white wine. Continue simmering while you put in 2 crushed garlic cloves, 9 ozs. of skinned, de-pipped rough-cut tomato flesh and the rough-cut flesh of 2 lbs. peeled egg plant. When all is tender, pile onto a heated dish and surround by—ideally—heart-shaped bread *croûtons*. Season lightly with salt and pepper and sprinkle overall with finely chopped parsley.

We are great ones for making life easy for ourselves in the dining-room. Empurpled strugglings with a carving knife are definitely not for us and so we long ago determined to uncover the mysteries of boning—a word which seems to strike terror in the hearts of home cooks.

Only two days ago we experimented with a young student who had never done a scrap of boning in his life. We showed him a boned leg of lamb, in order that he could handle the bone and study its contours. Then we made him replace the bone inside the sad sack of untied meat from which it had been removed. Then we gave him an unboned leg and left him to his own devices, aided only by a smallish, very sharp classic French knife—the kind we use for every scrap of cutting in the kitchen. He was comparatively slow—his first one took him nearly fifteen minutes, but he had no difficulty whatsoever. Indeed his comment was, "I wouldn't have believed it was so easy."

Once either a piece of meat or a bird *is* boned, a child can sew up one end, push in the chosen stuffing and sew up the other end. Anyone who can tie a neat parcel can tie up boned, stuffed items in whatever shape they require. Please have a go. Remember that if at first you find little scraps of flesh remain clinging to the removed bone, you can always scrape these off afterwards and stuff them back inside. No one will ever know and nothing will be wasted!

We timed ourselves at one of our regular Saturday luncheon buffets last week. We were carving two boned, stuffed cold ducks. All we had to do was cut slices—like chopping up a Swiss roll— and it took us exactly 4 minutes to cut each bird into 12 portions. Isn't that worth a little boning?

If, at your first attempt, you find yourself starting off quite cheerfully and then get utterly fogged when you are probing about in the middle, pause—and *think of rolling back a stocking top*. Treat the boned flesh in exactly the same way. Roll back as you work. It will look an unholy mess by the time you reach the opposite end. Don't give it a thought! Just remove the bone, congratulate yourself, unroll that flesh "stocking-top" and you will be able to admire your own handiwork with justifiable complacency. Then buy shoulders or legs of veal when you are feeding fairly large numbers. Bone them and transform them into dishes of far greater elegance than mouldy old shoulders which always signify being slightly hard up and "managing" to us.

· Rouleau de Veau ·

Start off with a *Rouleau de Veau* which, incidentally, can be served either hot or cold and looks most appetising as a fat slice with all the filling neatly tucked into the middle. We always try to use nuts in these stuffings and choose from the general range at our disposal: beech nuts, walnuts, brazil nuts or—the most perfect of all—pistachio nuts (which you encounter in the very best *mortadellas* as you will know very well). Going back in reverse order of *luxe* and quality our stuffings begin (once or twice in a lifetime) with *pâté de foie gras* and truffles (no nuts in this instance) and descend through the better sieved *pâtés* to simple minced or even fine-chopped *pâtés familials*. Take your pick. Eke out your chosen *pâté* with either soft breadcrumbs or ground almonds (!) and use the recipe we will now share with you as an *aide mémoire* or guide to creating your own fillings on whatever level is financially acceptable.

For a medium, boned shoulder of veal work 8 ozs. of *pâté* in a bowl with 3 ozs. fine, soft breadcrumbs, 2 ozs. ground almonds, 3 ozs. pistachio or rough-cut Brazil nuts, 1 large egg, 2 rashers of finely diced streaky bacon (to supply the saltiness), a quarter teaspoon of milled black peppercorns and enough strong stock or cooking sherry to bind all to a moistly firm paste. Brandy or Armagnac *can* replace the sherry with felicitous results! Sew up the narrow end of the boned shoulder, remembering that you should use a double thread and meat needle or an ordinary large darning needle. Make a huge knot at one end and leave at least 3" at the knot end, dangling down. Then when you remove the threads after cooking, you just pull gently on this culinary bell pull and the entire length of thread comes away—as it must do without any possible margin for error. Put half the given stuffing inside the shoulder flesh patting it down firmly. Take either two lengthwise split hard-boiled eggs or 2 skinned, cored, lengthwise-quartered pork kidneys and lay them down on the stuffing "bed" evenly distributed to trellis the inner surface. Pack in the remaining stuffing. Sew up the broad opposing cavity and tie down the length exactly as a rolled boned silverside of salted beef is tied when delivered to you by your butcher. If this explanation leaves you in the slightest doubt, go and examine any rolled, boned, tied piece of meat on the butcher's slab and all will be perfectly clear.

Having tied up your beautiful parcel, wrap it in covering butter papers, then in extra strength kitchen foil and re-tie securely. Immerse in stock in a roomy pot, stock pot or jam kettle, cover and simmer for about $1\frac{1}{4}$ hours. Cool in all its wrappings. Refrigerate in them too, then uncover for cold service. When serving hot, unwrap carefully in a meat baking tin or similar container as some of those precious juices will run out. Conserve them at all costs and pour them round the un-strung *rouleau* on its serving dish. If you should feel any further sauce is needed *Sauce Madère* will fill the bill nicely, especially if you replace the sherry with Madeira as your moistening agent for the stuffing.

The variations on this *rouleau* theme are almost endless. Moreover if you prefer you can roast the tied *rouleaux*. Put in meat baking tins. Run $\frac{1}{4}$ pt. stock and $2\frac{1}{2}$ fl. ozs. cooking sherry or Madeira around the *rouleaux*. Roast under a tenting of foil or a deep inverted meat baking tin, at Gas Mark 4-5 and baste regularly. When the meat is cooked like this, a skewer driven into it should reveal bubbles of straw-coloured juice escaping. At that point, set the *rouleau* on its heated dish, add a tablespoonful of brandy to the pan liquor, bubble it up fiercely over a flame until it is syrupy and pour overall.

Before we leave this versatile treatment do remember you can use legs and shoulders of lamb (with lambs' kidney), legs or shoulders of pork (with pork kidneys) in precisely the same way and what is more, all or any can be cooked, consigned to the freezer and thawed out for cold buffet service. It is, we suggest, a pity to re-heat frozen *rouleaux* for they never taste quite the same but cold they are very, very good.

· Paupiettes de Veau ·

The prime factors in entertaining without staff or with the absolute minimum are easiness of service and dishes which can be at least in part pre-prepared leaving as little as possible to do at the last moment. Therefore, *Paupiettes de Veau* must share pride of place among meat dishes. You or your butcher will need to bat out large veal escalopes and cut them into $4'' \times 6''$ rectangles allowing 6 escalopes for 12 *paupiettes* which are enough for 6 people. Alternatively, you can use leaf-thin slices cut from the eye of veal fillet, then batted and trimmed into shape. Spread each rectangle (to within $\frac{1}{4}''$ of the edges) with liver *pâté* used as

C.H.B.   I stuffing, roll up and tie into neat little sausage roll shapes with fine trussing string, remembering to tuck in the ends neatly so that the stuffing does not escape during the cooking. Turn them in flour and fry them briskly until browned all round in equal parts of well heated oil and butter. Range them inside a lidded heat-resistant casserole or pie dish, add 3 very small shallots for each serving (18 for six), add ¾ pt. basic brown sauce or *Sauce Espagnole* and 3 fl. ozs. cooking sherry. Cover and cook at Gas Mark 4, middle shelf, for 30–35 minutes. Remove *paupiettes*, cut away the strings, range down a heated dish, arrange the shallots as an en-circling border and rub the remainder through a sieve over the *paupiettes*. Finish, optionally, with a sprinkling of milled parsley.

· Sauce Espagnole ·

For the *Sauce Espagnole*, melt 1 oz. butter in a thick pan, add 1 oz. flour, stir to a smooth *roux* and add 2 pts. strongly-reduced stock gradually, beating well between each addition. Add 4 ozs. of rough-cut tomatoes and the *Mirepoix*. Simmer until reduced to half quantity, rub through a sieve and use. This is the mixture which we make in bulk three or four times a year and then freeze in small, medium and large waxed cartons so that it is always available to draw on at speed. The *Mirepoix* contained in it con-sists of 1 medium carrot and 1 medium onion, both grated coarsely and cooked for about 3 minutes in 1 oz. of butter and 1 fl. oz. oil. Add in half a crushed bay leaf, the chopped white of a 4″ stick of celery heart and a small sprig of thyme. Simmer for a further 3 minutes and use as explained above.

· Paupiettes de Veau à l'Italienne ·

There is another delicious version of these called *Paupiettes de Veau à l'Italienne*. Proceed as for ordinary *Paupiettes de Veau* and when you have ranged your paper-thin rectangles of raw veal on your working surface, cover each one with a fractionally smaller rectangle of very thin, lean raw ham or gammon. Place a fat finger of Gruyère cheese within ½″ of one 4″ edge, roll up and proceed as given in the previous recipe. Cut down the cooking time to between 25 and 30 minutes at the same tempera- ture and oven position.

Once we mention the magic words veal *escalopes*, we open up a very easy area of cookery for fraught cook-hostesses. All the ones we suggest are made *en papillote* and the *papillotes* are just rectangles of aluminium foil. Always brush the dull interiors with melted butter. Then lay down a single *escalope* for each person. Add everything else, fold up in very loose parcels with very firmly secured ends and cook in rows on baking sheets at Gas Mark 4-5, middle shelf, for about 20 minutes. For service and because these parcels are messy at the table, unwrap in the kitchen, slide onto a serving dish and keep warm until required at Gas Mark ¼ under a loose top-tenting of kitchen foil.

· Escalopes de Veau en papillote Dvořák ·

Now let us survey the various treatments and their menu names. We will begin with *Escalopes de Veau en papillote Dvořák*. For each serving mix a heaped tablespoon of whipped cream with tomato *purée—to taste—*and season with salt and pepper. Fold in as many hair-thin strips of pimento as the mixture will take. Pile down the length of the escalope on its buttery foil. Sprinkle over-all with a dessertspoonful of fine, soft breadcrumbs, wrap up and cook. The breadcrumbs off-set any tendency the cream may have to separate during the cooking time and acts as a thickener for the finished sauce.

· Escalopes de Veau en papillote Ardennoise ·

In early autumn try *Escalopes de Veau en papillote Ardennoise*. Season the raw *escalopes*. Mix a tablespoonful of soured cream per portion with as many milk-fresh peeled walnuts as it will hold, spread over the meat, dot the top surface with a few peeled, halved grapes and cook as explained.

· Escalopes de Veau en papillote au Vermouth ·

And you must have that very special treatment for *Escalopes de Veau en papillote au Vermouth*. The secret of this one is the *jus de viande* which is the French technical term for real *consommé* reduced by relentless simmering until it is positively syrupy. To every 5 fl. ozs. add 2 fl. ozs. of dry vermouth. Season the raw meat, cover the top with 1 fl. oz. finely diced, lean and fat of bacon and the same of chickens' livers. Moisten with two tablespoonsful of the meat syrup, season with more pepper and proceed as usual.

· Jambon au four Brillat Savarin ·

Of all the ambrosial dishes which can be made with ham for large numbers, nothing quite equals the *Jambon au four Brillat Savarin*, from his birthplace, the little town of Belley. It must be made with a whole, small, sweet ham. We always choose one which is very short and thick, never one that is long and rather narrow. Soak it for at least 24 hours, preferably in rain water and ideally with a large handful of wisps of hay. At the same time take a tin of Fowler's black treacle into the refrigerator to get really cold and very thick indeed. Then make up about 3 lbs. of flour into a thick paste of good rolling consistency with either rain or tap water. Dry the soaked ham carefully and have it beside you as you work. Roll out the paste to about ½″ thickness, coat the ham thickly with the stiff black treacle and dredge it all over with soft brown (pieces) sugar. Enclose it as speedily as possible in the paste, being careful not to stretch this and even more careful to wet the paste edges and see that they are completely sealed over each other. Bake for 3 hours at Gas Mark 4 on the middle shelf by which time the paste should be very hard indeed. Break it away and use it for the compost—it is no good for anything else. Put the ham into a meat baking tin, pour a bottle of dry-ish Graves over it and put it back one shelf below centre at Gas Mark 3 for a further 45 minutes. Please try to baste it at least 4 times at 10 minute intervals.

During the initial ham baking time start to make your sauce. Put 2 ozs. butter and 2 fl. ozs. of oil into a large frying pan. Coarse grate 1 big onion, ¾ lb. of carrots and the white of 2 big leeks. Brown them lightly over a moderate heat. Then add 8 ozs. of picked, washed spinach leaves and 4 ozs. of sorrel or you can use all spinach. When these have subsided to a pulp, scrape the mixture into a large saucepan and stir in 1½ pts. of good meat stock, 2 crushed garlic cloves and ½ pt. dry Madeira. Add a flat teaspoon of salt, 2 crushed black peppercorns and allow the mixture to simmer for about 2 hours. Watch it and give it an occasional stir lest it burns. Then strain it and leave it dripping for a while so that the last drops fall through from the weight of the pan residue.

This is a dish which you serve from the side yourself because at the last moment you put the ham on its dish, preferably one with prongs in so that it does not skid about all over the place. Add one-third of the sauce's bulk in double cream, boil it up so that it reduces until thick and send it through with a ladle in an appropriate container. Cut the slices of ham onto each plate, let them err slightly on the thick side, spoon the sauce over and serve with wedges of hot French bread.

· Langue Oporto ·

Passing from the sublime to the perilous, we think it is fair to say that other than vegetables, nothing suffers quite so much at the hands of English cooks as good ox tongue. It has the added virtue of being inexpensive, yet more often than not it turns up at the table bearing a marked gastronomic resemblance to one of our parents' description of a decrepid horse: purged of all earthly passion and probably been out to grass for the last forty years. The average boiled tongue with parsley sauce served in this country is boiled to a stringy and tasteless death and served under an unkindly mantle of chalk-white sauce made twiggy with ineptly chopped parsley.

Please be kind to tongue and give it a chance to show what it can do. Demand one which has not been salted. Drop it into boiling stock, not cold tap water, so that the flavours are sealed in the meat and are not drawn out completely into the liquor. Simmer it for no longer than it takes for the skin to come away easily. Skin it while it is still hot. Place a pint of basic brown sauce or *Sauce Espagnole* (p. 130) in a pan with 4 fl. ozs. of cooking port and ¼ lb. peeled, pipped grapes. Heat all through together, rub through a sieve and stir in 4 tablespoonsful of double cream. Taste and correct seasoning. Pour just enough of the sauce on the bottom of a heated dish to cover the base, slice the tongue and lay the slices on this base. Pour the remainder of the sauce overall and see whether *Langue Oporto* does not taste better than purged tongue in wallpaper paste and parsley sauce!

· Cold Tongue with Piquant Sauce ·

If you want to serve tongue cold, just refrigerate it as soon as it stops steaming and then slice it. There is no necessity to press it unless it is being put whole on the table which is not what we suggest. Arrange the slices on a flat dish and cover them with a sauce made by folding 3 finely chopped hard-boiled eggs and

2 tablespoonsful of capers (which have been carefully pressed through a small sieve to expel their surplus vinegary moisture) into *Sauce Vinaigrette*.* A further method of presentation for this *Cold Tongue with Piquant Sauce* is to cut the whole tongue up into chips and toss them with the given sauce with a great many pulled sprigs from a well-washed head of endive in English, which just to confuse you is called *chicorée* in French.

We have been looking back over this selection of meat dishes pruned from our own menu books. Speaking purely personally for a moment, we cannot help chuckling over the inescapable fact that you succeed best as a hostess if you fit the dish to the personality where you are not conversant with the palate. This is of course a generalisation and we are well aware of the inevitable limitations, but wealthy globe-trotting Americans do seem to be most impressed by a tarted-up hunk of steak and this choice is endorsed all too frequently by the young who have not had the advantage of any globe-trotting at all. They are quite unruffled by the fact that the hostess will have to leave the room to cook her main course dish; if the end product is large enough and tender enough, she will merely be a "doll". As such a thought is anathema to us and has been all our adult lives, we make a point of installing a cooker with a good grill in the dining room and so can amuse our guests with a bit of justifiable chi-chi and be with them throughout the meal.

The average middle-aged Frenchman will be ravished by the sight of almost blue lamb on his plate, but is unlikely to enthuse about any meat which is not accompanied by a sauce. Men who have been professionally involved with wines for a number of years will wax lyrical only when the sauces are sufficiently restrained and subtle not to over-top or in any way eclipse the accompanying wines.

The most rewarding people in the world today are women of any nation who like cooking themselves and have to do it anyway. Any pains are worth taking for them. More often than not they do not give a fig for their figures and are therefore good trenchermen as well. We take off all our hats to each one we have ever had the pleasure of feeding.

Feuilleté de Ris de Veau
Omelette de Ris de Veau Savoyarde
Crêpes de Ris de Veau Savoyarde
Soufflé de Ris de Veau · Cervelles Feuilletés
Sauce au Beurre noir · Cervelles au Beurre noir
Omelette aux Cervelles · Rognons de Veau en brochettes
Rognons de Veau grillés
Foie de Porc farci au façon de Périgord

twelve · **INNARDS**

If you have such a rooted aversion to what our offspring vulgarly call "guts" that you cannot even bear to cook them, flip straight over to p. 147 and miss this chapter altogether! If you are pro-innards please stay with us.

Frankly, if we were forced to make a choice between steaks, chops, grills and all the other hunks of meat; or calves' liver, veal, beef and pork kidneys, sweetbreads and brains we would choose these every time. We would also temporise, and make it essential that pig's fry became readily obtainable once again. Where has it gone we would very much like to know and WHY? We have a nasty suspicion that the pared-down modern methods of mass butchers have excluded it as not being worth the bother which we find *shocking*. However, this is typical irrelevance because even cooks like us who have a fine disregard for the "done thing" just because it either is or is not "done", would not venture to suggest that pig's fry is a suitable media for a main course when entertaining; so let us progress with the items of "Hoffal" which are!

The crowning glory of "*Les Abats*" to French cooks is *Ris de Veau*, the large double ones which butchers have a tendency to label "breads". We have already shared such delectable recipes with you as *Brioches de Ris de Veau** and *Escalopes de Ris de Veau Maréchal** but you have never had our *Feuilleté de Ris de Veau Hotel de France*, which omission we will now repair.

However, first let us recapitulate on the preliminary treatment of sweetbreads which is constant throughout all methods of final cookery. For 2 lbs. of sweetbreads allow 3 pts. boiling water and 4 ozs. flour. Mix the flour to a smooth paste with cold water, pour some of the boiling water onto this paste, stir carefully and when thinned down and absolutely smooth pour into the remainder of the boiling water in a large, deep pan. Restore to boiling point over moderate heat, slip in the raw sweetbreads, allow to simmer for two minutes, remove from the heat and allow to become cold in the *"blanc"* as this paste mixture is called professionally. Then fish them out and refresh them in cold water. All this is very easy, so here comes the crunch. You must now remove every scrap of skin, fat and muscle from the sweetbreads.

· Feuilleté de Ris de Veau Hotel de France ·

When using for *Feuilleté de Ris de Veau Hotel de France* separate the sweetbreads into little pieces (easy!), make your sauce, turn the pieces into the sauce and fill to within 1" of the rim of six individual casseroles or heat-resistant bowls. When once again down to below blood temperature, cover with little lids of only fairly thinly rolled puff paste. This can be either bought, frozen or home-made. At this stage the covered containers can be refrigerated for up to 24 hours. Just before service brush the tops with strained, raw, beaten egg and bake one shelf above centre at Gas Mark 7 until richly browned on top.

Like this the pots were placed before us many years ago at the Hotel de France, La Chartre-sur-Loir. The waiter then ran a small knife deftly around the rim of each pastry lid, lifted it onto each plate, scooped out the sweetbread mixture and left us to gorge.

The sauce for this dish is made in the following manner. Place ½ lb. strained, very thinly sliced, tinned *cèpes* in a pan containing 4 ozs. very hot mixed oil and melted butter in equal proportions, fry gently for 5 minutes turning occasionally. Sprinkle on 2 ozs. flour and work up to a pasty consistency with the back of a wooden spoon. Dilute with ½ pt. dry white wine (or stock and wine in equal parts), stirring well between each gradual addition of this quantity. Add ¼ pt. single or coffee cream, again stirring between each gradual addition. Fold in the separated sweetbreads and continue simmering for a further 5 minutes. Taste, correct the seasoning and use as explained above. If preferred, mushrooms (fresh, dried or frozen) or dried, re-constituted *morilles* may be used instead of *cèpes*.

· Omelette de Ris de Veau Savoyarde ·

Have you ever eaten a sweetbread omelette? If not prepare to make one now. Just use the method given above for achieving tiny pieces of sweetbread in a thick, rich sauce. Make your omelette with 6 eggs *à la Mère Poularde** and when the omelette is almost done—or still wet on the surface as you look down on the pan—draw a spoonful or two of the sauced sweetbreads over this surface, flip over, turn out and quickly mask it with covering spoonfuls of the same sauced mixture. Make sure your grill is very hot because now you will work fast; swill the top-covering with a tablespoonful of *double* cream into which you have stirred a teaspoonful of kirsch. Cover with half a dozen transparently thin slices of Gruyère cheese and brown as fast as possible under a fierce grill before carrying in triumph to the table. For your menu name this Lucullan affair *Omelette de Ris de Veau Savoyarde.*

· Crêpes de Ris de Veau Savoyarde ·

Having once mastered the sauced, sweetbread part of *Feuilleté Hotel de France*, you can use it in a multiplicity of ways. Make two leaf-thin pancakes per person, store them in the usual professional way* and make up the sweetbread in sauce mixture as before. Just before service have assembled on the working surface beside your cooker (with grill heating up furiously), a heat-resistant oval "flat" (metal or glass), a pile of those transparently thin Gruyère leaves, a small bowl of double cream (with tablespoon), a small bowl of softened butter and the Kirsch bottle with a teaspoon, with the pancakes and filling warming up in the oven at Gas Mark 1, and the pre-heated grill piping hot, rub the "flat" with butter. Lay in a pancake, spread one half thickly with sweetbread mixture, flip second half over and continue doing this until your dish is filled from end to end with stuffed pancakes. Spoon more sweetbread mixture overall. Flavour the cream to taste with Kirsch, just using enough to make a film over the sweetbread covering. Cover the surface speedily with Gruyère leaves and brown as fast as possible under the grill. The name becomes *Crêpes de Ris de Veau Savoyarde.*

There is, of course, an alternative method which you have to employ when numbers exceed half the amount of stuffed, sauced pancakes that you can get onto a "flat" *which will fit under your grill.* This is it. Fill pancakes as described above *with cold sweetbread mixture,* cover with remainder, and just add kirsch-flavoured cream and Gruyère leaves immediately before slipping into the oven under a light covering of foil for 15 minutes one shelf above centre at Gas Mark 4. Whip off the foil, step up the heat to Gas Mark 6 and give 7–8 minutes final cooking so that the top becomes *croustillant* and lightly browned.

· Soufflé de Ris de Veau ·

After all that creamy coloured cookery let us take whole, prepared sweetbreads and turn them into a *Soufflé de Ris de Veau*. Poach 1 lb. in a *blanc* until meltingly tender, emulsify with 4 fl. ozs. dry Madeira, correct seasoning with salt and pepper and allow to become perfectly cold. Then make up your basic *soufflé* mixture—no, this is a new one, the results of some very careful experimenting and just to be perverse, after all the carry-on we have made over omitting egg yolks, this one becomes the exception to the rule *by including them*. Assemble 1½ ozs. butter, 1 oz. flour, 3 separated standard egg yolks, 9 separated egg whites, salt and pepper to season, 11 fl. ozs. milk, 4 fl. ozs. dry white wine, and 3¾ ozs. finely grated Parmesan. Please do not try making this *soufflé* with any other cheese. Start work a maximum 10 minutes before cooking at Gas Mark 6, one shelf above centre, for 15 minutes. Do not look startled; a *soufflé* should be crisp on the outside, *but wet in the middle*. If cooked right through it ceases to be a *soufflé* and becomes a puddin!

Melt the butter in a thick saucepan over a moderate heat, add the flour and work into a smooth paste. Add the wine gradually, beating between each addition, then add the sweetbread purée and grated cheese alternately and on no account add a single scrap of the milk until all of both these items have been absorbed. Then thin down with given quantity of milk until thick, smooth and creamy. Remove from heat, beat in egg yolks, then fold in very stiffly whipped egg whites lightly and at speed. Turn into a 9″ diameter buttered soufflé mould, level off the top and away into the oven with it immediately. You can of course serve this mixture as individual soufflés baked in buttered, individual casseroles or other heat-resistant containers, in which case you would bake for between 8 and 10 minutes *depending upon the size of those containers*.

· Cervelles Feuilletés ·

Now let us tackle brains or *Cervelles* as you will call them on a menu. To begin with, you remove the fine films of skin and veins which mask each little lamb's brain and blanch them in the manner of sweetbreads (p. 137.) Then you can begin making *Cervelles Feuilletés* which have no resemblance whatsoever to the sweetbread

Feuilletés except that both use puff paste. Having blanched and rinsed the brains, pat them dry in a clean cloth, arrange them in a flat platter, cover with a sheet of buttered greaseproof paper and lay a flat baking sheet above them. Place heavy weights on top—we have used at one time or another large tins of fruit, a pile of books, two hunks of marble which we fished out of a junk heap and classic weights!

Roll out some bought or home-made puff paste very thinly. Cut into 6" diameter circles. Brush the pressed brains all over with melted butter. Place one in the centre of each circle. Season with salt and pepper and then bring up the edges of the paste circles all round and gather them together just a little above the enclosed brain so that there is sufficient space inside for the sauce which will be spooned in later. Pinch in the "waists" or "necks" of the raw paste. If this causes difficulties, brush with a little raw, strained, beaten egg; but be sure when you have done this to drive a raw chip-piece of potato into the gathered up centres which you can remove after baking so that you can drip in the sauce. Brush your pastry "posies" with egg. Bake one shelf above centre at Gas Mark 6 until puffy and golden brown by which time your *Sauce au Beurre noir* must be ready. Withdraw those "chips"—gently please—and drip a teaspoonful or two of the sauce into each central cavity. Serve surrounded by cut lemon and hand more *Sauce au Beurre noir* separately.

· Sauce au Beurre noir ·

Let us not confuse ourselves over this preparation. Black butter is butter which is cooked in a very small pan over a mode-rate to strong heat until it turns brown. Once it turns black, it has surrendered all hope of becoming *Beurre noir* or Black Butter and merely becomes burned butter which must immediately be con-signed to the compost bucket! The classic ruling is for wine vinegar to be used in its basic (*Beurre noir*) composition and more to be added when it evolutes into *Sauce au Beurre noir*—we beg leave to disagree. Our defence for deviation is as follows:

The basic classic instructions for Mayonnaise and for *Vinaigrée* contains the same vinegar directions—yet—as we all know—strained lemon and/or orange juice may be substituted with equal success and a more bland flavour. Furthermore both become use-less if these substances accompany wines—with which vinegar is on even worse terms than lemon and orange juice whose acidity displeases them greatly anyway, so in such circumstances grape juice replaces all three! Why then, we ask (if rhetorically), should we not substitute lemon juice which is just as much an improvement to *Beurre noir* as to Mayonnaise and *Vinaigrée*? Anyway that is what we recommend and you will do best to try both and see which causes your palate to respond with greater benevolence.

So here we go, melt 4 ozs. of the very best butter very slowly in a small pan. When melted raise the heat sufficiently to cause a froth or foam to rise to the top. Skim this off until the butter is a clear transparent yellow. Go on simmering, adding a teaspoonful or two of lemon juice and continuing until the clarified butter is *brown*. Reduce heat to a mere thread. Squeeze every scrap of moisture from two heaped tablespoonsful of capers, stir these in, add 1 (optional) heaped tablespoonful of finely milled or chopped parsley heads and send to table in a sauce boat.

· Cervelles au Beurre noir ·

So having got that off our respective chests, let us progress with great ease through the making of *Cervelles au Beurre noir*. If you have read this chapter from the beginning, we feel sure *you* could tell *us*! However . . . first you blanch, refresh, skin and dry the brains, then you press them (p. 137 and p. 141), then you turn each little, cold, flattened piece in (a) flour, (b) beaten, strained egg, (c) fine soft breadcrumbs. Finally you shallow fry the prepared pieces using equal quantities of oil and butter and making sure these do not rise, when foaming cheerfully, to more than half the depth of the immersed pieces. When they are nicely browned and delicately crisp on both sides, a medium/slow process to ensure they are cooked right through to their tender little middles, dress them on a napkin on a heated dish. Surround with sprigs of fried parsley and hand *Sauce au Beurre noir* separately, definitely omitting the parsley in this instance as using it twice in the same dish would be shaming.

· Omelette aux Cervelles ·

You can also make a delicious omelette with brains. The one we have in mind is *Omelette aux Cervelles*. The only difference between this and the *Omelette de Ris de Veau Savoyarde* is the filling, so we will explain that and then ask you to turn to p. 138 for the rest. Prepare the brains as usual and fry 4 very gently in equal parts of oil and butter to use as a filling for a 6-egg omelette. Cut them up quite roughly in the pan. Pour on 4 tablespoons of dry white wine and one of brandy, *flambé* and put out the flames with 6 tablespoons of single cream. Taste and correct the seasoning. Cut the tender tips up neatly from a dozen stems of asparagus. Stir ten of them into the sauce, pour the filling into the omelette, fold and turn onto a buttered heat-resistant salver or small flat dish. Pour just enough cream to coat the top, dab the cut up stalks and the remaining two asparagus stems over the top, sprinkle with grated Parmesan cheese, dot with tiny flakes of butter and brown fast at highest position under a pre-heated grill.

· Rognons de Veau en brochettes ·

One of the kidney recipes which we have already shared together is a *Rognons Flambés** which is eminently suited to either luncheon or dinner parties. Equally useful for such occasions are *Rognons de Veau Bercy**, *Rognons de Veau Feuilleté** and *Timbale de Rognons à la crème** but we feel confident that you will not yet have encountered *Rognons de Veau en brochettes* served with rice and *Sauce Béarnaise**.

For 8 people assemble 1 lb. of veal kidney in the piece, 6 rashers of No. 3 cut de-rinded back bacon, 6 ozs. of raw unsalted pork fat off the rind, 8 bay leaves, a shallow container of fine breadcrumbs, salt and pepper, 4 ozs. melted butter, stock and 8 skewers. Pour enough boiling stock over the kidney to cover it and thus stiffen it. Leave it in the stock off the heat until cool. Slice up into neat segments being careful to remove the central core. Meanwhile cut the bacon into large dice. Tear each bay leaf in halves. Slice the piece of pork fat thinly and cut in matching sized pieces to the bacon. Cook the bacon in a small pan in the melted butter until it is firmed but soft. Drain thoroughly and load your skewers in the following sequence: kidney, bacon, kidney, pork fat, bay leaf, kidney, bacon, kidney, pork fat, bay leaf. Season lightly with salt and pepper, brush with the remaining melted butter, turn and coat thickly with fine crumbs. Brown gently under a moderate grill. Cook 1½ lbs. rice* in the classic manner, shape into a fairly high, slightly sloping rectangle on a heated dish and arrange the 8 skewers on top, alternating them, tip to head, down the line. Hand the *Béarnaise** separately.

· Rognons de Veau grillés ·

There are many occasions when planning a menu, we succumb to the temptations of a really rich creamy, sauced fish course. This usually creates a dilemma: with what shall we follow it? A simple service of *Rognons de Veau grillés*, using veal kidney of course, meets the bill very well. You must allow 2 lbs. for 6–8 people and it is better to obtain this in two pieces. Split each piece down the centre without cutting right through to the opposite side, cut out the core very carefully with a pair of scissors so as not to pierce the kidneys through, then drive two long, slim skewers crossways over the upper part and through the edges in such a way as to hold them down flat during the grilling. Dilute about a dessertspoonful of French mustard with about 2 tablespoonsful of stock, brush the kidneys on both sides with this, then brush them with melted butter and finally season them with salt and pepper. Grill them briskly on each side for 2 minutes, then reduce the heat and cook them more slowly until when pierced for testing, they ooze a little pink *jus*. Withdraw the skewers, set on a small metal flat or salver and surround with watercress. If the preceding course has not been too outrageously rich, you can hand *Sauce Bercy** as an accompaniment.

· Foie de Porc farci au façon de Périgord ·

Now for a little beauty which is comparatively new to us; *Foie de Porc farci au façon de Périgord.* Buy a pig's liver weighing about 2 lbs. which will cost you . . . well, how can we tell how much further prices will rise? . . . but we paid 9/6 in September 1969. With a small, sharp knife, split it from one edge right through to the other without severing the opposing edge. Mix together in a bowl 2 ozs. of melted, strained, raw, unsalted pork fat, 1 finely grated shallot, 1 crushed garlic clove, 2 standard eggs, 1 rounded eggspoon of finely chopped fresh or dried crumbled thyme, ½ teaspoon of salt and ½ a flat eggspoon of black peppercorns. Mix thoroughly together and work in sufficient fine soft breadcrumbs to form a thick paste. Fill into the liver. Place in a buttered casserole (or ideally coat sides and base with melted pork fat). Encircle with 18 very small onions. Moisten with 5 fl. ozs. tomato juice and 5 fl. ozs. of very strong stock. Cover and cook on the middle shelf, Gas Mark 4, until no pink shows when you prod the fat part of liver with a fine skewer or needle. Lift out, set liver on a dish for slicing at the sideboard or slice in the kitchen and arrange neatly. Encircle once again with the little onions, rub the pan residue through a sieve overall, sprinkle lightly with parsley and serve with absolutely plain steamed potatoes or *Pommes Vapeur*.

thirteen · **PLUCK IT AND SEE**

As there are more classic ways of cooking a chicken than any other bird, may we come to an understanding straight away that none of the recipes in this book are intended for those tasteless eviscerated fowl which according to their condition when they are purchased, were born with their innards in a polythene bag. Quite frankly they are simply not worth cooking and of course the same applies to ducks and turkeys which have endured the same mayhem.

When you can get your hooks on $3\frac{1}{2}$–4 lbs. free-range fresh poultry and want to make special occasion poultry dishes, invest in a casserole type container which has only just come onto the market in this country. It is called, quite simply, a Roman Pot (stockists p. 000). This cook's treasure is not only superb for the cooking of any fowl, but also the one perfect way of cooking for anyone unfortunate enough to need a saltless and fat-free diet. You just put the chicken in the pot, put on the lid and put the pot in the oven, middle shelf Gas Mark 5. Each pot carries meticulously accurate cooking instructions.

· Chicken Roman Pot Style ·

Whenever we want pre-cooked birds for final saucing and serving hot or for dividing and serving cold under aspic or a *Sauce Chaudfroid*, we cook Roman Pot Style. Then, immediately the bird comes out, share with us a little trick you are not told in the instructions. Lift the bird out, slip a grill rack over the pot, put the bird on this and leave it for 10 minutes. Thus the gorgeous natural juices drip down into the pot and accumulate. For those on a fat-free diet you then pour off those juices and when they are cold, remove the little cap of poultry fat which will have formed on top. For the less vulnerable you merely use the fatty juices in your sauces.

For family dishes which take care of themselves in the oven, nothing beats an old-fashioned earthenware casserole except perhaps that remarkable earthenware container which has been in use for nearly a thousand years. It is called a *Tripière*. It looks like a cross between a lidded bedpan and a flying saucer. It was used to serve *Tripe à la mode de Caen* to William of Normandy and his nobles at the banquet held in Caen the night before they invaded England circa (1066). The construction of this utensil is such that no single scrap of flavour can escape in fumes during the cooking time, because, remember, next time you sniff rapturously and exclaim, "Something smells good, it's making me hungry," that smell is flavour . . . wasting itself before you can wrap it round your palate!

It is a sad reflection on our life and times that chickens have become just about the best main-course value for money today. If you doubt the validity of that statement, compare the costs of serving a 3¾–4 lbs. chicken, which will serve six comfortably, to that of six veal *escalopes*, fillet or tournedos steaks, or six portions of sweetbreads, veal kidney or plain carved slices from any leg of meat.

· Poulet Forestière ·

Fanny taught a simple chicken casserole dish called *Poulet Forestière* in one of her early further education television programmes. This has proved one of the most popular we have ever given and—remember—there are probably more recipes available for cooking chicken than for any other main course dish. So we now deviate and instead of chatting through our recipes as we normally do together in these books, we set it out baldly in the English Trad. Manner.

Assemble one prime 4 lb. chicken; 10 de-rinded rashers No. 4 cut, back bacon; ½ lb. thinly sliced, unskinned mushrooms; 4 ozs. butter; ¼ pt. fairly dry white wine; ¼ pt. single cream; salt and pepper; top-of-the-milk.

Skin and divide the chicken into 2 leg, 2 thigh, 2 halved *suprêmes* (or breast) and 2 wing pieces (*see* diagram p. 150). Lay each skinless piece centrally on a bacon rasher. Spread each with a few mushroom slices. Season lightly with salt and pepper. Wrap up in bacon rashers and arrange side by side in a shallow, heat-resistant casserole spread with 2 ozs. butter. Scatter remaining mushrooms overall. Moisten with wine. Dot surface with flakes

from remaining 2 ozs. butter. Cover with kitchen foil and cook
in the oven, middle shelf, Gas Mark 6, for 30–40 minutes depending on size of portions. Remove chicken portions and arrange on
serving dish. Strain liquor and arrange cooked mushroom slices
between chicken portions. Cover with kitchen foil and keep warm
at Gas Mark ½. Place strained liquor, top of the milk and cream
in thick pan over low heat. Reduce by simmering to a thick
creamy consistency. Taste and correct seasoning. Either border
with a thickly ridged piping of Duchess potatoes* or surround
with small triangles of fried bread.

· Poulet Véronique ·

This can be used as both a recipe and a treatment. Change
the mushrooms to peeled, de-pipped, white or black grapes and
otherwise do exactly what *Poulet Forestière* dictates, and you will
achieve *Poulet Véronique* instead.

· Poulet Normande ·

Change the mushrooms to ½ lb. of thinly sliced, tart, little,
peeled cooking apples and add in ¼ lb. of the most finely and
delicately sliced peeled onions you can achieve. Roll up a few
onion rings and slices of apples with each chicken portion in a
rasher of bacon and substitute ¼ pt. rough, sharp cider for the
given ¼ pt. dry-ish white wine. This time the result will be *Poulet
Normande* . . . at least you can title yours *Poulet Normande* but,
in order not to mislead you, we must point out that, strictly
speaking, it is *Poulet Normande familiale* and not *classique*. For
family occasions you can, of course, use stock or part stock, part
wine or cider. When using the cream spare a thought for whipping
cream which can do all the jobs classic "double cream" can do
with the added advantage of costing less.

· Suprême de Volaille ·

Under the heading *Suprême de Volaille* or breast of chicken,
we have a huge main course repertoire at our disposal provided
you accept that one 2¾ lb. chicken will be needed for every two
portions or *suprêmes*. This leaves you with three breast-denuded
chickens on your hands when you are giving a dinner for six.
Frankly we have found this to be financially acceptable on the
basis that the thighs and legs can subsequently be transformed into

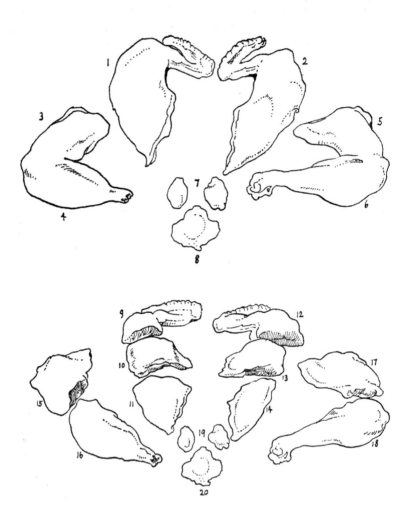

How to skin and divide raw poultry (opposite)

family style *Poulet Forestière,* or *Normande,* for one subsequent filling main course dish, and some used after the party is over as *Faute de Mieux Kievs* or *Poulet Hongroise.* Frankly it is difficult to make a short selection, the range of uses for such pieces of chicken is so enormous! Even then you are left with the carcase and certain bones, so into the stock-pot they go and absolutely nothing is wasted.

If you are to achieve all these things and many more, with ease and speed, you will have to know how to joint a chicken into neat pieces and above all how to take out the *"suprêmes".* Here is your *aide-mémoire.*

· How to Skin and Divide Raw Poultry ·

Implements: 1 pair game scissors or ordinary (sterilised) garden secateurs; 1 small sharp pointed knife.

STAGE ONE. Pinch all skin between thumbs and first fingers of both hands with quick little upward pinch/pull movements. This loosens the skin so that you can subsequently rip it away more easily. Finish by loosening the skin at the wishbone end by pushing your thumbs up between skin and flesh to about the end of your second thumb joints. Split this skin centrally with the knife and rip it off. Place the handle end of the knife over the tip of each leg on top of that first inedible little joint. With a little pad of tea cloth over it bang the other hand down onto this and discard the two joints—they are not even fit for the stock-pot. Do the same thing on the first joint of each wing tip or *aileron.* Cut away each leg and thigh piece from the carcase.

STAGE TWO. Lay on the table as illustrated in Nos. 3/4 and 5/6 in the upper pictured suite of portions and then using the same cloth/knife movement, go straight through the rounded centre of these two portions with your sharp knife so as to achieve the divisions shown in Nos. 15/16 and 17/18 in the lower pictured suite of portions. Remove parson's nose (unskinned), No. 8 upper diagram. Turn bird over and remove the two oysters, No. 7 upper diagram. Return the bird to its normal position on the table. Take up game secateurs. Cut straight through breast bone from end to end and with your knife cut through the muscle which holds the fat end of the *suprême* or breast (where the wing begins) to the carcase. This will give you Nos. 1 and 2 in upper picture. Divide these as shown in lower picture with secateurs so that you achieve

9/10/11 and 12/13/14. Your bird is now divided into ten pieces, excluding the two oysters (Nos. 19 in lower picture) and parson's nose (No. 20).

If you only want to remove the two *suprêmes* from a skinned chicken follow the picture on p. 150 in conjunction with the instructions in the first part of *Poulet à la Kiev* below.

· Poulet à la Kiev ·

Having cleared the culinary decks for action we can now embark upon our *suprêmes* recipes. The greatest of these is *Poulet à la Kiev* which is so shamefully mis-handled by professional chefs in Britain. This great classic was brought to England by the late, great restaurateur known affectionately to everyone as "Papa Vecchi". He, some of you older folk may remember, ran the Hungaria Restaurant in Lower Regent Street very successfully for a number of years and finally moved on to the Belfry Club before he, alas, moved on to other spheres. "Papa" wrote "The Tavern Is My Drum" and "Papa" also brought the original "Kiev" from Kiev before the first world war. He taught us. In fact this lesson constitutes the only one Fanny has ever had.

Two days before we gave a matinée and an evening performance at the Royal Festival Hall to an audience of around four thousand, the late Miss Evelyn Garrett, woman's editor of the "Daily Telegraph" and a beloved friend and mentor, telephoned us to ask in that wickedly soft and misleading voice of hers, "Could you change the menu a little for us and make *Poulet à la Kiev* at the Festival Hall?"

Constitutionally incapable of admitting that anything is impossible, we idiotically agreed. We telephoned "Papa" and asked for aid. Of course we got it. Fanny went round after luncheon to the Belfry and there was shewn how this delicacy is constructed. She made twenty-three, came home clutching the half-breastless chicken on which lay the uncut *suprême* for the twenty-fourth. She cut this and made yet another in our own kitchen. Late that night Vecchi telephoned. "I sold those twenty-three Kiev," he chuckled, "25/– each, not bad eh?" and we made them for the "Telegraph" at the Festival Hall the next day.

Follow the instructions given in Stage One (p. 150) for skinning and dividing raw poultry. Then with thumb and first finger of left hand press the flesh down taut over one side of the wishbone.

With the point of a small sharp knife scrape down this bone until it breaks through the flesh. Slip the point of the knife behind this bone and slide the knife down against it to base. Cut through the base and repeat with second side of wishbone. Take the two severed ends of the wishbone in the fingers and gently ease up and back giving final twist to bring it away whole. Run knife from tip of breastbone (parson's nose end) against breastbone and right through flesh to wishbone end and pare back the flesh of this breast and wing piece right down to the joint which attaches the wing bone to the carcase. Cut through the joint at this point and continue paring behind the joint until the whole section comes away in one piece. Repeat on opposite side of the bird. These two severed pieces of wing-breast flesh are hereafter called the *suprêmes*.

Turn each *suprême* singly on its back so that the under-side of flesh is exposed. Examine it carefully until you find the long tapering strip of flesh lying inside the breast flesh. Lift it up gently and pull it from the main section. Lay on a wooden board and with a heavy metal meat batter, or substitute, dipped into cold water, gradually bat down until it is almost transparently thin and roughly the shape of a small veal *escalope*. Place a 1 oz. square of butter in the centre. Season surface lightly with salt and pepper and fold up like a minute parcel so that the butter is completely enclosed. Set aside.

Now comes the tricky bit. Starting at the wing end of the *suprême* make a sharp incision from centre at this end to within $\frac{1}{4}''$ of the tapering, opposing end. Do *not* cut through. Using tip of knife work with blade parallel with side of the *suprême* at centre to within a $\frac{1}{4}''$ of the edges all round. Run your finger through it to ensure that you have thus obtained a large, neat pocket. Turn your little butter parcel so that the folds are underneath and push it into the pocket, ramming it as far into the wing bone end as possible. Take the lip on one side and pull it right over the parcel. Then draw the opposite lip over the top. Pick up gently in your fingers and draw it out into a long, *straight* tadpole with a tapering tail. Then, always keeping the *kiev* straight, roll it in sifted flour, dust off surplus, coat completely in strained, raw beaten egg, drain off surplus and bury in very fine, soft white breadcrumbs. Pat in a crumb overcoat, straighten once more and refrigerate as many as required until 7 minutes before serving.

Have ready a pan of slightly smoking hot oil. Place *kievs* with fractional space between each on base of frying basket. Plunge into oil, allow 30 seconds, turn off heat and allow *kievs* to cook to a rich golden brown for exactly 6½ minutes more. Lift out and serve immediately.

After that exhaustive explanation let us take you into the realms of slightly less complex *"suprême"* cookery. Once this entire section of breast and wing has been taken from the fowl, whether it be chicken, pheasant, pigeon or guinea fowl, it will lend itself to any of our suggested treatments.

· Suprêmes de Volaille aux Pointes d'Asperges ·

We shall begin with the assumption that one of these fine days you will need to prepare a super-delicious dish of chicken for a small wedding luncheon or other very special occasion at which a dozen people will assemble at the table. This is when *Suprêmes de Volaille aux Pointes d'Asperges* will fill the bill very nicely indeed. You will need 12 *"suprêmes"* or chickens' breasts; 3 lbs. scalded, unskinned, finely-chopped mushrooms; 4 ozs. preferably unsalted butter; 1½ pts. dry white wine; salt and pepper to season; ¼ pt. *Hollandaise†*; 1 pt. double cream; 1 teacupful fine, soft breadcrumbs; 4 heaped teaspoonsful milled parsley; and 3 dozen asparagus spears.

Rub butter around base and sides of two heat-resistant containers the size and depth of 2 meat baking tins (approximately 11″ × 13″). Season breasts lightly with salt and pepper. Lay down in containers, divide wine equally between the two. Cover lightly with foil and cook middle shelf Gas Mark 6 for maximum 20 minutes (with breast pieces or *suprêmes* from 3½ lb. chickens). Remove, chill and pack into lidded plastic container, cover and freeze. Pour liquors into thick pan, add mushrooms and simmer for 7 minutes. Strain and pack mushroom pulp into waxed carton and freeze. Simmer strained liquors down to ¼ pt. of syrupy fluid. Pour into waxed carton and freeze. Thaw overnight before wedding and make *Hollandaise*. In the morning mix mushroom pulp with crumbs and parsley. Season to taste with salt and pepper and spread neatly over undersides of each breast. Set top sides uppermost in neat pattern on chosen dish. Place reduced wine/chicken/mushroom flavoured liquor in small pan and reduce again, carefully, until it is a very thick syrup. Chill over bowl of ice (for speed) and whip cream as thickly as you dare. Fold in chilled syrupy liquor, then the cold *Hollandaise* spoonful by spoonful but do not whip madly or mixture might curdle. Pipe this in rosettes all over each breast. Surround with little bundles of cooked, cold, shortened asparagus (allow 5 fat or six medium sticks per person). Serve well chilled.

If you fail to whip cream sufficiently, reduce liquor sufficiently, or make *Hollandaise* thickly enough, the finished mixture will not be stiff enough to pipe. Should this happen, just spoon smoothly over each breast piece. No one will ever know what was originally intended! In this case try to have a few tarragon leaves to lay in Vees over each sauce-coated breast.

· Suprêmes de Volaille aux Champignons à blanc ·

There is another lovely, easy one of Escoffier's which he calls *Suprêmes de Volaille aux Champignons à blanc*. Assume we are cooking for four, and then you can add or subtract at will. There is something so intimidating about recipes given in huge costly quantities! Assemble your four prepared chickens' breasts, a dozen very neat, medium-sized de-stalked mushroom cups, ¼ pt. of dry-ish white wine and a little hazelnut of butter. Chop up the mushroom stalks roughly. Sling into a small pan with the wine and butter. Simmer very gently for 10 minutes. Strain through a sieve, being careful to press out every drop of the liquor. Pour this into a shallow pan and turn the mushroom cups down onto it. If there is insufficient liquor to come at least half way up the inverted cups, add a little more stock—white stock of course! Poach these tenderly—four minutes on each side, please—lift out, drain and keep warm. Pour the liquor into a shallow casserole or other heat-resistant container. Lay in the chickens' breasts, cover (foil will do) and cook in the oven centre shelf for not more than 15 minutes at Gas Mark 4. Fish out the chicken, arrange—wing ends outwards and tapering ends inwards—on a heat-resistant dish leaving a little empty circle in the centre. Set the poached mushrooms into this central space, cups downwards and arranged in a neat little mound.

Measure your mushroom poaching liquor which, by now, should have reduced itself to a mere ¼ pt. If it has not done so, just simmer it down in a small pan. Add in ¼ pt. of *Velouté** and work the two together over a gentle heat until faultlessly blended.

If in doubt rub through a *tamis*—the fine, classic, cone-shaped sieve which does the job pluperfectly for you. Return it to the pan, stir in ¼ pt. of thick cream and when all is bubbling merrily, take the pan off the heat. Beat the mixture a little to expel surplus heat, beat in 2 egg yolks very swiftly, and whatever else you do pray do not add the slightest scrap of butter after you have added the egg yolks or the mixture will surely curdle! Just pour enough of it neatly and carefully over all and hand any surplus separately in a (warmed with boiling water first!) sauce boat.

· Suprêmes de Volaille Hongroise ·

Escoffier also has a way with these *suprêmes* which he names *Suprêmes de Volaille Hongroise*. Even his directions are simple for this delicious version which does not require any vegetables to be served with it. Poach the required number of *suprêmes* in clarified butter very gently and until tender but *not dried up*. As a generalisation the people of this Island tend to over-cook chickens, hence the French label *à l'Anglais* for birds which are beige and dry instead of faintly pink at the bone and juicily succulent. Remove, season with salt and powdered (rose) paprika and set them upon a dish of pilaf rice with tomatoes. Swill the poaching pan with a few tablespoonsful of cream, add 4 fl. ozs. *Sauce Hongroise* for every *suprême* and pour overall at the moment of service.

· Sauce Hongroise ·

We gave you the method for the pilaf rice in the first of this trilogy, "The Cook's Book". All you are now required to do is stir into it skimmed, de-pipped tomato flesh which has been poached very gently in butter. Allow 6 medium tomatoes to every 8 ozs. of rice. The *Sauce Hongroise* is simply a matter of frying a tablespoonful or two of finely sliced shallots or onions very softly indeed with equal quantities of oil and butter and working in as the onions become tender 1 teaspoon of powdered paprika to every 4 ozs. onions. Moisten this amount with ¼ pt. dry white wine, add a faggot of herbs, simmer until mixture is reduced by one third, and finish with ¾ pt. ordinary *Sauce Velouté**. At the last sieve your sauce (ideally use that *tamis*) and stir into it a few flakes of butter to give it a very grand sheen.

· Suprêmes de Volaille Italienne ·

Suprêmes de Volaille Italienne is a good one to serve after some preceding dish which has been very creamy in character. You turn each breast of chicken in beaten egg, pass through a mixture of equal parts grated Parmesan cheese and very fine, soft white breadcrumbs and then you *sauté* these gently in a shallow pan with equal parts oil and butter. When they are cooked, you must have ready on a large heated dish six ovals of *Polenta à l'Italienne*. Lay a *suprême* upon each oval and moisten overall with a little butter cooked with a few drops of lemon juice until it is not brown in colour.

· Polenta à l'Italienne ·

To make the *Polenta*, place 35½ fl. ozs. water in a pan and bring to a fast rolling boil. Add 1 oz. butter and 1 flat teaspoon salt. Reduce the heat so that the water bubbles very gently indeed. Sift 8 ozs. semolina in gradually, stirring all the time and continue stirring until it is very, very thick indeed. Add 3 heaped tablespoons grated Parmesan and stir again until this is wholly blended. Turn onto an oiled marble slab so that it forms a ½″ thick layer. When cold cut into suitable ovals for the *Suprêmes de Volaille Italienne*. Slip the serving dish under a grill so that the top surface browns lightly and use as instructed.

· Suprêmes de Volaille en papillote ·

When you are really beset, have planned on one of these recipes, prepared the *suprêmes* but some drama develops, make them up into *Suprêmes de Volaille en papillote* and thus level yourself off on your time schedule. Stiffen them rapidly by turning them in hot butter for 1 minute on each side. Whip them out, all buttery, and place them in the centre of rectangles of parchment or kitchen foil, over a large spoonful of thick cream. Season them with salt and pepper. Wrap them into very loose parcels. Sling them into the oven Gas Mark 5, one shelf above centre, for 15–20 minutes depending upon the size of your *suprêmes*. Boil up ½ pt. of double cream for every 4 *papillotes* in the oven. Let it turn beige with simmering. Whip out the *suprêmes*, lay them on a heated dish and tent them with foil lightly so that they keep hot on the floor of your oven at Gas Mark ½.

Pour the accumulated juices and cream liquor into your boiling cream and pour it into the top of a double saucepan over hot water. At the moment of service add two tablespoonsful of brandy to the cream mixture, pour over the *suprêmes* and send to table otherwise naked and unadorned. As a good hostess, and when serving these, pick up a scrap of bread crust from your side plate and dunk it in the creamy mixture so that your guests may feel free to do the same. *Ça vaut la peine.*

Having dealt in the preceding recipes with the use of chickens' breasts in five different ways, let us in the interests of economy turn to ways in which the remainders can be used without anyone being even slightly suspicious that they are being given left-overs. In effect this means we can give you any good recipes for chicken pieces which you can employ at will with or without the *suprêmes*.

· Poulet Stanley ·

High on our list is *Poulet Stanley*. Mince 10 ozs. of Spanish onions finely. Blanch for 7 minutes in a little fast-boiling water. Strain and press out surplus moisture. Turn over 1½ ozs. butter and 1½ fl. ozs. oil which have been heated together in a roomy pan. Lay over this bed a neatly skinned and divided 3½–4 lb. chicken. If you have used the breasts elsewhere make up to this weight with leg and thigh pieces. Season with salt lightly and with pepper. Pour on ½ pt. double cream, cover with a lid and cook very gently giving the pan an occasional vigorous shake for 20 minutes, making sure that the heat beneath is moderated sufficiently to stop the contents sticking and burning. Lift out the pieces and set them aside in a warm place. Add a brimming teacupful of basic *Sauce Béchamel** and a level soupspoonful of tomato *pureé*. Stir well, allow to simmer for a few moments and rub through a sieve. Finish the sauce after sieving with a mere eggspoonful of curry paste, a flat teaspoon of paprika powder and the strained juice of a lemon. Now be careful and add that lemon juice drip by drip unless you want to curdle the whole affair! Pour the sauce over the cooked chicken. Tent lightly with foil and slip into the oven at Gas Mark ¼, bottom shelf, where, if required so to do, it can wait up to 45 minutes. Surround with little crescents of puff pastry for service.

· Poulet Hongroise ·

Heat 1½ ozs. each of butter and oil in a roomy shallow pan and fry briskly in this mixture the neatly skinned and divided 3½–4 lb. chicken. Once again for *Poulet Hongroise* you either use with the *suprêmes* or make up the weight with leg and thigh pieces. Remove the chicken pieces and set aside. Add ½ lb. rice and if necessary a spoonful more of oil and butter. Keep turning with a slice until the rice is nice and yellow. Pour on ¼ pt. good clear, strong white stock. Add a flat eggspoon of salt, the same of paprika, 1 raw grated onion, a faggot of herbs or *bouquet garni**, 3 medium, de-pipped, peeled, rough-chopped tomatoes and 1 flat soupspoon of concentrated tomato *pureé*. Add a further pint of stock, cover and allow to cook gently for 3 minutes. Turn the whole lot into a casserole, add the chicken, mix it round and slip into the oven at Gas Mark 4–5 one shelf above centre for 30 minutes.

During this period have an occasional peek under the lid to see whether or not the liquor is becoming absorbed before the chicken and rice are completely cooked. Should this be so, add still more stock at the rate of 5 fl. ozs. per addition, stir well, re-cover and continue cooking. You should end up with tender chicken, grain-separate perfectly cooked rice and an homogenous mixture which is moist and succulent but in no circumstances whatever is allowed to resemble a pond.

· Poulet Paysan ·

You must also have one we have just used for a Sunday luncheon in the garden which virtually made itself during the morning as everyone was far too busy to give any dish their attention. Skin and divide a 4 lb. chicken as explained on p. 151. Stiffen the pieces briskly in about 2½ ozs. of singing butter. Add 24 young, peeled shallots, turn them for about 4 minutes. Turn the whole lot into a casserole with 4 rashers of streaky bacon diced large. Add a pint of stock, a *bouquet garni** and a little seasoning of salt and pepper. Cover and cook at Gas Mark 3, middle shelf, for 40 minutes. Add 24 very small, scraped, new potatoes, turn them into the liquor, cover and when the potatoes are tender, lift all the solids with a skimmer onto a heated dish. Blend 2 heaped teaspoonsful of potato flour (*fécule de pommes*) with

3 fl. ozs. of sherry or water, stir into the residue pan liquor, pour over the chicken and serve the entire main course on one dish. Alternatively, if you must be grand, sieve the sauce over the solids and sprinkle with finely milled parsley.

· Faux Poulet à la Kiev ·

To complete this small circuit let us explain to you how you can turn left-over raw thighs or legs of chicken into some quite elegant little items. Start with a small sharp pointed knife. Lay either leg or thigh piece inside uppermost on the table and make a straight incision through to the bone from top to bottom lengthwise. Then scrape back carefully until you have excavated the bone altogether. Lay a chip-sized strip of Gruyère or Emmenthal cheese in the middle, cover with a slice of ham and roll up like a bulgy sausage. Secure the two open sides together with a wooden cocktail stick and lay on a buttered heatproof dish. Pour 1 pt. of Madeira sauce over 8 of these sausages and serve as a *Faux-Poulet à la Kiev*.

Alternatively, proceed exactly as explained with the boning bit, spread real or tinned substitute *pâté* over the interior, cover with a slice of tongue and cover with 8 little speared-through sausages spiked with wooden cocktail sticks. Set on a buttered heat-resistant container with, poured overall, 1 pt. *Sauce Mornay* (p. 66) into which you have blended 2 finely chopped hard-boiled eggs. Bake when required under a very light tenting of foil, one shelf above centre, Gas Mark 4, for 20 minutes. Withdraw from the oven after first 10 minutes, remove cocktail sticks when the items are boneless and surround if liked with a border of piped Duchess potato*, remembering to apply a thin film of melted clarified butter very gently to the top surface of the potato mixture.

· Pigeons de Laboureille ·

We made a passing reference to pigeons earlier on in this chapter so now let us give them a little proper attention. They are the least expensive of all game, so we are justified in asking you to use only the breasts or *suprêmes* (see p. 149) for dinner parties, and to use up the remainder in the stock pot or as a family salmi.

Having removed the breast sections as pictured on p. 150 and explained on p. 151 you have a wide range of treatments at your disposal. We have given you the most generally known *Pigeon* *aux Olives**, so now let us talk about a couple of lesser known treatments.

In the Perigord, a small cook's paradise, we gleaned *Pigeons de Laboureille* which will not do you any harm either. For 6 breast pieces dice up 4 ozs. of raw, unsalted pork fat very small, and place in a thick, heated frying pan. When they begin to sizzle over a good medium heat, lay in the breasts and allow these to fry for 2 minutes on each side. Mix together 7 fl. ozs. of a lusty red wine and 4 tablespoonsful of brandy. Warm gently in a little pan over a low heat. Turn up full flame under your pigeon breasts, pour in warmed mixture, tip pan to flame to ignite and shake vigorously to keep flames burning for 1 minute. Turn off the heat. Place the breasts, cut-sides downwards in a fairly shallow casserole. Strain on the liquor (thus withdrawing the frizzled pork dice); toss in a faggot of herbs, add 2 ozs. coarsely grated carrots and the same of celery heart. Of course if you possess a mandolin, cut these vegetables *en julienne*. Sprinkle with salt and pepper. Add 4 fl. ozs. of (a) *consommé* or (b) strongly reduced, cleared stock, cover and cook at Gas Mark 4, one shelf above centre, under a well-fitted lid for about 30 minutes.

Arrange the pigeon portions on a heated dish. Remove herb faggot and rub sauce through a sieve (ideally a *tamis*) overall. Surround with little triangles of fried bread which strictly speaking should always be fried in melted pork fat for this dish. The alternative presentation, which is easier when the dish is handed round for guests to help themselves, is to cut and fry six rectangles of bread, set a pigeon breast upon each one and then pour the sauce overall.

· Pigeons aux Petits Pois nouveaux ·

In the spring, when irritable farmers are creating a nice glut of inexpensive pigeons by their Pigeon Shoots to clear these marauders from their young crops, turn the previous dish into *Pigeons aux Petits Pois nouveaux*. Give the breasts precisely the same treatment as above but first give 2 lbs. of freshly shelled peas the *Petits Pois en Casserole** treatment. When they are tender, fish out those pulped lettuce leaves, strain off the liquor, simmer this down to a mere teaspoonful in a tiny pan and then emulsify or sieve with the cooked peas. Taste, make any seasoning correction thought necessary (with salt and pepper) and pour the *pureé* onto a heated serving dish. Keep warm until pigeon breasts are cooked. Dress them out on a bed of sieved peas, surround with triangular *croûtons* (passed through egg and milk and deep fried) and hand the sieved *Laboureille Sauce* (previous recipe) separately in a sauce boat.

· Salmi de Pigeon familial ·

Before we move on you may want to have a reliable *Salmi* recipe for using up the residues of large quantities of pigeon. Remove the leg/thigh portions from the carcases, turn in seasoned flour and fry briskly in good clean dripping or rendered down pork fat until portions are a good golden brown. Season with salt and pepper and pack in layers into a deep casserole with alternate layers of very thinly sliced onion. Tuck in a *bouquet garni** amidships during this layering. For every six pairs of leg/thigh portions mix together $1\frac{1}{2}$ pts. of good strong stock, $\frac{1}{4}$ pt. lusty red wine and 1 flat tablespoon of concentrated tomato *pureé*; stir well and pour overall. Cover and cook gently centre shelf at Gas Mark 3 until flesh parts willingly from bones. Fish out the herb faggot and remove the pigeon pieces. Remove all flesh when cool enough to handle. Reduce pot-liquor to half quantity by simmering, emulsify or sieve, return to pot, fold in flesh, taste, correct seasoning and serve from the (napkin-wrapped) pot.

· Identification of Our Feathered Friends in Prime Condition ·

Grouse. Spurs undeveloped; plumage shiny and gay; quill feathers will come away easily when tugged if bird is young.
Partridges. Reject all with rounded wing feathers—look for the long, sharp pointed ones and for yellow legs.
Pheasants. Legs smooth; plumage bright and shiny; spurs short.
Pigeon reveal their age by their vents—when it is discoloured, reject.
Poultry. Breastbone and toes pliable and soft; legs smooth; spurs short (on cockerel); beaks yellow (on ducks) and these must break easily, be pliable and feet must be yellow and supple.
Turkey. Flesh white; black legs very smooth; feet moist and pliable.

· The Roasting of Game and Poultry ·

Grouse. Here we must confess that we only ever spit-roast these treasures. Wrap the breast in a thin piece of raw unsalted pork fat. Tie securely. Impale on the spit which has been pre-heated for at least 10 minutes. Put 2 crustless squares of bread into the drip pan below for each impaled grouse, so that the drips of blood and pork fat fall onto them. Turn them at half time, then remove them and finish toasting under the grill. Put a halved grouse upon each cut-side downwards. Time on the spit is so variable according to the type of spit that we can only say that the skewer test should give you a fairly strong pink bubble of *jus* and not a pale one for the average taste; but if the idea of encountering pink near the bone repels you, soldier on for another 5–7 minutes. For oven roasting the grouse may be wrapped in either rashers of bacon or pork fat. When bacon is used, cover the birds for the last 10 minutes of roasting time. Otherwise the bacon will be charred! Time for roasting one shelf above centre at Gas Mark 6, 20 minutes for underdone, 30 for pink at the bone or 35–40 for cooked completely through.

Partridges—see Grouse. Reduce roasting times to minimum 20 and maximum 30 and 25 for the pink stage.

Pheasant. Such a dry bird unless carefully treated, so be generous with the pork fat or the bacon rashers. Very small birds will need 30–35 minutes, one shelf above centre, at Gas Mark 6; very plump ones will need 40–45 minutes. Spit-roasting—follow our preceding instructions for partridge and grouse.

Pigeon—do not roast. Only the breasts or *suprêmes* are really worth bothering about at all. If the remainder is left unroasted, the little legs and thighs can be cooked *en salmi* or made into an absolutely splendid stock for soups.

Poultry. Rub a 3½–4 lb. bird fairly liberally with softened butter. Season with salt and pepper. Place in a meat baking tin and roast at Gas Mark 6 until breast skin is nicely browned, (1 shelf above centre). Tent this with a scrap of foil. Reduce heat to Gas Mark 5 and continue cooking until the bird is tender. Test, as with all the others, by driving a metal skewer, steel knitting needle or trussing needle through the fat part of the thigh. If the bubble of juice which emerges is just faintly pale pink, the bird will be tender and moist; if colourless, the bird will be beige and dry.

Turkey. Rub liberally with coarse salt and coarsely ground pepper and then with butter. Wrap prepared turkey loosely in foil. Bake at Gas Mark 4–5, allowing 40 minutes for the first pound and 20 minutes per pound thereafter, up to 14 lbs. For every additional pound between 15 and 20, allow 15 minutes per lb. For every additional pound between 20 and 25, allow 10 minutes per lb. For open oven roasting allow 15 minutes to the pound after an initial 30 minutes for the first pound at Gas Mark 4–5. Always remember to cover the upper breast of the bird with a piece of kitchen foil after the first 30 minutes of roasting and until the last 15 minutes. Baste regularly. We have given you no oven position as it will depend upon the size of the bird, but we can at least make the point that the breast bone should clear roof of oven by 2" whenever possible. When rising above this level, cover breast with 2 thicknesses of kitchen foil as soon as skin is lightly browned.

Steaming · Oven Casseroling · Casserole de Petits Pois
Petits Pois Lucullus · Tartelettes de Petits Pois Berrichonne
Petits Pois Printanier · Laitues braisées au Jus · Poaching
Courgettes pochées au Beurre · Corn on the Cob
Beignets de Maïs · The Cooking of Chicory · Endive à la crème
Endive au Parmesan · Endive en chemise rouge · Grilled Tomatoes
Tomates Elvia · Cervelles de Veau · Tomates Gourmandes
Beignets d'Aubergines · Gâteau Rothschild
Pommes de Terre Grand'mère · Galettes · Champignons
Petits Pains · Individual Golden Sandcastles
Individual Pommes Anna · Gâteau Anglais
Gnocchi de Pommes de Terre
Soufflé de Pommes de Terre
Pommes de Terre Robert · Pommes de Terre Roxelane
Ma Galette · Cheese and Potato Flan
Gratin de Pommes de Terre · Pommes de Terre Helder
Salade Christiane · Salade Gabrielle
Salade de Romaine Bernoise
Crudités aux Fonds d'Artichauts
Fonds d'Artichauts aux Raisins

fourteen · BE DAMNED TO DROWNING

All too often we hear the remark, "I find the smell of vegetables when they are cooking so off-putting." In this context smell is sin because good vegetables are never boiled and the smell stems from just that. We steamed some small courgettes today—a totally odourless process until the lid was lifted for testing when a faint, fresh, earthy tang arose from the steamer. We also diced (unskinned) and then steamed some of our own hothouse cucumbers—under a plate because there was not a well-fitting lid to hand—and again . . . no niffy permeations throughout the house, but all the goodness and flavour carefully retained for the diners to enjoy at the table. Of couse, both these vegetables came straight from garden to pot to tum, so those who are unfortunate enough to buy their vegetables from average greengrocers must just stiffen up their sinews and prepare to wage war-unto-the-death against the salesmen who try to palm them off with tasteless rubbish.

The majority of vegetables die twice before they come to table, firstly by being "grown on" which is a habit conducive to mayhem; and secondly by being drowned!

Gardeners who are not also cooks are all too prone to surrender flavour to their besotted zeal to grow enormous whatever-it-is. This size-mania applies to both the enthusiastic amateur and the commercial grower; the former for sheer vanity and the latter for sheer greed. The larger the heavier, the heavier the less to the pound and the higher the ratio of profit, which practice can only persist because housewives are far too complacent about what they will accept in exchange for their money or their menfolks' hard earned lolly. If *everyone* refused to buy the overgrown, the blown and the stringy, as a Continental chef once remarked on hearing complaints from the restaurant, "There would have to be the pulling up of the sockses."

Not only are these Brobidnagian veterans offered to us as

scandalous value for money; but our labours are doubled while
the flavour and texture is shamefully diminished. A young French
bean needs only topping and tailing whereas a stringy one has to
be stringed! A crisp, stringless runner bean sails through a little
bean slicer, a stringy one clogs up the works. When broad beans
are left until the pods drag the plants down and the beans themselves—fat, pallid and unhealthy—are enclosed in leather over-
coats, cook must divest them of these outer garments before sending them to table—double waste of both time and weight value
per pound. Broad beans which are young and tender go from pan
to dish to table and the lot is polished off. These are also quite
easily digestible, whereas the old leathery, flavourless ones are
positively anti-social in the noisy effects they produce in the unfortunate stomachs which receive them. They should cook very
quickly, as indeed they do when they are young; but when they
take a wet week in the pan they merely pass from being tough and
raw to being tough and pappy.

One of the most scandalous practices is the growing-on of tiny
Brussels sprouts until they are large enough and sufficiently
blown to be nothing better than cabbages for "borrowers"!
There is a very vulgar name for good small ones in French
restaurants which it would not be seemly for us to quote here;
but please take our word for it that no self respecting chef would
ever accept anything but little green bullets over the lintels of his
kitchen door.

Consider the sad story of the vegetable marrow. The English
grower labours under the delusion that unless the wretched thing
is grown-on until it is the size of the Graf Zeppelin, it is a reflection upon his horticultural skill, whereas if he would allow these
to be picked when they were the size of a pork sausage, he would
go on cropping and having little fresh ones from early summer
until the first frosts. Thus cook would have flavour to dish up, the
fuel bills for cooking would be down and the family would be
taking in considerably less than 92 per cent water; added to which
of course there are no great cores of pith and pips to excavate and
consign to the compost buckets.

If, as we hope you will always do, you study the great Escoffier,
you will discover that he instructs us all to remove the hard cores
from carrots before cooking them, a charming little chore for the
single-handed housewife with five kids! Pick 'em young, pick 'em

often, scrape instead of peel, steam instead of boil and, in summer, have two great steamer orgies of bulk steaming so that you can consign your surplus when cooked and cold to polythene bags and the freezer. (Of course you will not freeze them raw.) This way you get the best out of the best.

Even so there are vegetables which actually improve with size. Jacket-baked new potatoes are horrid while the big old ones are marvellous; but then the whole subject of the potato really needs considerably more attention than it ever gets. Anyone who has ever tried to make *pommes soufflées**—those tiny little, completely hollow, miniature cushions which blow up with their *second* frying—will know that these stubbornly refuse to blow unless you get the right kind of potato. This is in fact the red-skinned Dutchman and nothing else ever produces an equal percentage of success. Similarly, an old fashioned, flavoursome King Edward makes the best mashed potato or *Pommes Duchesse**, whereas a soapy potato always makes the best potato salad*. Best of all are new potatoes for the job. Wash them, steam them, skin them while hot and give them a jolly good rinse under the cold tap to soap them up. These should be soapy, then they will slice without cracking and crumbling.

The globe artichoke is another special case. We grow these and are busily cropping the newly established plants in our new garden which we started from seed when we moved in. We first take a young crop of very small ones for the simple and obvious reason which the Italians know better than any other nation. When steamed, they can be eaten whole with *vinaigrée* or *vinaigrette*. Conversely the big chaps—the best of which come from the Médoc area of France—are the true *Artichauts Vinaigrette* which you are offered all over France. These should have the scissors clipped across their tops to cut off the peaky part of the cluster which forms each one. Then, ideally, they should be tied firmly with fine string but not so firmly that the string cuts in when cooking makes them tender. The purpose of this, like planting a lily bulb slightly on its side, is to stop too much water getting in. As soon as an outer leaf comes away at the gentlest pull, into a pan of iced water with them, squeeze them out in a cloth and they will be—perfection!

Then there is the sad case of ill treatment to beetroots. Here you must be the judge as to whether we are talking rubbish or common sense. In England the standard practice is to skin cooked beetroots and slice them in rounds so that all the grainings show on each slice like the graining on a section of a tree trunk. The French practice is to cut them vertically exactly to the size and shape of chips. Try both and if the chips do not taste far better to you—when diced with a little oil and *wine* vinegar and given a top-sprinkling of parsley—go back to tree trunks and do not bother.

Cauliflowers take a pasting too. Cauliflowers should be cut as soon as the flower is round, tight and white and not left until the stem of each "bloom" forces its way upwards to the light leaving spaces in between.

Small round turnips can be absolutely delicious, but those whacking great jobs you get offered can only be called a gastronomic experience if you like eating balls of fine crochet cotton. We reach a peak of foolishness with all this, when we face the inescapable fact that the large and inferior are always more difficult to cook for women whose days become increasingly busier.

When you are being selective, when you have lugged home quality-vegetables, do not condemn them to death by drowning them. There are three basic and absurdly easy ways of cooking vegetables: steaming, poaching and oven casseroling. Setting aside the exceptions, stop boiling, please.

· STEAMING ·

Since we actually have a letter from a reader asking us to explain our extraordinary and mystic references to "steaming" and wondering if this meant putting the relevant food in front of a steaming kettle; we will deal with this briefly in case there are others to whom the process is equally esoteric.

A steamer is a generally aluminium, straight-sided pan with perforations in the base. The item for steaming is placed in this container which is fitted over a base saucepan a little under half-filled with fast-boiling water. A lid is placed over and the water is maintained at a steady, but gentle bubble and the item left until it reaches the requisite tenderness. All steamed items need a little attention after cooking and before sending to table. They *must* be seasoned and should be either tossed in butter, or sparked up with herbs or both, or sauced in some way to enhance, not submerge, their natural flavours.

Before leaving this subject let us round it off for the beginner cook by pointing out that one steamer is better than none but two or three are even better. Why? Because two and three can then be fitted over one and thus, for example, a steamed pudding put in the first one, potatoes in number two and carrots in number three and no foodstuff will offend any above or below by its close proximity. For the very small household there are also dividers and thus a little of three different items can be steamed in one container if each is put separately within the confines of its divider—lacking one, make thick foil partitions yourself.

· OVEN CASSEROLING ·

The chosen container for oven casseroling should be lidded. When little Willie sends the lid flying and you have swept up the pieces, use a double fold of tightly pressed-on kitchen foil. It will take a shade longer but will do the job very well. Today the range is very wide: heat-resistant glass or china, earthenware or copper—of course you choose. The principle is to put butter, or a moistening agent, with the vegetable, cover with the lid and let it make its own natural juices during slow cooking time . . . as a generalisation Gas Mark 4 lowest shelf and up to Gas Mark 6 (when roasting large joints) on the floor of the oven. Now let us be more specific, with no apologies for repeating ourselves because there is a long season throughout the year when you should indulge yourself as follows:

· Casserole de Petits Pois ·

Take 2 lbs. of shelled peas in prime condition, the outside leaves of a lettuce which has been trimmed and, of course, washed, 3–4 tablespoons of dry white cooking wine, 1 flat eggspoonful of salt, 1 generous pinch of milled black peppercorns, 1 walnut-sized piece of butter and 1 flat teaspoonful of castor sugar. Line out your chosen casserole with two-thirds of the outside lettuce leaves. Place the peas on this little bed, add the remaining ingredients and finish with a "lid" of the remaining lettuce leaves. Put on the proper lid and cook as explained. What will have happened is this: the water in the lettuce leaves and the natural juices in the peas will have come together with the other ingredients and made a small quantity of thin but delectably flavoured fluid. The lettuce leaves will become a nasty brown pap. Dredge up and discard.

· Petits Pois Lucullus ·

For grander occasions transform this dish into *Petits Pois Lucullus*. Strain off the liquor, place in a small pan and reduce by simmering fiercely to one-third its original bulk. Measure and add the same quantity of double cream, return to the pan, re-simmer until creamy. Pour over the peas in a serving dish or pile the cooked peas into little savoury short paste tartlet cases. Spoon a little sauce over each, arrange the now *Tartelette de Petits Pois Berrichonne* on a heat-resistant serving dish, tent lightly with kitchen foil and re-heat at Gas Mark 1; *but please do not* spoon the sauce over just before re-heating or the pastry cases will b soggy at the base.

· Petits Pois Printanier ·

There is a further variant on this theme, *Petits Pois Printanier*, which is ideal if you are serving *escalope de veau* or the baby slices called *piccate*. Add one dozen of the white only of small spring onions to every pound of shelled peas, otherwise proceed exactly as for *Casserole de Petits Pois* until they are cooked. Then just dredge out the lettuce leaves and serve in the pot or remove the lettuce leaves, strain off the liquor, dissolve about 1 rounded tea-spoonful to every ¼ pt. fluid, of potato flour (*fécule de pommes*) in 2 fl. ozs. of either tap water—if you must—or ideally dry white cooking wine. Remember that, unlike cornflour, you can stir the potato flour and the cold liquid together and immediately add it to the hot liquid in the pan. It will thicken almost instantly without lumping as you stir. It has the added virtue, unlike cornflour, of thickening sauces like sweetened red currant juice without clouding or dulling. Moreover, it is totally tasteless and odourless —marvellous in fact on a humbler level, when you have made a family casserole and find as you are about to serve it that it is a little too thin. Blend a teaspoon of potato flour in cold water and stir in gradually until the requisite thickness is obtained. If the fluid in the casserole is really hot it thickens in seconds and you can carry your dish straight to the table without anyone even guessing that you had boobed in the first instance.

· Laitues braisées au Jus ·

Cos lettuce makes another delicious and slightly different vegetable when casseroled as *Laitues braisées au Jus*. Assemble 4

firm cos lettuces, 2 fatty rashers of No. 3 or 4 cut bacon, 1 large
shallot or small onion, 1 medium carrot, 1 gill of really strong
stock, ½ oz. butter, 1 heaped tablespoon of chopped, fresh parsley,
salt and pepper to season. Butter a pie dish large enough to contain the washed, trimmed whole lettuces with the tops just folded
under. Lay the bacon on the buttered pan, sprinkle with half the
finely chopped carrot and onion, put in the lettuces, sprinkle with
the remainder of the carrot and onion, swill with the stock and
cook on the middle shelf for approximately 45–50 minutes, Gas
Mark 4. Lift out the lettuces, halve or quarter lengthwise according to their fatness, arrange on a narrow serving dish. Pour the
stock into a small pan, simmer until reduced to half quantity,
season with salt and pepper, pour over lettuces and sprinkle
parsley overall. You can, of course, improve this even more if you
use half a gill of strong stock and half a gill of dry Madeira, i.e.
Sercial, in which case the title of the dish becomes *Laitues braisées
au Madère.*

· POACHING ·

The greatest response to poaching comes from cucumbers and
courgettes or *zucchini*, generally lumped together under the heading
"Baby Marrows".

· Courgettes pochées au Beurre ·

For *Courgettes pochées au Beurre* use pork-sausage-sized courgettes, slice off tops and tails and slice into ¼″ thick rounds *unskinned*. Melt enough butter in a small, very thick pan to cover the
bottom to a depth of a generous ⅛″. When the butter has melted
and is sizzling, gently tip in the prepared courgettes, cover with
plate or lid and shake vigorously to coat the top halves with
butter. Pan should be a maximum half full whatever its size. Now
reduce heat to very low and get on with whatever else you are
doing in the kitchen; just remember to give an occasional shake to
the pan to ensure that the gradually softening base slices are not
allowed to stick and become dark brown. In 10–15 minutes the
courgettes will be ready. All they need is a sprinkling of salt and
pepper, a spoonful of milled parsley and a final shake as you turn
them onto their dish for service.

You can do the same thing with baby carrots, scraped and
sliced, and also with unskinned, fairly coarse dice of cucumber

and all three are as delicious as they are simple to cook. Given the patience to keep shaking without forgetfulness, baby onions are succulent if given the same treatment, but, if they are not absolutely minute, they should ideally have 10 minutes steaming first and then the butter-poaching treatment to achieve perfection.

· Corn on the Cob ·

There are, however, certain vegetables with which you really do not get the best from any of these three treatments and some, making the exceptions to the rule, which must be boiled. Corn on the cob is an excellent example. The cobs, when every particle of outer leaf and silken tress has been removed and the stem cut off level with the first grain, should be tossed into a very roomy pan with plenty of fairly fast-boiling, slightly salted water. Cook them until a single grain is tender on your teeth. Drain and either chill for later use; brush liberally with melted butter, sprinkle all round with salt and pepper and brown under a brisk grill, or dry them while still hot and give them the same treatment immediately. If serving these at a dinner, do remember to drive a wooden cocktail stick into each end so that the eater can pick up the sticks and not the cobs. Butter down tight-fitting wrists of dinner dresses is unwelcome to most women and even with the cocktail sticks to hold, finger bowls are essential.

· Beignets de Maïs ·

Nor must we forget that little fritters of fresh, not tinned, corn are a delicacy as an accompaniment to something like *Poulet à la Kiev* (p. 152) or Spatchcock Poussin. For these *Beignets de Maïs* cook the corn exactly as explained. Strip off the grains, scratching downwards with a very sharp knife until they all fall away from the husk. Make sure they are completely chilled before using. Make a thick flour batter by adding one standard egg to a bowl containing 3 heaped tablespoons of sifted flour. Add a tablespoonful of olive oil and a very little top-of-the-milk, sparingly, as you beat, until you achieve a mixture which flops idly off a lifted spoon. Fold in the corn. Heat a thick iron frying pan or griddle *dry*. When contact with a piece of raw, unsalted pork fat causes this to sizzle, slightly polish the surface with your bit of pork fat until it is thoroughly greased. Reduce heat to medium low, drop generous dessertspoonsful fairly wide apart over the surface, pat them down with a pork fat rubbed metal spatula, have an occasional peek to see that you flip each one over the moment the underside is golden brown. At this point reduce heat to very low to ensure that the second side cooks through thoroughly before becoming too dark.

Another temperamental vegetable is what the Flemish call *whitloof*, the Belgians and French *endive* and the English chicory; hence the confusion that some of you may have encountered at Continental greengrocers who set up shop in England. You ask for what you think is chicory and you get what to them is *endive*, because in French the terms are switched. A great number of people detest what we call chicory because of its bitterness, not realising it is very easy to dispose of this in the cooking. Here is what you do.

· THE COOKING OF CHICORY ·

Place the heads in a roomy pan containing plenty of cold water, adjust heat to medium and allow water to come to the boil. Strain the chicory, throw the water away, cover liberally with fresh boiling water and add 2 lumps of sugar to every pound of chicory. Simmer until tender and you are off to a flying start with the chicory divested of its oppressive bitterness. Then it can be presented *à la crème, au Parmesan* or *en chemise rouge*.

· Endive à la crème ·

Lay the well drained heads in a slightly buttered heat-resistant dish. For half a dozen heads allow a ¼ pt. of double cream. Boil this until it begins to thicken, remove from the heat, stir in a tablespoon of Hollandaise sauce*, add to the chicory and serve.

· Endive au Parmesan ·

For this presentation put the chicory into a dish as described for *à la crème*, cover with a strongly flavoured cheese sauce made with Parmesan cheese, cover the top with transparently thin slices of Gruyère or Emmenthal, place in the oven one shelf above centre at Gas Mark 5 for 10 minutes and serve.

· Endive en chemise rouge ·

For the third variant of your chicory "in a red dress", again cook the chicory exactly as explained at the beginning. For the sauce you will need, for six heads, 6 medium ripe tomatoes, 1 oz. butter, salt and pepper to season, 2 small heads of fresh mint and 4 of tarragon. Melt the butter in a small pan, add the rough-cut tomatoes, the finely chopped herbs and simmer gently to a rough pulp. Sieve, season and pour over the chicory.

One of the greatest chefs who ever lived was Edouard Nignon. He wrote in his introduction to his great work *Eloges de la Cuisine Française*—in French and therefore we will translate— that the culinary art is by no means epitomised in the making of sumptuous and classic dishes but rises to a peak when the talent of the cook makes a memorable experience out of humblest *pot-au-feu*; the simplest culinary formulas can be more enhanced by a touch of artistry than even the most highly complicated dish.

To any Frenchman served by the great growers of Provence the tomato is as cheap as it is commodious, yet at the hands of a hash-slinger masquerading as a chef this unfortunate item is either sliced up with the skin on and used raw to garnish a grilled steak or halved and shoved under the grill until the skin wrinkles and collapses and the flesh is reduced to a flabby pulp.

· Grilled Tomatoes ·

At the moment of writing we are watching a new student preparing half a dozen tomatoes for the grill. He has halved them and then nicked north, south, east and west through the skin for a $\frac{1}{4}''$ so that it will not split and collapse but merely open out slightly under the heat like the early development of a flower. For the twelve halves he has worked up 2 ozs. of butter on a chopping board with as much finely snipped fresh chives from the garden as the butter will hold. Then he has mounded this paste equally over the twelve cut surfaces, sprinkled overall lightly with proper *gros sel* or French kitchen salt and proper peppercorns ground in a mill and tonight he will cook them slowly under the grill to accompany loin of pork. This recipe is so simple that it scarcely justifies a title, so now let us go to the other extreme and give you Edouard Nignon's *Tomates Elvia* which is fine enough to be served as a separate vegetable course or entrée.

· Tomates Elvia ·

Halve 6 large, firm tomatoes. Remove cores and pips, place tomatoes in a shallow container, fill them with a simple *vinaigrée**

and leave them to marinade for 2 hours. Pour off and retain the
vinaigrée for future use in salads and place ½" thick slice of cold
cooked veal brains in each. Bring three, four or five 1½" long
asparagus tips to a peak, tips rising centrally, inside each and
above the veal brains. Level off to the rim of each hollowed tomato
half with mayonnaise*. Skim the bottom of a round serving dish
with *vinaigrée*, arrange the tomatoes in a circle and fill the centre
with a bunch of well picked, stalked fresh watercress. Chill and
serve.

· Cervelles de Veau ·

None of this tells you how to cook the brains or *Cervelles de
Veau*. Wash them under a thin stream of running cold water and
carefully remove the fine skin and veins of blood. Place them in a
shallow pan, just cover them with the best possible cleared stock
at boiling point, simmer extremely gently for 4 minutes, leave
them to become cold in the liquor, clap them between two plates
with a heavy weight on top and use as instructed.

· Tomates Gourmandes ·

From the same source we also obtained delicious *Tomates
Gourmandes* which go wonderfully well with little *piccate* of veal
served in their own *jus*. Hollow out the required number of
tomatoes just cutting a large enough "lid" from the top to get a
teaspoon inside. Season the interiors lightly with salt and pepper.
Then split one or more large egg plants lengthwise. Heat a tablespoonful or two of oil with 1 or 2 ozs. of butter in a large shallow
pan and slap the prepared egg plants cut-side downwards into this
mixture. Fry gently until the flesh is pulped, scrape from the
skin, mash with a fork, season to taste with salt and pepper and
fill into the tomatoes. Dust the tops thickly with grated Parmesan.
Place in a heat-resistant container and cook for 20 minutes on the
middle shelf of the oven at Gas Mark 3–4. Small tomatoes will
really need the lower temperature and large ones the higher.

In that recipe we said "prepared" egg plants so this is as good a
moment as any to explain what we mean. These can be bitter and
it is standard practice in our kitchen to extract the bitterness
before cooking. Score the halved, lengthwise-cut surfaces lightly
and closely with a small sharp knife, sprinkle liberally with salt
and leave for 30 minutes, by which time the upper flesh will have

started to turn brown and the salt will have transformed itself
into little beads of moisture. Wipe carefully with a clean, dry cloth
and proceed with the cooking.

· Beignets d'Aubergines ·

Supposing you are slicing the egg plants for *Beignets
d'Aubergines*, on no account remove the skins—as with cucumbers
—just lay the slices on a flat surface *without* any scoring of course,
sprinkle with the salt and wipe off the moisture thereafter as
explained for the halved ones. Then pass them through vegetable
fritter batter* and deep fry to a rich golden brown in slightly
smoking hot oil. Dress on a napkin-covered dish and either
sprinkle lightly with paprika or decorate with little edible sprigs
of parsley fried till they crisp up in slightly smoking hot oil. Do
be careful if you are doing this in your best party frock at the last
moment and be sure to pat dry in a cloth after washing and
removing surplus stalks from your parsley, as water and oil do not
mix and in this context can only lead on to sizzle and splash! These
beignets are eminently suitable as an accompaniment to *Côtelettes
d'Agneau Erwin Schleyen†*.

· Gâteau Rothschild ·

At this point let us bring together the tomatoes and aubergines we have been discussing and use them in one of the most
distinguished vegetable *mélanges* we have ever found. The circumstances were amusing. We were lunching at Baron Philippe's
Château Mouton-Rothschild. *Gâteau Rothschild* was served. The
Cradocks rhapsodised, the Baron's charming cook was brought in
with the coffee and invited to tell us how she made it. This did not
please Madame who pursed up her lips and filtered the information through with manifest reluctance. Anyway we got it and the
fact that it takes a bit of time and trouble is we think offset for a
special occasion by the other glowing fact that it can be completely assembled the day before, refrigerated and slipped into the
oven just prior to service.

In this country *Gâteau Rothschild* is primarily a late summer dish
when the main vegetable components are at their lowest price and
the herbs are fresh. You assemble 1 lb. of split, de-pipped, de-
pithed pimentoes; 1 lb. skinned, finely sliced tomatoes; 1 lb.
rough chopped, unskinned egg plant; 1 lb. finely sliced shallots or

small onions; optional 2 crushed garlic cloves; ½ lb. finely sliced unskinned mushrooms and their stalks; 4 ozs. grated Parmesan; 6 ozs. fine soft breadcrumbs; pepper and salt; oil; butter; 2 hugely heaped tablespoonsful finely chopped or milled parsley and 1 flat dessertspoonful of fresh finely chopped oregano (or else leave this out altogether). You begin by dissolving enough butter and oil together in a big, thick frying pan. Then slice the prepared pimentoes into narrow ribbons and simmer them very gently until tender. Press in a sieve with the back of a wooden spoon exerting sufficient pressure to expel the oil and some of the natural juices thrown by the pimento. Turn the vegetables onto a plate, return the oil mixture to the pan, re-heat it and repeat the procedure with the shallots or small onions, adding a little more butter and a little more oil as it becomes necessary. Keep this and all other vegetables separate after frying. Repeat with the tomatoes and garlic, if it is desired, then the egg plant and finally the mushrooms because these will absorb your final quantity of oil and juices. If you look at your little piles of vegetables, you will see that each one has oozed a little surplus greasy fluid, blot this up with a little bit of kitchen paper and discard.

Mix the oregano with the tomatoes and, in a separate container, mix Parmesan with breadcrumbs and parsley. Season each vegetable lightly with salt and pepper and shape the pimentoes into a flat disc on a preferably round heat-resistant serving dish. Sprinkle lightly with the cheese mixture. Make a second layer with the onions and with this and each additional vegetable layer, sprinkle the top lightly with the cheese mixture. When all are assembled in layers and you have achieved a vegetable *gâteau*, coat the top and sides with the rest of the cheese mixture and neaten off carefully.

It only remains to slip the dish into the oven one shelf above centre at Gas Mark 4 for 15 minutes. Then turn the heat down to Gas Mark ¼ and leave on lowest oven shelf until moment of service.

If you sit and think about it for a moment you will realise that it would be a fatal mistake to use this as the accompaniment for a richly sauced dish like, for example, *Poulet à l'Estragon**, *Ris de Veau aux champignons à la crème*, *Pigeons au Madère* or *Rognons flambés à l'Armagnac*. It is, however, splendid with little fat *Tournedos*, grilled kidneys and bacon, spatchcocked *poussins* or a saddle of lamb.

· Pommes de Terre Grand'mère ·

The last four main course items would be equally happy with the *Pommes de Terre Grand'mère* of Monsieur Puget who is currently cooking such beautiful food at Au Petit Brouant in Nice; but, unlike the preceding recipe, it should be assembled in its cooking/serving pot on the afternoon of the dinner and served straight from the pot.

Butter an 8–9″ diameter heat-resistant flan dish generously and assemble 2 lbs. medium, even-sized, peeled, old or new potatoes, a grated shallot or small onion, 4 ozs. finely chopped unskinned mushrooms, ¼ pt. single or coffee cream, 1 standard separated egg yolk and salt and pepper to season. Overlap enough ⅛″ thick sliced potatoes to cover the base of the prepared container neatly. Season lightly with salt and pepper. Overlap the remaining potatoes. Blend prepared shallot and mushroom together, spread evenly over the potatoes and season again. Blend egg yolk with cream and pour overall. Cover lightly with kitchen foil. Bake on centre shelf Gas Mark 2 for approximately 1 hour 15 minutes until the potatoes are almost tender. Remove foil, place one shelf above centre and continue baking until top is richly browned.

Potato dishes suitable for formal entertaining without the staff to back it are not always easy to choose, although there are 450 classic ways of cooking Sir Walter Raleigh's little discovery. Duchess potato mixture* is an admirable standby and there are several classic shapes which come well within the range of any careful, but not necessarily experienced cook. At the same time they can all be piped out onto buttered or oiled baking sheets in advance and refrigerated until they are baked to a delicate golden brown in time for the chosen meal. When baking the choice between brushing the tops very lightly indeed with strained raw beaten egg, its more aristocratic relation *Anglaise** or melted butter will be yours alone. We suggest that a standard domestic pastry brush is lethal as the bristles are so coarse that they obliterate your fine ornamental piped patterns however lightly you apply the chosen glaze. We buy ordinary paintbrushes which we sterilise and use.

· Galettes ·

Galettes are elegant, little, flat, round potato-cake shapes made by rolling 1½ oz. balls of prepared Duchess very lightly in flour and then flattening them to about $\frac{1}{4}$" thickness. Dip a knife in hot water and make fairly deep criss-cross scorings across the tops. Brush with *Anglaise** and bake one shelf above centre at Gas Mark 6 until well-coloured (about 8–10 minutes).

· Champignons ·

You use a plain $\frac{1}{2}$" writing pipe fixed to a nylon icing bag for *Champignons*. Pipe blobs the size of small tomatoes. Press down an oiled teaspoon centrally to make a small indent. Hold a knife dipped in cold water in one hand and with the other hold the pipe vertically over each indent. Pipe a "stem" about $\frac{1}{2}$" in length and lop each one off neatly with the wet knife. Brush with *Anglaise** and bake as for *Galettes*.

· Petits Pains ·

You also use the icing bag and pipe to make *Petits Pains*. This time, pipe finger lengths onto the prepared baking sheet, pushing harder as you reach the centre to make this bulge slightly, and more gently as you reach the opposite end of each one. Lop off with a wet knife. Pinch in the tips gently and use the wet knife to make a central incision the full length of each little "loaf", pressing the knife outwards left and right of the length. This forms a Vee-shaped gully. Score each side of the gully with the wet knife, egg wash and bake.

For *rosettes* the icing bag has a rose or crown pipe inserted. Hold this vertically above the prepared tin. Pipe down to make a rosette and jerk back to make a neat small peak on top of each, not a lolloping great peak like a miniature leaning tower of Pisa! You can also make *finger shapes* with the crown pipe by piping with the bag held almost horizontally, pulling as you pipe to the required length and lopping off the ends with the wet knife; or rings by piping small, hollow circles with either a plain or a fancy writing pipe, which is enough to start you inventing your own shapes.

· Individual Golden Sandcastles ·

The Duchess potato mixture will also make delightful little *Individual Golden Sandcastles* if you pipe the mixture with a plain pipe into liberally buttered and floured dariole moulds (top diameter $2\frac{1}{4}$") to within $\frac{1}{4}$" of each rim. Pat down neatly. Then fill a rectangular bun tin ($9\frac{1}{4}$" × $5\frac{1}{4}$" × $2\frac{3}{4}$") to half its depth with very hot oil. Inset the filled dariole moulds and bake on the highest shelf possible for 25 minutes at Gas Mark 8. If you have buttered and floured correctly and made really firm Duchess mixture, you will be able to turn out a dishful of golden brown crispy potato with soft, gooey insides! They never fail to impress, yet once you have familiarised yourself with the slightly unusual baking method you will find they are extremely simple to achieve. At the end of the 25 minutes cooking, they can be transferred to the lowest shelf at Gas Mark Low for a further 10–12 minutes, either unmoulded onto their serving dish or left in their moulds, without fear of deterioration.

· Individual Pommes Anna ·

They are, in fact, a Bon Viveur modification of Escoffier's *Individual Pommes Anna*. For this classic version begin by slicing a pile of absolutely transparently thin raw old potatoes onto a clean teacloth. Then pat the potatoes dry, turning them over and over to do this thoroughly. Sprinkle lightly with salt and pepper. Butter with great thoroughness 6 little dariole moulds and literally ram the sliced potatoes in pell mell driving them down hard with your thumb until moulds are filled to within $\frac{1}{4}''$ of the top. Cut more as needed. Stop ramming and lay slices very neatly to fill to rim as you will need a steady base when turning them out. Stand the dariole moulds in the bun tin as described above, but this time bake on the highest possible shelf for 35 minutes at Gas Mark 8

· Gâteau Anglais ·

Then you must share with us the French way of cooking potatoes called *Gâteau Anglais*. It may amuse you to know this is just a French version of good old English bubble and squeak! You start by making up a pound of basic Duchess potato.* You must also have a large breakfastcupful of cooked, quartered Brussels sprouts and a teacupful of cooked, peeled, roughly-chopped chestnuts. Mix these together with a seasoning of salt and pepper. Put enough melted pork fat into a thick iron frying pan or skillet to skim the base. Press the mixture down into a flat cake and leave over a low heat to form a crisp bottom crust. Just ease it up with a slice and have a peek from time to time. Once the crust has formed, put a large plate on the top of the pan. Grasp the sides with two fairly thick cloths and turn the whole thing over so that the brown side is uppermost on the plate. Trickle back any remains of pork fat. Slide in the half-cooked *gâteau* and do the browning all over again on the underside.

· Gnocchi de Pommes de Terre ·

You can also bring a little added zest to table in the shape of *Gnocchi de Pommes de Terre*. Sieve 1 lb. cooked potatoes. Beat in 1½ ozs. of butter. Season with salt and pepper. Then beat in 2 whole eggs, 3 ozs. flour and 2 dessertspoonsful of grated Gruyère or Emmenthal cheese. Turn the mixture out onto a thickly floured surface. Pat it down to a ½″ thickness and let it get very cold. Once chilled, stamp it out into rounds with a plain 1½″ diameter cutter, being careful to dip this into cold water before cutting out each one. Place these in a double layer on the base of a buttered fireproof dish. Sprinkle thickly with grated cheese (Parmesan whenever possible), moisten liberally with melted butter and bake at Gas Mark 5 one shelf above centre until the top is nicely browned. Incidentally, this is an excellent Friday dish because it marries well with almost every kind of fish dish from the simplest grilled plaice or sole to a lush *Homard Mornay*.

· Soufflé de Pommes de Terre ·

Indeed one may say the same for *Soufflé de Pommes de Terre*, easy for back-timing and simple as pie to make. Rub 8 ozs. of dry, floury, cooked potatoes through a sieve. Beat in 8 fl. ozs. thick *Sauce Mornay* (p. 66) and 1 tablespoonful double cream. Correct the seasoning with salt and pepper to taste and blend in an *optional* heaped tablespoonful of chopped chives or parsley. Then whip up 5 standard egg whites very stiffly indeed and do not add little pinches of salt to them. Just cut them into the potato mixture gradually. Beat fast. Level off in a buttered *soufflé* mould and bake one shelf above centre at Gas Mark 7½ for 15 minutes.

As you will realise from the suggestion of optional herbs, so you may go raving mad at present prices and add very finely diced truffles, or on a modest level minutely diced raw mushrooms, lean York ham or tiny, very crisply fried bread *croûtons*. Clearly you will not use the ham with fish but all the rest can team up with great amiability.

· Pommes de Terre Robert ·

So now we are with the oven, let us stay there for *Pommes de Terre Robert* and then march through a small army of potato recipes which you have not had from us as yet. First you sieve 1 lb. potato pulp scooped from jacket-roasted potatoes, then you beat in 3 standard eggs, a teaspoonful of finely chopped chives and seasoning to taste of salt, pepper and a pinch of nutmeg. Now melt enough butter to coat the base of an 8–9″ diameter heat-resistant dish. When this is sizzling, pat in the mixture to form a large, round flat cake. Brush the top with raw beaten egg and mark a criss-cross trellis of lines on the top with a sharp knife pressed in deeply. Put it one shelf above centre in the oven at Gas Mark 5 and bake until the top is a rich golden brown.

· Pommes de Terre Roxelane ·

When you can buy, or make, 6 standard *brioches*, you must try your hand at *Pommes de Terre Roxelane*. Behead the *brioches* and hollow out the soft centres. Then scoop out and sieve the flour from 6 medium old potatoes, which have been baked in the oven. Beat 4 ozs. butter into this *purée* and stir it over a low heat with a wooden spoon until it becomes stiff and dry-ish. Beat in 2 egg yolks. Correct the seasoning with salt and pepper. Whip up 2 egg whites stiffly, fold them in and fill the mixture into the *brioches*. Mound them up slightly, pop the lids on and bake on centre shelf Gas Mark 4 for 15 minutes under a light covering of foil. At this moment you take off the foil, brush tops and sides liberally with melted butter, step up the heat to Gas Mark 6 and finish the cooking until the exteriors are considerably darkened, approximately 12 minutes.

· Ma Galette ·

From the vast range of oven-baked composite potato dishes you must have one or two of what even the French on occasions err over by naming *gratins*, so we make our rather grudging apologies for repeating that a *gratin* has nothing whatsoever to do with cheese. A *gratin* must contain breadcrumbs or in other words be *gratiné* with breadcrumbs and top-moistened with melted butter, with or without benefit of herbs and paprika. We have two favourites of our own and the one we will start with called *Ma*

Galette comes from a very famous restaurant in the South of France. For it you must use a flattish, plate-shaped, heat-resistant dish. Butter this liberally. Steam 3 or 4 very large old potatoes or a dozen small new ones for 12–15 or 6–7 minutes respectively and then plunge into iced water. Slice them into about ⅛" slices. Whichever you use, cook a few more than you need and trim each one down to the smallest so that they are uniform sized. Now arrange from the outside inwards into slightly overlapping circles until the interior of the platter is covered. Beat 2 standard eggs with salt and pepper to season, 2½ fl. ozs. milk and 2½ fl. ozs. of ideally double but acceptably single cream. Pour very carefully over the potatoes. Tent loosely in foil and, while baking other items, cook slowly on the bottom shelf of the oven, i.e. Gas Mark 2. Once the potatoes are tender, which takes quite a long time, whip off the foil, put one shelf above centre at Gas Mark 4 and allow the top to become a rich golden brown. If the base buttering and the slight overlapping of the potatoes is done with care, this can be cut into very thin *galette* or *gâteau* slices for service.

· Cheese and Potato Flan ·

Everyone in this house seems to be very fond of a simple affair certainly not justifying the grandeur of a French title, save in the interests of a menu otherwise written completely in French. We call it Cheese and Potato Flan (*Flan au Fromage*). Quite the best cheese to use for this, some may be surprised to learn, is the yellow, sliced processed type. Cut each peeled-off layer into ½" finger strips. Begin by buttering one or more heat-resistant glass flan dishes. Cover with a layer of cooked potatoes sliced ⅛" thick. Sprinkle lightly with salt and pepper. Then trellis with criss-cross strips of cheese. Repeat. Beat 1 egg into 3 fl. ozs. of top-of-the-milk. Swill overall and bake uncovered one shelf above centre at Gas Mark 4 until the base, top and outer rim are all crisp and brown and the inside is cheesey goo.

· Gratin de Pommes de Terre ·

More elaborate but perfect to serve with a *Carré d'Agneau Persillé** is one we made for the first time a few days ago. We called it *Gratin de Pommes de Terre*. Butter the base and sides of a 9½" diameter by 2¼" deep earthenware or heat-resistant glass casserole. Sprinkle liberally with chopped chives and parsley.

Cover and build up to within ½" of the rim with ⅛" thick slices of
2 lbs. cold, cooked new potatoes. Season with salt and milled
black peppercorns. Sprinkle surface liberally with chives and 1
flat dessertspoon powdered paprika overall. Mix together 1 small
teacupful fine, soft, white breadcrumbs, 1 heaped tablespoonful
milled parsley and 2 ozs. grated Parmesan cheese. Whip 2 small
eggs in a bowl with ¼ pt. of milk and a light seasoning of salt and
pepper; add 1 rounded dessertspoonful of raw grated onion to the
milk mixture and half the breadcrumb mixture. Pour overall, dot
with a few small flakes of butter, sprinkle remaining breadcrumb
mixture overall, moisten with 2 ozs. melted butter and bake at
Gas Mark 3 middle shelf until nicely browned on top (approximately 40–50 minutes).

One of the best of this type of potato bake was created by
Edouard Nignon who must surely have been among the greatest
of vegetable chefs; yet it is only such a simple thing as the matchsticks of fried unsalted pork fat that impart the distinctive character to this dish. So little pork fat is used in this country (and so
little larding and barding done) that its neglect is one of our
perennial moans. Similarly, you will rarely find our kitchen
lacking a black and rather shrivelled looking piece of smoked
ham from which over the months we cut little pieces to toss into
brown sauces, casseroles and soups instead of the standard salt
seasoning. The flavour thus achieved is unique and, very long-
lasting, is well worth the outlay. Just keep it hanging in a cool
place in a slight draught and the maggots will not manufacture
themselves in it!

· Pommes de Terre Helder ·

For the *Pommes de Terre Helder* begin with a well-buttered
heat-resistant glass flan dish, 6½" diameter for 6 people, 8" for 8
and so on. Fry matchsticks of raw unsalted pork fat very briskly
in a dry shallow pan until richly browned. Cut laboriously with a
knife or in seconds with a mandoline enough raw potatoes *en
iuliennes* (in matchsticks) to make an inch thick pad on the base.
Then trellis this meanly with the matchstick strips of browned
pork fat. Cover with a layer of grated Parmesan and season this
with salt and pepper, if your pork fat is not already salted. Moisten
with about 2–3 tablespoons of melted butter and put uncovered in
the oven one shelf above centre at Gas Mark 4 until the top is

richly browned. Remove, cover with a plate and turn out. Return
to flan dish bottom side upwards and bake until the top is crisp.
Tip onto a serving dish. Surround the base edge with freshly
milled parsley and send to table.

· Salade Christiane ·

Nignon of course was also brilliant at salads, of the type
which can replace vegetables in the summer. *Salade Christiane*, for
example, should be presented in a glass dish sunk into an outer
large one packed with crushed ice. When fresh asparagus is in
season, cook short stemmed stalks, chill, trim and mound into a
pyramid with the tips rising centrally. Surround with overlapping sections of skinned, de-pipped tomatoes with the cores
removed. Moisten liberally with a good *vinaigrette** not too long
before service and sprinkle liberally overall with hard boiled egg
yolks rubbed through a sieve.

· Salade Gabrielle ·

For *Salade Gabrielle* toss into a wooden salad bowl 3 hearts of
lettuce torn up small, one head of *endive* in little sprigs, the leaves
from a small bunch of cress, slender petals of cored and de-pipped
skinned tomatoes and a small teacup of minutely diced, lean cooked
ham. At the moment of service pour on *vinaigrette** and toss well.

· Salade de Romaine Bernoise ·

In winter there is nothing to beat *Salade de Romaine Bernoise*,
provided of course you either plant the *romaine*, which we call corn
salad (stockists p. 292) in July to give you a regular winter supply
even when only the tips are peering forlornly through a blanket of
snow, or can buy it from your local greengrocer. Take one per
person, so six for six, of all but the discoloured outer leaves, pull
them apart to remove the little core and toss them into a bowl.
Season them liberally with salt, pepper, 1 tablespoonful good wine
vinegar and 4 tablespoonsful olive oil. Have ready 2 heaped tablespoons of coarsely grated Gruyère or Emmenthal. Add this, toss
the whole lot together and chill briefly before serving.

· Crudités aux Fonds d'Artichauts ·

Some of the finest salads for serving in individual portions at
dinners or luncheons are made with artichoke bottoms like

Crudités aux Fonds d' Artichauts which are simply equal quantities of *juliennes* of raw carrots, Jerusalem artichokes and raw white cabbage tossed until well moistened with equal quantities of mayonnaise* and *vinaigrette** and piled into little peaked domes on *fonds d'artichauts* (or artichoke bottoms) which of necessity in this country will come out of a tin in winter.

· Fonds d'Artichauts aux Raisins ·

Another little beauty is *Fonds d'Artichauts aux Raisins*, especially for teaming with a dish of chicken cooked with grapes. You peel and de-pip 6 tablespoons of white or black grapes, add halved, skinless segments of 3 small thin-skinned oranges and make a sufficient quantity of *vinaigrée** to toss them into a well saturated goo, substituting equal parts of orange and grape juice for wine vinegar or wine vinegar and lemon. This then becomes one of the occasions when wine can be drunk with salad, although if it is a very great one, it would be as well as to use only grape juice.

Omelette de Mon Curé · Omelette à la Mistral
Omelette d'Arbois · Omelette au Thon · Omelette aux Truffes
Oeuf Monstreux · Garniture à la Royale
Oeufs en vapeur à la crème · Oeufs en cocotte Florentine
Oeufs en cocotte Beaujolais · Oeufs en cocotte Pas de Calais
Oeufs en cocotte au jambon · Oeufs Mollets Halévy
Oeufs Mollets à la Reine · Oeufs Mollets Stanley
Oeufs Mollets aux Anchoise · Soufflé Feuilleté (Parmesan)
Soufflé Feuilleté au Foie gras · Soufflé Feuilleté aux Crevettes
Soufflé Feuilleté aux Ecrevisses · Soufflé au Liqueur

fifteen · **THE HEN AND YOU**

"*Bien vivre mes enfants,*" wrote a friend of ours not long ago, and being a Frenchman he added, "*et surtout bien manger*"!

There are five foundations upon which fine cookery is based: oil, cream, wine, butter and eggs. Sometimes we nearly come to blows in our household in an attempt to establish an order of precedence for the Magnificent Quintet. Right now eggs are in the van as we reflect, at the onset of this chapter, how desolate our kitchen would be if there were not those two big, bright, Provençal ceramic bowls brimming with "bought" eggs for "serf" cookery and farm eggs from just-up-the-hill, for everything especially nice. We do hope you noticed the word "bowls" for we would as soon put baby in the refrigerator as an egg, and we beg of you not to avail yourselves of those totally inadequate, potty little egg pockets tucked in by the lamentably uninformed non-cooks who make refrigerators.

Having got that off our chests, let us then put behind us the fallacy that there is any difference between brown eggs and white ones—other than their colours; but there *is* a psychological difference; very deep-rooted it is too and anyway brown eggs look nicer.

Nevertheless, when it comes to egg whites for whipping, we actually fall over backwards to ensure we have a supply of *stale* egg whites expressly set aside for this purpose. One ten-days-old whips far, far better than one fresh-off-the-nest. We even keep separated egg whites for this period, even though the eggs from which those whites came are already as much as a week old. They are better that way and that is all the reason either of us ever want to know about any edible substance or culinary method. Indeed our one cry is: Does it taste all right? never; is it dieteti lly sound? . . . or how many calories should I count for how many ounces? . . . or what is the vitamin content? Frankly we doubt whether we should recognise a calorie or a vitamin if we met them on the street. Our concerns are flavour—quality—sheer hedonistic pleasures at the table.

Egg dishes can so very easily meet all these gourmet requirements; at least they can if the "auld reekie" of staleness, that awful mousetrap pong does not come seeping through the cream, the cheese, the vegetable *purée*, the butter or the wine with whom our chosen eggs keep company.

In a book devoted to cook-hostesses we have no difficulty whatever in giving omelettes precedence over all other egg treatments. Not just plain, *à la Mère Poularde* on which we have touched previously and will recapitulate, but for some of the great variants which can be served at the beginning of luncheons or dinners. Also we must go back over our little discovery which makes a non-stick omelette pan out of the most battered and adhesive relic. Heat the pan dry over a low heat until the surface turns grey with exhaustion. Make up your chosen omelette mixture. Take a scrap of raw, unsalted pork fat and rub the hot sides and base very vigorously. Thereafter go ahead in the classic manner starting with the tossing on of a generous nut of butter.

· Omelette de Mon Curé ·

We are talking this time of the kind of omelettes which gladdened the heart of that fantastic old gastronome/gourmet, *Le Prince Elu des Gastronomes*, Curnonsky who chose to spend the war years with Madame Mélanie, the finest cook in all Brittany. Both are gone now, but still when three or four are gathered around a table with their *fines* and the smoke from cigars throws a faint haze across the candlelight, those who remember them recall their magnificent achievements. It was a good sight to see *"Le Prince"*, well into his eighties and as lusty as Horace Annesley Vachell, relishing every mouthful of an *Omelette de Mon Curé* with which any home cook could begin a meal for her guests, provided she has a row of sorrel in her garden. To those who have the gardens but not the sorrel we would point out that this is about as difficult to grow as cress-on-a-bit-of-wet-blanket. Also it comes up cheerfully year after year with no attention.

The ingredients for this omelette are given for 10 eggs, this being the correct number for six people; but as we are averse to making huge omelettes and much prefer to do the operation in

two parts, please try this way. By the time the first omelette is
served the second will be ready. Tear up 4 ozs. well washed and
picked sorrel quite roughly and cook exactly as spinach*. Put
dry omelette pan over lowest possible heat. Whip eggs up very
lightly with a fork but do not over-beat them—we do not want
scrambled eggs! Add light seasoning of salt and pepper and the
prepared, fairly finely chopped, sorrel. Step up heat to fullest
under pan (this is where you do the pork fat rubbing bit if pan is
sticky). Run 1½ ozs. softened butter into egg mixture, then beat
again lightly. Toss a generous nut of butter into the pan. Wait
until it melts and browns around the edges. Pour in half the mixture and work it fast, catching up the frills as they form around the
edges using *only the flat back of the fork prongs* and try to keep pan
shaking with the other hand while so doing. Just as soon as base
is set, stop stirring and shaking. Let it settle until mixture is just
very moist on top. Flip over first fold in pan, tip pan and dish at
sharp angles to each other and thus form second fold while
turning out. Criss-cross the top with a sharp knife and run 2 very
liberal tablespoonsful of thick hot cream into these incisions.
Serve fast for, as we have reminded you before, eggs go on cooking even on a warmed plate or dish and if an omelette is not eaten
while still very moist in centre (*baveuse*), it will cease to be one and
become a poultice! Toss a further nut of butter into the pan and
make second omelette in the same way.

· Omelette à la Mistral ·

If this fails to please you or is unsuitable for an otherwise
chosen menu try your hand at Lucien Filhot's *Omelette à la
Mistral*. Assemble all ingredients beforehand. Use exact omelette-
making, pan-treating formula as described above for all or any of
these omelettes. You will need 10 eggs for six people as a first
course, 14 eggs if making for a main-course at a light luncheon or
supper. The remaining ingredients for the 10 egg one are as
follows: 1 fl. oz. olive oil and 1 oz. butter or 2 fl. ozs. oil, 4
medium, skinned, de-pipped and roughly chopped tomatoes, 1
crushed garlic clove, 2 rounded dessertspoonsful of milled parsley,
salt, pepper and 1 flat teaspoon each of chopped tarragon, thyme
and basil; and, of course, extra butter. Heat oil and butter or oil.
Poach tomato pieces gently until soft and buttery. Fork up eggs as
usual, add extra 1½ ozs. softened butter in flakes, add garlic, herbs,

fork again and make omelette to *baveuse* stage. Spread tomato
mixture in centre and finish as for *Omelette de Mon Curé*.

· Omelette d'Arbois ·

One of our great favourites is for *Omelette d'Arbois*, in which
mussels are intermingled with mushrooms. Poach 4 ozs. unskinned, sliced mushrooms in butter in a small pan. Scrub, beard
and steam 4 pts. mussels until they open. Remove from shells.
Beat up and season 10 eggs, fold in the mussels and mushrooms.
Make the omelette as usual but try to turn out onto heat-resistant
(heated) dish or platter while wetter than usual on top. Coat fast
and completely with thick cream, sprinkle very lightly with
grated Parmesan and brown at fastest possible speed under fiercest
possible grill.

· Omelette au Thon ·

For an *Omelette au Thon* give precisely the same final treatment to a 10 egg omelette into which you flake 4 ozs. of tinned
tuna with its own oil—therefore omit, just for once, those little
butter flakes. Season with salt, pepper and, if possible, a rounded
teaspoonful of finely scissored frondy green fennel leaves—fennel
and dill we must never forget are fish herbs. Make omelettes as
usual, brown under grill and serve.

· Omelette aux Truffes ·

Now, supposing any of you are going to Spain—which has
more tourists from the United Kingdom annually than any other
holiday area in the world—you, like us, can enjoy the fantastic
luxury of an *Omelette aux Truffes*. We buy small tins at 20 pesetas a
tin and French ones—the best of course—cost at the time of
writing about 45/– each. Point taken?
This brings us back to that most fantastic of women cooks
Madame La Mère Poularde of whom we have written so often.
Her first omelette inspiration was the running of butter flakes
into the raw egg mixture so that the butter, melting slower than
the egg sets in the pan, causes little butter pockets throughout
which make all omelettes so much better that it has become constant practice with the greatest cooks. She then went on and
experimented with omelettes made without egg whites—just the
yolks and the whites replaced with double cream. This is how,

when you can get practically priced truffles, you make her truffle omelette. Weigh a mixing bowl, put a dozen egg yolks into it (use the whites up for angel cake, meringues, or German Custard). Weigh the bowl again and add ¾ of the egg yolk weight in double cream. Beat up with a fork. Slice the truffles from the little tins finely, then cut into slenderest strips and fold into egg and cream mixture. Season with salt and pepper and shake/make over only two-thirds heat beneath until mixture begins to coagulate. Stop using fork; continue shaking gently until top surface becomes, as always, *baveuse*. Turn out and eat in reverent silence.

· Oeuf Monstreux ·

Let us now talk about eggs in an entirely different context. We have something for you which we hope will be new to you all. Put 6 to 8 separated egg yolks into a thick polythene bag, let them settle in the bottom of the bag—cornerwise so that they assume, in the bag, the shape of a ball with a peak (corner) at base. Tie in the neck of the bag, hold over a pan of fast-boiling water and allow the yolks to poach until set. Then take out, cool and trim off the pointed bit to make a flat-based ball shape. Whip up *their whites as stiffly as possible* and put them into a much larger polythene bag, slide in the giant hard egg yolk until it sinks amidships and submerge the tied bag into fast boiling water to poach once again until set. Slip it from its polythene bag onto any chosen mayonnaise or *chaudfroid* Russian Salad vegetable mixture on a cold serving dish. You will appear to be a miracle worker to the guests who cut themselves a giant-egg slice but it is all very easy indeed, just a little different for a small buffet. If you are serving it at table as a first course write on your menu *Oeuf Monstreux*.

· Garniture à la Royale ·

If we are going to maintain our majority interest on the level of dishes for entertaining, we should spare a thought for some of the functions of eggs, particularly when separated, as an edible garniture for soups. Plain *consommé*, when well-made, is a delight in itself and a marvellous "opener" when rich dishes are to follow. Indeed, we have to this day a splendid restaurateur who, at the mere appearance of Fanny through the doorway at luncheon time, promptly sends a waiter scurrying for "Madame's morning tea"— a cup of sticky, straw-coloured, perfect hot *consommé*. Run either the whites or the lightly whipped yolks over a buttered plate till either reach the height of the outer rim. Place each plate over an inverted heat-resistant beaker in a pan of slightly heaving water. Tent the plate with kitchen foil, cover the pan and leave to set in the vapour. You will, after a few moments, be able to stamp out tiny fancy shapes for slipping into *consommé* at the moment of service *à la Royale*. These are the simple or basic *Royales* from which Escoffier developed so many great ones.

· Oeufs en vapeur à la crème ·

If 4 or 6 unseparated eggs are broken from their shells over a buttered serving dish and given the same steam treatment under little top coats of thick cream, seasoned with salt and pepper and top sprinkled with parsley, you can put *Oeufs en Vapeur à la Crème* before the most fastidious guest provided you take extreme care to see that they are not steamed for so long that they become *oeufs comme pierres*—like revolting, little, flat unresistant stones!

Indeed this is always the rub when it comes to eggs and steam; or eggs cooked in the oven. *Oeufs en cocotte* are dreadful if either leathery and dry or laced with globules of raw egg white. On balance—and as there are too many factors to be judged for anyone to be able to give you the exact time or oven position, it is easier to steam/poach on top of the cooker than bake in *cocotte* moulds in the oven. So this is the method we will stick to throughout the following little suite of recipes. Just be firm with yourselves about always covering the *cocottes* with foil before immersing up to a maximum half of the moulds' depth in water and over only just enough bottom heat to enclose them in steam. If the heat is too high you will end up with *oeufs en sauce à l'eau*.

· Oeufs en cocotte Florentine ·

Take heart over one point, if the whites are just softly set, the yolks will take care of themselves. Yolks break if tested with crafty little prods through their covering of sauce or whatever; whites will not carry any tell-tale marks so prod to the sides of each *ramequin* to determine if they are *au point* or *bien cuit* which, as with steaks, is a synonym for *ruiné*!

We will start with *Oeufs en cocotte Florentine*. Butter the interior of each *cocotte* mould carefully. Line the base with spinach *purée*. Break an egg into the centre. Mix a further tablespoon of spinach *purée* with a tablespoonful of thick cream, a pinch of nutmeg, salt and black pepper, sprinkle with grated hard cheese, cover and poach. When the *white* is set, whip out and drive a finger of deep fried, very thinly rolled bought or home-made puff paste into one side of each *ramequin* and serve immediately.

· Oeufs en cocotte Beaujolais ·

Maybe you would prefer *Oeufs en cocotte Beaujolais*. Mix together 5 fl. ozs. young, red Beaujolais and 5 fl. ozs. double cream. Butter the interior of 4 or 5 *cocottes* and just cover the base of each one with finely diced, fried bacon. Break an egg into each, fill to just below the rim with the cream mixture, scatter the tops liberally with soft white breadcrumbs, dot with minute flakes of butter and poach as explained.

· Oeufs en cocotte Pas de Calais ·

Alternatively use shrimps for *Oeufs en cocotte Pas de Calais*. Butter the *cocottes*, base and sides. Cover base thickly with shrimps. Cover with a thin layer of thick cream into which you have stirred chopped chives. Break an egg into each container and cover with more thick cream seasoned with salt and pepper. Cook as for previous recipe. At which point we hasten to remind you that in every instance of double cream, this can be replaced by a good thick white sauce.

· Oeufs en cocotte au jambon ·

Then there's *Oeufs en cocotte au jambon*, for which you use both white sauce and cream. Make a small quantity of *Sauce Mornay* (p. 66), line buttered *cocottes* out thinly with this very thick sauce. Cover with finely chopped cooked ham, break an egg into each; cover this with more Mornay, but this time add chopped ham to the remainder. Pour over eggs, sprinkle with grated cheese and cook as for all the rest.

Brushing aside this treatment and moving onto the almost inexhaustible range of *Oeufs Mollets* we shall have to recap a little on the basic process. *If* the eggs are lowered with extreme gentleness into boiling water, maintained at a steady but not fierce bubble for exactly 4 minutes, fished out and plunged into a bowl of iced water they will be exactly right. Then you must pick each one up separately straight away. Tap the shells gently and *all round* on the inside of the sink and shell by easing away the first little bit of shell and holding this gap under a thin stream of cold tap water. The water will then force the inner skin away and, by inserting itself between this and the tender cooked egg white, force the rest of the shell to come away easily without any unsightly nicks or perilous cracks.

· Oeufs Mollets Halévy ·

Then you can use them for such charming little dishes as *Oeufs Mollets Halévy*. Line the inside of a baked savoury short paste tartlet case with diced cooked chicken turned in a little *velouté* sauce*. Slip in the soft-boiled egg—fat side downwards—and fill in the sides till level with the rim of the case with more *velouté*, this time enhanced with a spoonful or two of whipped cream and a touch of tomato *purée*. For *Oeufs Mollets à la Reine* emulsify equal parts of cooked white chicken meat and double cream, add 2 tablespoonsful of aspic at the syrupy stage for every 8 ozs. of this mixture, correct seasoning with salt and pepper and use with a soft-boiled egg to each tartlet case exactly as for *Oeufs Mollets Halévy*.

· Oeufs Mollets à la Reine et Stanley ·

Ring the changes again with *Oeufs Mollets Stanley* but this time, when the eggs are shelled, have ready the required number of baked tartlet cases lined out with *Sauce Soubise**. Use this to fill in the sides and sprinkle overall with curry powder.

· Oeufs Mollets aux Anchois ·

Any of the above *Oeufs Mollets* can, if you prefer, be given an entirely different "container" treatment. Stamp out a small round of crustless bread passed through egg and milk (1 egg to ¼ pt. milk) and fry at once to a good golden brown. Pipe a little ring of Duchess potato* around the rim of each. Sprinkle thickly with grated cheese. Mix a teaspoonful of thick cream with a flat egg-spoon of anchovy *purée* and spread over the inside of each *croûton*. Stand an *Oeuf Mollet* on this base and criss-cross the top of each egg with a lengthwise-split, washed and wiped anchovy fillet. This will give you *Oeufs Mollets aux Anchois* and you can use these Duchess potato *croûtons* for any of the previous *Oeufs Mollets* variants instead of the tartlet cases.

If you want none of these, perhaps we can tempt you with a *soufflé*. In the first place let us get it quite clear that by planning, anyone can serve a *soufflé* as the first course when entertaining; *provided the recipe really works.* We discovered recently that Barbara Cartland took the pains in her memoirs to recount the, to us simple, fact that we served *Soufflés en feuilletage* to 64 guests at a garden dinner party in our last home and only left the garden for 10 minutes. To give you some reassurance, let us tell you how we did it and see if it will help. First we shall have to confess we always have a great many domestic gas cookers in our kitchens. We made and pre-baked until beige the puff pastry-cases for these *soufflés*. We had ordinary baking sheets of the complete *mise en place* set out beside our cookers before dinner began. The only exceptions were the milk and the egg whites. The whites were measured off and placed under foil in refrigeration. The milk sat there too. For each *soufflé* we had two saucepans: one small one ready for the milk to heat through slowly, one larger one into which we tossed the butter the moment we turned on the heat. Thus, with Fanny making the *soufflé* sauces and Johnnie whipping the egg whites by electric mixer, the *soufflés* went into the oven one after the other at a rate of knots.

We always plan large parties at small tables for either 6 or 8 which are laid up for these numbers but place cards are set out leaving one cover at the head empty. Thus between us course-by-course we can move round from table to table and spend one course with each set of guests so that no one feels neglected. We were not therefore missed when at the end of a course we got up and 10 minutes later returned to other tables. Because we had made it our business to know exactly how long each soufflé required in the oven, the people who were serving the food to us only had to whip each one out as the pinger pinged. Yet we have seen written by an alleged expert in a very famous national newspaper's magazine, the bald statement that you must cut soufflés and omelettes out of your menus if you are doing the cooking yourself.

Do not get cross with us because we had so many cookers and helpers to serve on the occasion we have cited because you can do it alone for 6 or 8 people with either one big *soufflé* or individual ones. We will deal with the big ones first. You will need bought or home-made puff paste for the case and this is how you go to work.

Cut a $7\frac{1}{2}''$ diameter circle of greaseproof paper; butter and flour it on one side. Butter and flour the sides of a $7\frac{1}{2}''$ diameter sliding-based cake tin. Fit the prepared paper over the base. Roll out a long strip of puff paste fairly thickly so that you can cut a $4\frac{1}{2}''$ wide strip $\frac{1}{2}''$ longer than the circumference of your tin. When it is cut, fit it against the buttered and floured interior allowing a mean $\frac{1}{2}''$ to settle on the bottom and push this down all round onto the base. When this strip is in and the ends overlap slightly, just wet the edges with cold water and press the joins in neatly. Gather up the trimming, roll them out thickly and cut a $7\frac{1}{2}''$ diameter puff paste circle. Press this down on the base of the tin. Butter and flour *the base and the outside* of a $6\frac{1}{2}''$ diameter solid-based cake tin. Place a $6\frac{1}{2}''$ diameter circle of greaseproof paper (buttered and floured on both sides) in the centre of the raw puff paste base in the large tin. Slide the prepared smaller tin in so that buttered and floured base sits on the paper. Bake one shelf above centre at Gas Mark 6 until the pastry edge rising between the two tins is a pale biscuit colour.

Slide out the small inner tin, remove the inner greaseproof paper and allow to get cold. You can wrap it up in foil, keep it in a cool place for 48 hours without the slightest qualms and then you can fill it with any savoury *soufflé* mixture that pleases you and re-bake with the raw mixture inside at Gas Mark $7\frac{1}{2}$ one shelf above centre for precisely 18 minutes. By this time your *soufflé* mixture will be crisp and brown on the top and very moist and creamy in the centre . . . and that is the way a *soufflé* always should be.

When the party is on, you circulate drinks in the sitting room and remove yourself 25 minutes before service because you cannot possibly need more than 7 minutes to make up the mixture and get it in the oven if you have set everything to hand in the way that we have already explained.

If you want a *Soufflé au Parmesan* with a really super texture, mix $\frac{1}{2}$ pt. of milk with $\frac{1}{4}$ pt. of double cream and refrigerate. Measure off 9 fl. ozs. of raw unbeaten egg white, cover with foil and refrigerate that too. Set beside your cooker on a baking sheet 3 ozs. grated Parmesan cheese; $1\frac{1}{2}$ ozs. butter; $1\frac{1}{2}$ ozs. sifted flour, sieved with 1 scant flat teaspoon salt; 2 heavy pinches of milled black peppercorns; 1 scant flat teaspoon of dry English mustard and a generous grate of nutmeg. Do not forget to put the two saucepans in position on the cooker top.

Let us assume you are working alone. The pastry case (having been eased out after baking to make sure that it does not stick and then having been banged back again into position in the tin) awaits you on a flat baking sheet. You plunge into the kitchen, light the oven at Gas Mark 7½ and check that the shelf is in the right position. Whip the foil off the egg whites and tip them into your mixer bowl but do not switch on. Pour the milk into the small pan over a low heat. Toss the butter into the big pan over a low heat and while it dissolves, see that your serving plates are heating in warming drawer or on floor of oven and turn on the mixer. Toss the flour, nutmeg, pepper and mustard onto the butter and step up the heat to medium high. Blend to a smooth paste with a wooden spoon. Add about a quarter of the milk mixture from the saucepan, about a quarter of the cheese and leave all alone until the milk/cream begins to bubble. Then start stirring, increase pace, beat very thoroughly and repeat with remaining 3 additions of fluid and cheese. As soon as the sauce is smooth (the flour cooks its taste out during oven baking time) snatch it off the cooker and beat it once more to reduce the heat as you cross to the mixer. Switch this off and with a plastic spatula dollop a huge lump of egg whites onto the sauce. Beat in fast and roughly. Repeat with second dollop. Then invert entire contents of saucepan over remaining egg whites in mixer bowl. Beat quickly and lightly until only a few small peaks of egg whites remain. Scrape the lot into the pastry case—do not worry if it domes up—and slip it into the oven.

Set your ringer or pinger and take it back into the sitting room to slip behind a vase of flowers. Then about 4 minutes before a crafty peek at the pinger tells you it will go off, take your guests into dinner. Nip back to the kitchen and do not forget at this point what we have forgotten to tell you until now! Have a large jam jar or a tall tin ready on the table, take out the *soufflé* in its tin, place on top of jar or tin and press sides of tin down gently—this is the easiest and swiftest way to get the whole thing out. Place it on a serving dish and carry it to table.

All that remains is to give you a number of variations on the above cheese *soufflé* mixture and you can ring the changes to suit yourself and your chosen menu.

· Soufflé au Foie gras ·

Just remember one important point—the given quantities of flour, butter, fluid and egg whites will be constant for all our suggested variants. For *Soufflé au Foie gras* make up your fluid quantity with 2½ fl. ozs. sherry or dry Madeira, 2½ fl. ozs. single cream and ½ pt. of milk. Delete the cheese and its seasonings. In place of these use a 4 oz. tin of *pâté de foie gras truffé* or any modest substitute for this *recherché* ingredient, and cream it down beforehand with 1 tablespoonful of brandy and 1 tablespoonful of single cream. Refrigerate it. Then when you make up the filling mixture, add the creamed *foie gras* in four gradual additions exactly as given for the cheese, and add the chosen sherry or Madeira first and alone, beating this in before you add any of the milk/cream mixture—otherwise the whole sauce will curdle and you will be very cross with us.

· Soufflé aux Crevettes ou aux Ecrevisses ·

Say you prefer a *Soufflé aux Crevettes*. Achieve the given quantity of fluids with ¼ pt. dry white wine, ¼ pt. single cream and ¼ pt. milk. Replace the cheese with 4 ozs. shelled, chopped shrimps and season the flour with pepper only—there will be enough salt from the shrimps. The same procedure using diced prawns instead of shrimps will give you a *Soufflé aux Ecrevisses*.

Please forget all about that puff paste case if you think the whole thing far too complicated and exhausting; all the given *soufflé* mixtures can be baked without any pastry, just turned straight into well-buttered 6½–7″ diameter *soufflé* moulds and baked at Gas Mark 7½ one shelf above centre for from 17–17½ minutes instead of the 18 minutes needed inside the puff pastry cases.

· Soufflé au Liqueur ·

Furthermore, *if* you like to slip away from the table a fraction before your guests have finished whatever it is that you are serving before the main course, you can get your *soufflé* in, dish up the main course and get through it comfortably before the *soufflé* is baked. If you think 17–17½ minutes is too little time, reduce the heat to 7 and win yourself an extra 3 minutes in the dining room. Use the same basic given ingredients and quantities

—flour, egg whites, milk/cream—but see that you put a vanilla pod in with these latter while resting in refrigeration and boil them up with the pod when starting to make up the mixture. Remove vanilla pod when milk has boiled, wipe and store for future use. Instead of the original cheese use 3½ ozs. castor sugar and when the *soufflé* comes out of the oven, dust the top thickly with sifted icing sugar and hand *any chosen liqueur* separately in a shaker for *Soufflé au Liqueur*, or, for example, *au Kirsch, Cointreau, Grand Marnier, Curaçao* etc.

Zephyrs au Parmesan · Le Fromage Blanc · Cheese Ice Cream
Hot Cheese Puffs · Crème de Camembert · Liptauerkäse
Cheese Creams · Our Cheese Straws · Camembert en Gelée
Cheese Beignets

sixteen · WINE'S BEST FRIEND

Wine's best friend, as you scarcely need reminding, is of course cheese, which is why the cheese board must always precede the pudding, so that the last glass of good red wine makes its happiest marriage with its favourite table companion. Not for nothing did La Mazille write, "No *gourmet* has ever lived who has not proclaimed the indispensability of cheese at either small or large dinners".

This can be a sliver of Gruyère if this happens by the grace of God to be in prime condition when sold you so far from its Swiss home. If you are drinking Burgundy, or one of the lustier clarets, you can offer England's own Blue Stilton, Roquefort, Bleu Bresse or Gorgonzola, provided this is not too salty and has a creamy, crumbly texture. If it is soapy, do not have anything to do with it at all.

· Zephyrs au Parmesan ·

Matching lightweight to lightweight you will be more likely to succeed with a *petite Suisse* if the wine of your choice were a modest *vin rosé*, but there is one made-in-seconds cheese delicacy which can safely be offered as a hot cheese course with any of the wines we have mentioned or with a lusty red Beaujolais (forgive us for mentioning the colour, but there are still so many people who have not discovered the great pleasures of drinking white Beaujolais). All our *Zephyrs au Parmesan* ask of you is a pan of slightly smoking hot oil, salt and pepper, 2 very stiffly whipped egg whites and 2 ozs. of Parmesan cheese. Grate the cheese very finely, mix with a large pinch of salt and 2 of pepper. Fold into the prepared egg whites and with a teaspoon scoop up little blobs and drop them into the very hot oil. Each one will blow up like a baby Blériot balloon and turn a richly golden brown. Heap the *Zephyrs* onto a napkin-covered salver, sprinkle with paprika powder and serve immediately.

· Le Fromage Blanc ·

These small delicate items are all the majority of us need—if we have already been well fed! La Mazille extolled the virtues of two simply home made cheeses. One, *Le Fromage Blanc* undoubtedly merits our attention. In his own words (translated!) place 4½ pts. of good sweet milk in a thick shallow pan and put in a fairly warm place. La Mazille stressed of course that the milk must never be allowed to boil. We use a working surface immediately adjacent to one of our cookers with half the pan over the edge of the cooker and almost reaching a very low flame. "Throw in a teaspoonful of rennet," the author continues, "and leave to coagulate. After one or two days (ours took two) you turn the curd into a four-fold bag of muslin and suspend it by string and over a bowl for an hour." As the whey separates—very slowly open the muslin over a sieve and work it well with a wooden spoon or fork. When it resumes dripping through muslin and sieve, beat in half a dozen soupspoons of boiling cream which will complete the smooth texture. Then it may be enjoyed either with finely scissored chives forked in and seasoned with both salt and freshly milled black peppercorns, or it may equally well be eaten with castor sugar and fresh wood strawberries. Very evocative and absolutely true.

· Cheese Ice Cream ·

If you really want to surprise your guests and save yoursel the trouble of working on this course at the time of your entertain ment, serve our *Cheese Ice Cream*. Johnnie moaned on about the lack of this kind of ice cream for many years and, finally, Fanny settled down to what she calls a trial and error session. There emerged the recipe we have been using ever since.

Make a good sauce by dissolving 1 oz. butter in a smallish pan and working in 1 oz. of fine sifted flour. When the *roux* is formed and has cooked for at least 2 minutes work in ¼ pt. of dry white wine gradually, beating well, as always, between each addition. Repeat the process with ¼ pt. milk or ¼ pt. single cream. Then add ¾ oz. of very finely grated Gruyère cheese and 1¼ ozs. finely grated Parmesan. Remove pan from heat, beat in 1 separated egg yolk and then 2½ fl. ozs. of double cream. Taste, correct seasoning with salt, pepper and a pinch or two of nutmeg. Remember when doing your final seasoning that freezing diminishes the potency of both sweet and savoury flavours so err a little on the generous side.

Divide mixture between 1 dozen tiny *casserolettes* or miniature *soufflé* moulds and freeze under a tight covering of foil until a very few moments before service. Alternatively, show off with a large cheese ice cream. Oil an ornamental mould, pour in the mixture and freeze until 10 minutes before service. Dip into very hot water, unmould and surround the base with a little wall of coiled pretzels. Incidentally, we think the *appearance* of the finished ice cream is dull—a flattish creamy beige—and we have taken to adding a few drops of harmless green vegetable colouring to make it more pleasing to the eye.

· Hot Cheese Puffs ·

No one will take any exception to a few *Hot Cheese Puffs* (*Feuilletés de Fromage*) either. When pressed we quite unashamedly make them with the one and only frozen puff paste we think worth buying. We roll this out really thinly indeed and cut into 3", 3½" or 4" squares. Into the middle of each square goes a cube of Gruyère which has first been sprinkled extremely sparingly with cayenne pepper and—surprise!—a drop or two (no more) of lemon juice. Wet the pastry edges with beaten egg, not just with water. Fold corners over to centre and pinch together to ensure an absolutely sealed mini-parcel. Brush with egg and bake on a wetted baking sheet at Gas Mark 6 one shelf above centre until palely golden brown. We know this is a lower temperature than we normally advocate for puff paste, but it is absolutely essential that the cheese is completely melted inside so do not be tempted to exceed Gas Mark 6. Put into a napkin-lined container, cover and send to table.

We have deprived ourselves of three other very suitable party recipes in this book by publishing them already; *Crème Ecossaise**, *Crème de Roquefort** and Stilton Cream* but we have not yet shared with you a really appetising way of using a Camembert. These cheeses are, we think, shockingly bad travellers. They behave like tourists and show themselves off in the worst possible light in England. Therefore we argue it is perfectly justifiable to submit them to some "tiddling up" which we would certainly regard as heresy in their place of origin.

· Crème de Camembert ·

This "tiddling" bears the name of *Crème de Camembert*.
Choose a Camembert which is, at least, springy to the touch and
not too deeply chalk-encrusted. Scrape off as much as you can
from the outside wall without penetrating this and then submerge
the cheese in dry white wine. Let it marinade for 24 hours. Then
lift it out, wipe it, place in a mixing bowl with 4 ozs. of unsalted
butter. Whip both down together to a smooth cream. Chill in
the mixing bowl and when quite chilly to the touch, re-shape into
a semblance of the original form. Coat top and sides thickly with
ground almonds and press 8 pretzel whorls around the outside
"wall". This tases best served with the very thinnest of crustless
brown bread and butter rolls.

· Liptauerkäse ·

When serving wines of no importance you can even risk a
Liptauerkäse or square of Liptauer Cheese. There is one particular
brand of bought cream cheese (stockists p. 291) which we especially recommend for this job. Use 8 ozs. and blend in its own
weight in butter, 2 rounded teaspoons of Edelsüss paprika, 2
heaped teaspoons of fresh, scissored chives, 2 rounded teaspoons
of caraway seeds, 2 finely pressed and finely chopped capers, 2 flat
teaspoonsful of French mustard and 2 extra finely chopped whole,
large anchovy fillets. When all are smoothly blended, shape on a
small dish into a neat rectangle, surround with pretzels, stud the
top-surface with neatly trimmed radishes and hand knobs of hot
black bread inside a napkin-lined basket.

· Cheese Creams ·

Back again with cold cheese dishes we turn to Victorian
receipt books for *Cheese Creams*. Take ½ pt. of double cream, ¼ pt.
of aspic at syrupy stage (p. 75), ¼ lb. very finely grated Gruyère,
a shake of cayenne and an eggspoonful of French mustard. Whip
up the cream, whip in the syrupy aspic. Add the remaining
ingredients and turn into those darlings of the Victorian era, little
fluted paper cases. Tuck into the freezer compartment of your
refrigerator until you are ready to serve them and then sprinkle
minute quantities of very finely chopped sage on top of each
cheese cream.

· Our Cheese Straws ·

Now let us share a secret we are generally too polite to reveal, that the average cheese straw is a dry and rather nasty little object, as hackneyed as it is uninteresting. We got so abysmally wearied of the little horrors that we set about making them really worth eating. Now we use them for two different courses—piping hot they are handed with clear soups and, again piping hot, they go round in lieu of a cheese course. For *Our Cheese Straws* roll out a ½ lb. slab of that frozen puff paste extremely thinly. Brush half the rolled out surface with melted butter, then sprinkle thickly with grated Parmesan, then very meanly with cayenne pepper and finally give a restrained sprinkling of grated Gruyère or Emmenthal cheese. Moisten overall with flicks of melted butter, fold unsprinkled paste half over sprinkled one and roll down lightly but firmly. Cut into fingers—twisting each one or baking flat is purely a matter of personal taste—and lay on a lightly floured baking sheet. Brush tops with raw beaten egg and sprinkle with finely milled walnuts. Bake one shelf above centre at Gas Mark 6 until puffed and golden and see if they do not taste better, look better and go down better with your guests than those mouldy old conventional cheese straws.

While browsing through old notes we came upon a cheese dish made by Annette. She, you may remember, was the remarkable woman who went to Somerset Maugham as a kitchen maid and subsequently cooked for him, the world, his wife and half the crowned heads of Europe for nearly thirty years.

Annette was, as Fanny's brother remarked caustically, "closer than a dead heat" when it came to sharing recipes; but by some alchemy she and Fanny got themselves onto the same wave length. This startled everyone—Fanny included. But she *was* admitted to Annette's rather dreadful little kitchen and finally bound herself to Annette by very special ties for she naughtily persuaded Annette to pose for a photograph beside the truly monstrous old gas cooker which W.S.M. flatly refused to declare obsolete. That picture—taken by Johnnie—was duly published. Within days, as Annette told us gleefully when next we saw her, a brand new gas cooker was installed. Thus the power of the press on a distinguished but very close old writer for whom, outside the cooker episode, we had great admiration and respect!

C.H.B.   o

· Camembert en Gelée ·

Let us get back to the recipe which sparked off this disclosure. Annette called it *Camembert en Gelée*. You do exactly as we described for *Crème de Camembert* on p. 208 until the point where the cheese is put to chill in a refrigerator. Then you make a straw-coloured aspic (p. 75), test it for a firm but delicate set (we do not want a surround of straw coloured India rubber!), rewarm it to the syrupy stage and pour it into a 6½" diameter wetted *soufflé* mould. Set base aspic to a depth of ¼". Place the cheese inside and pour in more syrupy aspic until the cheese is completely engulfed, top, bottom and sides. When set, unmould onto a small salver and surround the base with a narrow edging of aspic whipped to a froth with a fork.

· Cheese Beignets ·

Now let us conclude this section with *Cheese Beignets*. These appeared on our parents' and grandparents' tables. They are very easily achieved. Sift 4 heaped tablespoonsful of flour into a basin, make a well in the centre, tip in 1 tablespoonful of oil, 2 separated egg yolks, a generous pinch of salt, a small teacup filled to the brim (without pressure) with grated Parmesan cheese, a heaped high teaspoonful of milled fresh parsley and a really whacking pinch of freshly ground black peppercorns. Using *light ale* work this mixture up to a thick paste which just flops reluctantly from a lifted spoon, beating very thoroughly indeed between each addition. Do not bother to "rest" this batter. You can of course, but whatever approach you use to our recipe, fold in 2 stiffly beaten egg whites immediately before you start frying. *If* you put in the egg whites too soon, you have only yourself to blame if no-one wants seconds and what remains, after "firsts" have been taken, is doomed to the dustbin. Drop small spoonsful into slightly smoking hot oil and let them puff up and turn a glowing golden brown. Heap into a rather random pyramid on a napkin or doiley covered salver and send to table with a few sprigs of fried parsley for garnish and a top scattering of either paprika or celery salt.

Puff Pastry · Feuilleté de Fraises ou Framboises
Doigts de Feuilletage · Mille Feuilles · Mini Croquembouche
Petits Choux en Surprise · Pâte à chou au Café · Paris-Brest
Gâteau St. Honoré · Profiteroles au Chocolat
Chocolate Sauce · Crème Chibouste · Orange Custard
Profiteroles à l'Orange · Crème à l'Orange · Orange Cream Sauce
Les Petites Tartelettes de Fraises ou Framboises ou Abricots
Charlotte Russe aux Fraises ou Framboises ou Ronce-Framboises
Sauce Mousseline Froide · Real Pêches Melba · Sauce Melba
Our Iced Fruit Soufflés
Gâteau de Pêches, Abricots, Fraises ou Framboises
Cream Cheese Filling · Strawberry and Raspberry Fools
Fraises Romanoff · Fruit Water Ices · Spoom au Citron
Lemon Water Ice · Italian Meringue
Italian Meringue Petits Fours · Chocolate Refrigerator Cake
Mont Blanc aux Marrons · Orange Cream
Biscuit Glacé Grand Marnier · Cheese Cake
Soufflé au Chocolat · Soufflé aux Fruits Confits
Blanc-Manger · Blanc-Manger à la Princesse
Black Cherry Compôte · Sweetened Almond Milk
Crème Bachique

seventeen · **CROWNING GLORY**

Nearly every guest, male or female alike, experience a slight sense of anti-climax at a dinner party if they are not given what is always referred to in the family as a "glamorous pud". If there is nothing else on the buffet, the fruit salad or *compôte* will vanish; but in our experience, it will disappear *last of all* when an array of glamorous puds is provided as well. As we all know, this most certainly does not apply to children who are far more interested in savoury items.

We entertain a great many men who are dedicated to wine drinking and to appreciating and understanding fine wine; yet it is these men who are always first with little grunts of pleasure when a rich party pudding comes to table; but, we must stress, never in any circumstances do we serve cheese after pudding or serve savouries at all. They have had a mouthful of cheese after the main course and a last mouthful of good red wine with the cheese, so they are ready for this last pudding pleasure. The huge range of cold puddings on which we can draw enables cook to get them out of the way and into either refrigerators or deep freeze before doing any main cooking preparations. Thus she can devote herself to them single mindedly and then forget them until they are whipped out and garnished on the day.

Let us deal first of all with puff paste and tackle this tricky subject in some detail together. We will stand or fall by your opinion of our categorical statement that however experienced you are at making pastry and however much care you are prepared to take, your puff pastry, will be as good as, but no better than, the flour which you use in the making.

· Puff Pastry ·

Many years ago now we did a test. We started three 1 lb. 1 oz. batches of three different kinds of flour consecutively on our lengthy road to a high risen and million leaf flaky *puff pastry*. The recipe we used for all three was as follows: 1 lb. 1 oz. of three-times sifted flour which had been stored in a very dry place; 1 lb. of unsalted butter; the strained juice of half a lemon topping up 1 tumblerful of icily cold water. Each batch of flour, one English, one French and one Swiss, was sifted into three mounds on a very large marble slab, each was worked up swiftly to a dough by pushing each mound into a ring on the surface, adding the water bit by bit into the well in the centre and working it gradually with the flour from the encircling wall with a small table knife in each hand.

When the doughs were formed into identical, light, firm pastes which were not so overworked that they became like elastic, each one was rolled out into a long, thin panel; the cold butter for each was squeezed in a clean cloth so as to expel every drop of moisture from it; each was then shaped into a neat flat rectangle so shaped as to be $1\frac{1}{2}$–$2''$ smaller than the width of the long paste panels and then each was placed in position in the centre of each panel. The flap above the butter was brought over the butter, the flap below the butter folded over to the top and the edges were pressed at left and right with the roller to seal them in with the thus-joined paste edges. Then without moving each panel, we drove a thumb into the top at centre, folded each into waxed paper and refrigerated it for 30 minutes. In the same way, after 30 minutes, each one was taken out, put on the lightly floured marble with the thumb mark top in the same position, rolled out into another long thin panel with light jerky movements, folded again into three, half turned on the table, re-rolled, folded again into three, the edges locked in with the pin and the top marked with a thumb mark. All three were then returned to refrigeration for 30 minutes and this procedure was repeated five times more.

Half an hour after the last time, the paste was rolled, cut and stamped out into a series of different shapes. These were placed on three baking sheets, each one of which had been run under the cold tap before the paste was put on and all were baked in three identical ovens at Gas Mark 8 one shelf above centre. None were egg washed—we will talk about that later—because we were not attempting to assist the glamorous look of any one of the three by this procedure. When they were taken out of the oven, the ones with English flour were not bad at all, but more beige in colour than golden and white. The French ones were better and had risen more but only the Swiss flour batch was perfect, flew apart when cut and was golden and white in colour. We are not expecting you to go chasing over Europe for Swiss flour; we tell you all this merely to console you if yours does not meet the highest standards. This cannot be achieved, although of course the results would be delicious.

There is a small restaurant a few miles from Nice called La Belle Route, where the *chef/patron* excels in a puff pastry item which calls for either fresh raspberries or strawberries. Try it with the most superb canned or frozen ones and it will become a soggy mess, so mark this down as a soft-fruits-season buffet or dinner party pudding.

· Feuilleté de Fraises ou Framboises ·

It is called quite simply *Feuilleté de Fraises ou Framboises*. It only requires first class puff paste, the soft fruits, whipped cream, confectioners' custard* and sifted icing sugar.

Begin by rolling out a long narrow $\frac{1}{2}$" thick panel of the paste. Trim the edges meticulously to give you the required number of $4\frac{1}{2}$" × $3\frac{1}{4}$" rectangles. Then with a small, pointed knife draw an inner rectangle $\frac{1}{2}$" from the edges all round and to within $\frac{1}{8}$" of the base. On no account let the knife go right through! Brush the top of the inner rectangle and the outer "frame" with raw, unbeaten egg white, sprinkle thickly with castor sugar and bake on a wetted baking sheet (run under cold tap), at Gas Mark $7\frac{1}{2}$ (pre-heated oven for this one please), one shelf above centre. When paste is fully risen and golden brown on top remove from oven, run the knife round the inner line and lift off each "lid". Scoop out any surplus of soft flabby inner paste. Return the cases but *not* the lids to the oven at Gas Mark 2 until they are just dried out and do not glisten with moisture anymore.

When cold, spread confectioners' custard thickly all over the inside. Heap to the brim with the chosen fruit, dust thickly with sifted icing sugar and pile whipped cream on top. At the moment of service rest the "lid" lightly on top of each one. The addition of a few drops of kirsch, or apricot brandy is optional but delectable.

· Doigts de Feuilletage ·

Then there are those ridiculously simple *Doigts de Feuilletage* which raise the status of a bowl of fruit *compôte* immeasurably.

Roll out puff paste trimmings to a $\frac{1}{4}$" thickness and cut from them the required number of $4\frac{1}{2}$–5" long fingers. Take each cut finger and twist it from end to end, giving the paste a slight pull as you twist. Lay these on a wetted baking sheet. Brush over the tops as thickly as possible with raw, unbeaten egg white and cover the tops with as much castor sugar as the raw white will absorb. Bake at Gas Mark 6, one shelf above centre, being careful, as with all puff paste items, to give an occasional peek to see if they are rising evenly or starting to lurch in a slightly tipsy manner. If they are so misbehaving, just push them back into their proper shapes. Do not be afraid . . . this will not cause them to sink.

· Mille Feuilles ·

Nearly everyone longs to make good *Mille Feuilles*—not those flat fingers with rum chocolate on the top and a lick of jam and cream inside them. The same ruling should be applied to them as to eclairs. If it is possible to eat either in the fingers without getting into a scandalous mess, they are really not worth eating! So let us share the one most loved by our family and friends which we gave the Daily Telegraph Kitchen Committee members in 1968 at one of our many cook-ins together.

Roll out your puff paste into a $\frac{7}{8}$" thick panel $4\frac{1}{2}$–5" wide. Slap this onto a wetted baking sheet (no egg wash please) and bake one shelf above centre at Gas Mark $7\frac{1}{2}$ until the paste has risen well and the top is a pale biscuit colour. Have ready the longest, sharpest knife in your possession. Snatch the puffed panel from the oven and with such a knife slice off the "lid" as thinly and carefully as possible. Lay this inside uppermost on a cooling rack and return the rest to the same brisk oven. In a few moments it will become pale beigey/biscuit coloured on top. Repeat the process. Then go on slicing off leaf thin layers returning the remainder to the oven until you possess seven puff paste panels.

When these are cold, spread the base layer *thickly* with vanilla-flavoured confectioners' custard* and cover with another layer remembering to reserve the top layer (which you removed first) for the final top or lid. Spread this with your best home made strawberry jam. Cover with no. 3. Spread this thickly with the best possible, stiffly whipped double cream. Repeat this trio as given and go to work on the lid. Cover it with lemon flavoured *glacé* icing. Leave this to form a faint film on top. Place a little softened cooking chocolate or chocolate chips in a paper icing bag without any pipe affixed. Pipe a thin trail down the centre of the lid lengthwise. Pipe alternate 1″ long slightly fatter "branches" down each side of this trail in 1″ apart positions. Take up a fine skewer, a steel knitting needle or a cocktail stick—whichever in fact you find is easiest to work with—and "run in" the chocolate by drawing your chosen implement through it undulating the implement slightly. Practise a little first if you think this sounds complicated. Spread a little *glacé* icing on an upturned cake tin. Do some main stems and wiggled branches onto it until you achieve the familiar appearance of the "run in" chocolate on the top of *pâtissiers' mille feuilles*.

We have found that this one of ours tastes far better the day after it is made and is almost as good for a further two days.

· Croquembouche ·

The trouble with us, as usual, when we start talking to the typewriter about cooking (because we always try to imagine we are talking to one or two of you in our own kitchen) is that one thing does tend to lead on to another through a remote culinary hare having been started up in our minds! This time it is a form of *Croquembouche* or French Wedding Cake which is a great deal easier to make in *feuilletage* and lasts for a good deal longer than the great classic. Being made of *choux* paste the *real thing* really only has a life of a few hours, which is why the nuns in France are so persistent in their visitations to *pâtissiers*. The remainder of the dawn bake is considered unsaleable by luncheon time. The nuns collect it for the poor. The noon bake is withdrawn before the doors close and given to the nuns.

We well remember spending a wedding morning in the kitchen of a Savoyard whose daughter was being married at two o'clock. No luncheon for him. He began his 6 ft. high *Croquembouche* with the very first piped bun while the bride was being given away by her uncle. His assistants piped out, baked and rack-cooled literally hundreds in graduated sizes while he built up the huge, traditional cone being meticulously careful as the pyramid rose to place the little buns one atop the other with large enough spaces between for the long green stems of sugar roses to be driven in between them. Each bun held firmly in position because each one was dipped in the caramel sugar which he, like every other professional, had made in advance. We will of course say nothing about the hours he had spent beforehand making the really exquisite Marechal Neil sugar roses. When the pyramid was completed a *sous-pâtissier* took a huge, pre-made bowl of icily chilled *Crème Chantilly* from the *garde manger* or cold room and everyone began filling it into giant icing bags as the bride went into the vestry with the rest of her family. Up, up rose the *Chantilly* inside the pyramid, until, finally, it was brought to the very top. In went the roses until the gold brown confection was studded with them. Then as the bride's car swept up the drive, Papa took his pan of caramel sugar from the oven and began dipping two back-to-back forks into it, and throwing or flicking them back and forth over a long wooden bar (like a broom handle). With each flick or throw more and more hair-like threads of pale straw coloured spun sugar fell from the forks.

Onto its pedestal went the *Croquembouche*. Over went the great cloud of sugar. A waiter rushed in with Papa's morning coat as he whipped off his *Coq de Cuisine*, apron and sweat cloth. A *commis* handed him a white carnation, Fanny fixed it in his buttonhole and as the bride entered the salon, Papa strolled out to share in the celebrations as the *Croquembouche* wedding cake was carried to its lace-draped table.

We tell you this, firstly because it enchanted us and secondly, to make the point—albeit laboriously—that this kind of *Croquembouche* is a tiny bit beyond the average cook housewife.

Not so the caramel sugar. Here it is for you to cherish. It took us three weeks to perfect the formula so that we could make it one day at home, let it go cold in its pan, haul it up to a television studio, reheat it there (three times in one evening) and spin sugar exactly as we have described at the precise moment we needed to do so on TV. In other words, *if* you make it accurately you can reheat it and use it again times without number and it will *not* turn pitch black in the pan and cost you a good container. But pray never lose sight of the all important fact that it *cannot* be submitted to more than gentle heat without the danger of it being a costly enterprise.

When you have tried it, you will be able to use it for those sugar-at-the-crack covered pairs of grapes, slices of tangerine, small strawberries, pairs of ripe cherries which constitute the most glamorous *fruits glacés* for your dinner party dish of *petits fours*.

You can use it to make the professional, ice-smooth, transparently thin tops to *Crème Brulée* (as opposed to the domestic method we gave you in the "Cook's Book") and Dobos Cake or to stick little circles of baked puff paste one above the other for a modest but delicious *Croquembouche Feuilleté*.

Here is the table for Fanny's Own Spun Sugar Mixture.

Sugar	Glucose	Water	Cream of Tartar
3½ lbs.	4 teasp.	1 pt.	1 heaped teasp.
1¾ lbs.	2 teasp.	½ pt.	½ heaped teasp.
14 ozs.	1 teasp.	¼ pt.	¼ heaped teasp.

Please Read This Next. The sugar must be granulated, the glucose liquid from the chemist, *not* in powder form. We insult you by this seemingly patronising explanation because our ears are still stinging from the dressing-down we received from a woman who said she had seen us make a pudding on stage with orange flower and rose waters. She had tasted the pudding and found it "divine", then she went home, followed the recipe faithfully and it was disgusting. Cross-questioning revealed that madam had bought orange and rose skin tonics.

Method for Spun Sugar Mixture. Place the sugar, water and glucose pell mell in a very thick pan and set over a very low heat. Stir carefully until the mixture forms a clear, grit-less fluid. Increase the heat very slightly and allow mixture to rise to 240° on a saccharometer. Toss in the cream of tartar and stir until the cloudiness vanishes. Reduce heat again to minimal. Half fill a large bowl with ice. Pour over just enough very cold water to submerge the cubes. Set a pastry brush to hand. Re-raise the heat sufficiently for the mixture to bubble steadily. Then, as the edges begin to throw a tiny rim of crystals against the wall of the pan, dip the brush into the iced water and brush them away. Wipe the brush and go on dipping/brushing/wiping until the mixture has turned to a very pale golden straw colour. Drop a flick or two into the iced water. If it forms a tiny crack-hard blob, withdraw the pan if wanting to make *petits fours glacés*. On the other hand if you want it for *Croquembouche* or for the skating rink lids to gâteaux and creams continue simmering. It never matters if you pull the pan off the heat and then return it.

As it resumes a steady simmer and begins to deepen very slightly in colour, dip a fork into it and flick it (over a paper covered surface). When fine hairs spin out from the shaken fork, stop again please. At this stage you can use it for Spun Sugar, for Nut Brittle, or for any of those skating rink top-surfaces. When you have used what you require, tent the cooled pan in foil and put it away in a completely dry area. Next time you want to use it slip it into the oven, middle shelf, Gas Mark ¼ with the oven left ajar and allow it to re-dissolve very slowly indeed. When it is hot, carry on as before.

· Mini Croquembouche ·

By this time we have strayed rather far from puff paste so let us retrace our steps and pick up with *Mini Croquembouche*. Set a 10″ diameter cake board on your working surface after making or while reheating and softening your spun sugar. See that the puff paste is not more than ⅛″ in thickness and stamp out about a dozen circles with a 4″ diameter fluted pastry cutter. Lay the paste on a wetted baking sheet and bake one shelf above centre at Gas Mark 7½. Meanwhile stamp out about a dozen 3½″ diameter discs; and the same of 3″, 2½″, 2″, 1½″ and 1″ discs. When all are baked and cooled, lay the 4″ discs in an overlapping circle, a maximum of ½″ from the edge of the board all round; dipping each one into the hot syrup first so that by the time you have placed the last one in position, the entire overlapping ring can be lifted up, locked together by the sugar syrup. With the next batch (3½″ diameter) dip and overlap so that the outer rim of the finished ring is ½″ inside the base edge of rings. Repeat with each given size of discs making the third (the 3″ set) and all subsequent rings 1″ inside the previous ring. This should leave you with a hole in the centre from the topmost ring to the base one. Whip up a pint of double cream, flavour it very lightly with sifted icing sugar and kirsch. Fold into this mixture ½ lb. rough-chopped crystallised pineapple cubes from the sweet shop. Fill into the centre and mound it up. Drive a few ½″ fluted, baked, sugar-dipped pastry circles into the cream here and there at the moment of service and dust overall with sifted icing sugar.

Of course, you can stab half *glacé* cherries and leaves of angelica at intervals around the rim if you can spare the time, and you can use half confectioners' custard and half cream for the central mound, but if you do this, be sure to make up each standard quantity of custard with 1½ ozs. of flour instead of the given 1 oz. or the whole thing will collapse and run!

Having pointed out the perils of advance-making *choux* paste items we would like to discuss for a moment the ways in which they can be drawn into a busy cook-hostess' pattern, without her having the professional speed of the chef in our little wedding story. Firstly, and before we give you the basic, classic *choux* paste recipes which are superior to the ordinary, all-purpose water *choux* paste, may we stress that your Mrs. Jekyll half makes the paste for Mrs. Hyde the night before her party. She then covers it with plate or saucer and leaves it on top of, if you like, but absolutely never inside the refrigerator. On top she places her baking tins, oil and brush for treating the tins immediately prior to piping and baking which are then done at great speed in the early afternoon.

· Petits Choux en Surprise ·

To illustrate how little need be done to finish your sweet item—be it for a cake or pudding occasion; let us begin with *Petits Choux en Surprise*. Once made and cooled, you need to have mocha ice cream† in your conservator, chocolate sauce† made and ready to slip into the top of a double saucepan over hot water and *Crème Chantilly* made and refrigerated in its serve-yourselves dish. You put the sauce into the double pan when you are ready "except for my frock". You have already shown whatever help you have how to fill the ice cream into each ready-split *choux* bun. Indeed if you are serving these at a dinner party you have actually put the three, four or five baby buns onto each pudding plate for the "help". After which it only remains to stress that the filling is only put in while everyone is hock-deep in the main course. Then the sauce goes into its sauceboat (ladle set beside it) and the bowl of cream is handed separately.

· Pâte à chou au Café ·

The basic mixture we would like you to try for this one is called *Pâte à chou au Café*. Assemble 1 oz. preferably unsalted butter, a scant 4½ fl. ozs. of cold strong black coffee, a scant flat eggspoon of salt, 2¼ ozs. of sifted flour and 2 standard eggs. Place butter with salt and coffee in small pan and allow liquid to boil by the time butter has melted. Tip in the flour, wait a moment until liquor seethes over it and remove from heat. Beat very thoroughly, add first egg and whip until smooth once more. Repeat with second egg, cover and leave until required. When baking, oil baking sheets, pipe mixture into very small balls with a ½″ or maximum ¾″ diameter plain pipe, spacing them fairly widely apart. Bake at Gas Mark 7½ one shelf above centre until browned, not merely beige. All *choux* paste is susceptible to the humidity in the atmosphere and the mixture needs to be baked crisp to avoid it turning flabby before it is served.

· Paris-Brest ·

Use the same method when making a *Paris-Brest*, one of the most simple *choux* paste *gâteaux* and utterly luscious. Use *Pâte à chou Ordinaire*. Assemble 1 oz. unsalted butter, a scant 4½ fl. ozs. milk, 1 mean flat eggspoon of salt, 2¼ ozs. sifted flour and 2 eggs. Proceed exactly as for coffee *choux* paste. Place the entire mixture in an icing bag with no pipe whatever. Oil a flat baking sheet and force out the paste into as fat a circle as possible. Brush the top with raw beaten egg, sprinkle thickly with flaked almonds and bake as for coffee *choux* paste, but expect the big sausage-ring to take up to 30–35 minutes to rise and brown. Cool it on a rack. Just before putting on your frock, split the ring all round. Remove the top. Fill the interior generously with *Crème Chantilly*, replace the top and dust overall very thickly with sifted icing sugar.

· Gâteau St. Honoré ·

From the same *choux* paste mixture you can progress to a simple version of classic *Gâteau St. Honoré*. When you are rushed, forget about the tiny buns with which the edge is trimmed. Just spread the made paste into a flattish circle on an oiled baking sheet and bake as for *Paris-Brest*. When it is brown and puffy, cool on a rack and split in two like halving a circular sponge. Fill the interior with *Crème Chibouste*, and warm up your stored Spun Sugar Mixture (p. 219). When this is melted, spoon it quickly over the entire top surface, but do this thinly or someone's tooth may go AWOL on a rocky thick bit! Cover the *Crème Chibouste* generously with whipped cream, sift icing sugar over it and clap on the gleaming spun sugar-coated top half. Alternatively, you can put the lid over the *Chibouste* and heap the cream on the top of the crisp sugar-coat, provided you do this immediately prior to service.

· Profiteroles au Chocolat ·

Before we move on to cream puddings let us remind ourselves that few flavours can compete with chocolate, and therefore rejoice that we can make *Profiteroles au Chocolat* with even greater ease than the foregoing items. Use the ordinary *choux* paste*. Pipe it all into very small blobs and bake as described. Cool on the rack and then fill each one, rather meanly, with chocolate flavoured confectioners' custard. Do this up to 2 hours before your guests are expected. Then pile them into a pyramid on a shallow salver. At the moment of service pour hot chocolate sauce all over them and serve whipped cream and sifted icing sugar separately.

· Chocolate Sauce ·

Everyone we meet has their own favourite chocolate sauce the majority of which, in our experience either turn to brown glue when ladled over ice cream, or else become rock hard in an instant. We boast neither of these naughtinesses occur with ours. Put 5 ozs. cooking chocolate or chocolate chips into a small pan with 2 level tablespoons soft brown (pieces) sugar and 2 tablespoons stock sugar syrup. Melt very gently over minimal heat. Beat in 2 ozs. of unsalted butter; add it in little flakes gradually while beating. When all is smoothly blended, add a dessertspoonful of strained orange juice and the very lightly and finely grated zest of half a small thin-skinned orange. Finish sauce with an optional dessertspoonful of either Tia Maria or Crème de Cacao. Turn into the top of double saucepan over hot water and let it await service over a mere whisper of heat.

· Crème Chibouste ·

Now for the *Crème Chibouste* to which we referred in our recipe for *Gâteau St. Honoré*. Place ¼ pt. confectioners' custard* in a small thick pan and put over an outer pan of hot water while you whip up the whites of 4 small or 3 large eggs very stiffly indeed. Sprinkle 1 oz. castor sugar over the surface. Whip egg whites again for 1 minute. Immediately take confectioners' custard pan from hot water and set over mild heat. Ladle in the meringue mix gradually remembering that for this mixture to succeed you must not stop whipping for an instant. As the last meringue dollop is whisked in, snatch from the heat, dump into a bowl of ice and whip on until the *Chibouste* descends to blood heat.

Our constant attempts to meet the demands for something different with strawberries, raspberries and loganberries prompted us to experiment with classic confectioners' custard*. We started with the knowledge provided for us by equally classic *Fraises Romanoff*, that oranges and strawberries bed down together with great amity. Joining these two thoughts together, we began by replacing the milk in classic confectioners' custard with fresh, strained or unsweetened, tinned orange juice.

The finished sauce has two separate stages. The first stage is, in fact, a slightly thicker version of classic confectioners' custard made with orange juice instead of milk. Like this it is used as confectioners' custard for insulating the base of puff paste or sweet short paste* baked cases which are intended to receive fruits various. This insulation, like the original, stops pastry bases from becoming soggy after finishing and before service. We then come to stage two—the addition of very stiffly whipped cream which turns the custard into a gorgeous orange cream sauce which can be piped to hold a firm peak and used as a topping for the cases various. So now for the basic recipe.

· Orange Custard ·

Assemble 4 separated egg yolks, 4 ozs. castor sugar, 10 fl. ozs. fresh strained orange juice or 7½ fl. ozs. tinned unsweetened orange juice with 2½ fl. ozs. of good old tap water, one vanilla pod and 1¼ ozs. sifted flour. Put the chosen fruit juice or juice and water with the vanilla pod in a small pan and allow to become very hot but not boiling. Beat the flour, egg yolks and sugar together in a bowl with a wooden spoon until very thoroughly blended. Pour on the hot liquid (removing the vanilla pod), stir well and scrape the contents with a rubber or plastic spatula into the top of a double saucepan over hot water. Continue stirring with a wooden spoon until the mixture becomes very thick and just flops idly from the spoon. Return to a bowl. Cover the top surface with a fitting circle of wetted greaseproof paper to ensure no crust forms while the mixture is cooling.

Before we tackle stage two, let us just run over some of the ways this Orange Custard can be used.

· Profiteroles à l'Orange ·

You can fill it into *choux* buns and hand orange cream sauce separately with them, thus achieving *Profiteroles à l'Orange*. You can stiffen the custard with gelatine using ½ oz. dissolved over a low heat with 4 tablespoons water for one pint of the made custard. Pour this made mixture into an oiled, ornamental mould. When set, unmould and surround with decorative pipings of orange cream sauce and serve as *Crème à l'Orange*; or you can serve the *Crème* surrounded by hulled strawberries in which case you hand the sauce separately.

· Orange Cream Sauce ·

So now for the *Orange Cream Sauce*, or stage two. To the given Orange Custard quantity add 8 fl. ozs. of very stiffly whipped cream and, optionally, flavour to taste with orange curaçao.

· Les Petites Tartelettes de Fraises ou Framboises ou Abricots ·

Turn back a little in your thinking and remember how the custard is used to insulate pastry containers. If you strew or pile strawberries over the custard, you then use the orange cream sauce mixture for top pipings. We are particularly addicted to individual tartlet cases, each filled to within ¼″ of the top after baking and cooling with the finished orange cream sauce. Then you simply heap small strawberries or raspberries on top and dust liberally with sifted icing sugar at the moment of service. They are delicious. The same thing done with halved, stoned, peeled apricots inverted like cups over the orange custard with a rosette of the orange cream sauce on top merits the title of a *bonne bouche*.

· Charlotte Russe aux Fraises ou Framboises ou Ronce-framboises ·

The annual struggle to meet the soft fruit recipe demand has become known in the family as "like Uncle Arthur's drills"; this will be as clear as mud to you unless we explain that Uncle Arthur was a wealthy relative by marriage whose source of income depended solely upon his producing annually some kind of drill which was capable of going deeper than the one he invented in the preceding year. The end of the line for him was when it stuck at the previous year's level and could go no further. We are getting perilously near to the end of the line but we are safe for another twelve months now with what we have called *Charlotte Russe aux Fraises ou Framboises ou Ronce-framboises* (literal translation: bramble raspberry—i.e. loganberry).

Begin with one of those invaluable standard heat-resistant glass flan dishes measuring 8½″ in diameter and cover the base with a ¼″ thick fitting circle of our standard fatless Swiss roll mixture*. Now make the following mixture. Whip 1½ gills (7½ fl. ozs.) double cream with 3 level dessertspoonsful vanilla-flavoured castor sugar until it hangs loosely from the whisk. Whip in 2½ fl. ozs. cold milk gradually until smoothly blended. Stir in ¼ oz. powdered gelatine dissolved in a small saucepan over a very low heat with 3 tablespoons cold water. Finally, whip in 1 *stiffly* whipped standard separated egg white, at which point the mixture should begin to thicken rapidly. Pour over the sponge in the container when it is thick enough to flop out and level itself off with a good shake . . . why? Simply because if you pour it when it is runny, it will wet the surface of the sponge which will spoil the texture and the flavour on the palate. By the time you have washed up your containers the mixture will be set. Tent in foil, refrigerate it for up to 4 days or, as we do now in bulk, freeze some to cover your entertaining expectations in this respect during the soft fruit season.

We are not qualified to say that skinned sliced-with-a-silver-knife peaches or nectarines off a south wall would not carry the life of this particular summer pudding further, but, there are few of us fortunate enough to have adequate crops! It is, however, marvellous later on in the season with mirabelles or cherry plums which in our experience can frequently be found in chalky areas growing as a common wild hedge.

When required move from refrigerator or thaw from deep freeze. Pile the top with hulled strawberries, raspberries or loganberries. In the case of loganberries only, give a liberal dusting of sifted icing sugar. Pipe with sweetened whipped cream or when feeling inordinately extravagant *Sauce Mousseline Froide*, which was a creation of the very great Mrs. Agnes Bertha Marshall.

· Sauce Mousseline Froide ·

Assemble 3 ozs. lump sugar, 2½ fl. ozs. cold water, 1 vanilla pod (to wipe, store and use again), 3 separated standard egg yolks, 1 tablespoon maraschino, 1 tablespoon brandy, 1 separated standard egg white, 2½ fl. ozs. stiffly whipped double cream, 1 standard tray of 12 ice cubes. Place sugar, water and vanilla pod in a small pan over a thread of heat and allow to dissolve without stirring— just shake the pan occasionally. If making large quantities it is helpful to have a bowl of iced water and a pastry or clean paint brush, as the sugar tends to crystallise slightly round the sides of the pan and you can defeat this by occasional flicks of the brush dipped in the iced water. Just run it round the upper rim to clean it off. Continue simmering until one or two tests can be applied: (a) a crisp, colourless pearl forms when a drop is shaken over a cube of ice, (b) when if you have a perforated spoon, you dip it in, blow the bubble and it will float away. Remove from heat, remove pod and place over ice. Whip in the raw egg yolks until mixture is thick and creamy. Whip in alcohols and then the stiffly whipped egg white. Finally, whip in cream and leave on ice in refrigerator until moment of service. Pipe over the chosen soft fruit and send to table with justifiable vanity.

· Real Pêches Melba ·

This summer we gave a series of terrace luncheon parties to introduce some of our closest friends to our new (and absolutely last) home. We found that the *succès fou* was real *Pêche Melba* which none of the very young had ever tasted. The poor little wretches honestly believed that tinned peaches, over bought vanilla ice cream, with dreadful imitation raspberry goos poured on top and the whole finished with ersatz cream *was Pêche Melba*. When we gave them the Real Thing they raved. Indeed one elegant and very well-to-do man of over thirty had four to our certain knowledge (we suspect a fifth but cannot be sure!). He has never stopped talking about it since. This Escoffier creation should be real vanilla ice cream made with confectioners' custard, double cream and vanilla pods, spooned into large *coupes* with fresh, halved, skinned peaches on top and surmounted by fresh raspberries rubbed through a fine sieve. The peaches are poached with infinite care in stock sugar syrup* strongly infused with vanilla pods.

At these parties for which we had gorgeous weather, we assembled all our puddings and their garnish in the kitchen and as the orders came in we sent out individual portions, popping such items as Iced Raspberry and Strawberry *Soufflés* into the freezing compartments of our kitchen refrigerators in between dollops.

· Sauce Melba ·

Incidentally, before giving you this recipe, let us emphasise that the real, sieved, unsweetened raspberry *purée* which IS *Sauce Melba* can be filled into waxed cartons and frozen for use, in winter. The peaches can be bottled in season after poaching in their vanilla syrup. With vanilla ice cream in the freezer *Pêches Melba* then become available all the year round and are a super standby for us all when we can afford to put them up for future use.

· Our Iced Fruit Soufflés ·

Now for our basic *Iced Fruit Soufflé* recipe. You will require ½ pt. of double cream, ½ pt. of stock sugar syrup*, ½ pt. of sieved unsweetened fruit and 5 egg whites. It is just money, not cooking this one! Stir cold, chosen fruit *purée* into the sugar syrup. Beat in the stiffly whipped double cream gradually. Add the stiffly whipped egg whites, whisk altogether and turn into prepared *soufflé* moulds—if wishing to serve at dinner parties. Otherwise, just pour mixture into lidded plastic containers and freeze until required. Just remember when using *soufflé* moulds that, unlike any proper hot *soufflé*, you *should* surround the outside of the mould with a band of cartridge paper securely fixed with paper clips as these are safer than pins! Cut these bands to rise 1½" to 2" above the mould's rim and brush each one with oil on the inside before affixing. With this mixture you can in fact ring the changes from strawberry *purée* through raspberry and blackcurrant, plum (various) and finally damson plum, but not those small, very sharp old damsons—too viciously sharp to give an unctuous result.

When serving the moulds, whip off papers, and in summer heap the top with the appropriate fresh fruit, give them a liberal top-dusting of sifted icing sugar and pipe the interstices with whipped cream, or go mad in the head with the extravagance of it and hand Orange Cream Sauce separately. Conversely, for buffets, take dollops from the freezer-containerful into *coupes* or sundae glasses, top with raspberries or strawberries, dust with sifted icing sugar and "finish" with a top spiral of thickly whipped cream.

· Gâteau de Pêches, Abricots, Fraises ou Framboises ·

Reverting for a moment to Sauce Melba it furnishes an exquisite sauce for pouring over slices of our *Gâteau de Pêches, Abricots, Fraises ou Framboises*. These *gâteaux* are made with our basic Swiss roll sponge mixture*, cream cheese filling and sliced skinned peaches, apricots or halved large or whole small strawberries or raspberries. Be sure to freeze some unrolled panels of this sponge mixture to draw on at speed in summer and winter. The cream cheese filling does not freeze well and so do this a day or two before using. To make it you use $\frac{1}{2}$ lb. of curd cream cheese, sifted icing sugar to taste, a tablespoonful of strained orange juice and $2\frac{1}{2}$ fl. ozs. stiffly whipped cream. Mix all together, beat well and spread over each half of a divided sponge panel or two rounds, which have been baked in a Victoria sponge tin. The filling must be spread at least a $\frac{1}{4}$" thick. Then you cover one of the two cream cheese spread sponges thickly with your chosen fruit. Dust it thickly with sifted icing sugar, clap the second half on top, pipe small rosettes of whipped cream over the entire surface, decorate with whatever fruit you have chosen and at the moment of service give a final dusting of sifted icing sugar. In our experience none of this is ever left to go back into the kitchen!

· Strawberry and Raspberry Fools ·

Fanny's mum used to make her own version of *Strawberry and Raspberry Fools* which the cooks in the family have copied ever since. Sieve the fruit, sweeten it to taste with sifted icing sugar, whip as near to half as much its own bulk in thickly whipped cream as you can possibly afford and then continue whipping relentlessly for at least 10 minutes. This is no trouble at all for anyone who can afford the very few pounds it costs to buy the very best and most practical electric mixer—the little hand one which can be hauled around on an extra long flex to pots and pans on and off your cooker. Have ready $\frac{1}{4}$ lb. of the raspberries or strawberries for every pint of fool. At the moment of service fold these in and ideally accompany these fools with a dish of dry *petits fours*. Incidentally, we think that blackcurrant *purée* makes one of the best fools, but we cut the sharpness with sifted icing sugar before freezing. Once again may we remind you that you will need still more of those unsweetened fruit *purées* in your freezer if you are planning on making such fools during the winter months.

· Fraises Romanoff ·

Before we go any further, let us pause and draw breath for long enough to share the details of one or two things about which so far we have only made passing references. *Fraises Romanoff* is a palate-cleansing strawberry dish suitable for serving after a very rich main course or cheese dish. Hull even-sized, not too large strawberries—the flavour is seldom as good in the very big ones. Put, say, 2 lbs. in a crystal serving bowl, dust thickly with sifted icing sugar, mix 1 liqueur glass of orange Curaçao with the strained juice of 2 very small oranges, pour overall and chill overnight. If serving out of doors, stand your bowl in an outer one of crushed ice or ice cubes.

· Fruit Water Ices ·

Now we can go on and try to tempt you into making room in your freezers for *Fruit Water Ices*. This is a generic or basic recipe. Assemble the strained juice of 1½ medium lemons, 1 lb. lump or preserving sugar, 1½ pts. boiled cold water and 8¾ fl. ozs. fruit *purée*. This last can be sieved raspberries, strawberries, loganberries, blackcurrants, fifty per cent each of black and white currants mixed, or of raspberries and red currants, or apricots, peaches and should you ever want to go totally insane, or be a millionaire, nectarines.

Heat up water and sugar together until the latter has completely dissolved. Chill. Mix lemon juice and chosen *purée* together. Rub them through a sieve onto the cold sugar syrup. If you want to achieve a more luxurious and subtle flavour for each of these fruits, then use kirsch with the black or white currants and raspberries, brandy with the peaches and apricots, or orange curaçao with the strawberries. Extract 1 or 2 tablespoons from the given quantity of boiled water and replace with the liqueur after boiling the reduced water content with the sugar and chilling the resultant syrup. The best way of freezing these is to pour the finished mixture into plastic lidded boxes or waxed cartons. It is

more space-saving to use large cartons as, there always being an
exception to every good rule, fruit water ices can, like ice creams,
be removed from the freezer, mulcted of any part of their contents and the balance returned to the freezer. As we are saying this
and *giving* you our assurance, we have to make the very important
point that to do this with meat or fish dishes is to invite tragedy!
Say to yourself, "Once out of the freezer fish, meat, poultry and
vegetable dishes must not go back."

There are actually four basic methods for making water ices:
Sorbets or Sherbets, the proper names for the fruit water ices we
have just dealt with; *Granités* which answer the same purpose as
Sorbets; *Spooms* and *Marquises*.

Spooms can be made with the basic fruit water ice recipes
(above). They can also be made with champagne and such wines
as Samos, Muscat and Zucco. All right! We are only mentioning
them to put you in the picture; we readily accept that they are
ridiculous to attempt with the current iniquitous taxation laws.

· Spoom au Citron ·

Say you want a lemon-flavoured special *Spoom au Citron*.
Make up a pint of Lemon Water Ice mixture—it is honestly not
worth making less as you will see in a moment—and very
gradually and carefully induce ½ pt. of Italian Meringue mixture
by light blend/beating until the whole mixture is a snowy foam.
Rush it into the coldest area of your freezer and on no account let
it sit about after finishing and before freezing.

· Lemon Water Ice ·

For the *Lemon Water Ice* assemble 8 ozs. lump sugar; 1 pt.
water; 4 lemons and 2 egg whites. Dissolve all but 6 lumps of
sugar with the water, bring to the boil and maintain at a slow
rolling boil for 10 minutes. Meanwhile rub the 6 lumps on 2 of the
lemons until the lumps begin to crumble and go yellow. Add these
to the simmering syrup. Squeeze all the lemons and then strain the
juice. Stir syrup over ice until cold. Add juice and blend again.
Fill into ice trays, place in freezing compartment of refrigerator
or deep freeze and leave for 20 minutes. Bring out and whip down.
Put back for a further 20 minutes. Then divide the frozen mixture
in halves. Whip up egg whites and add to one half. Finally, add
remaining mixture, blend altogether and freeze until required.

· Italian Meringue ·

So what is *Italian meringue*? It is the opposite of Swiss meringue. Chalk white, needing no baking, crisp, firm and close textured instead of pale biscuit colour and crisp/collapsing to a gorgeous central toothy-goo! It is made of boiled sugar in water and very stiffly whipped egg whites. We ask you not to attempt this mixture unless you have either another pair of hands to aid you or a table electric mixer which is, in this instance, the equivalent.

Given these begin by measuring 17½ fl. ozs. cold water into a 6–7" diameter saucepan and adding 1¼ lbs. granulated sugar. Set these together in the pan over a very low heat indeed and make sure every grain of sugar is dissolved before you raise the heat. Meanwhile place 4 separated egg whites in bowl and switch on mixer, or exhort mate to start whisking vigorously and steadily. When the pan syrup is clear, raise heat till it achieves a steady rolling boil. Maintain this and after the first 3–4 minutes test it with a *perforated metal spoon*. Dip spoon into syrup, bang down and blow through it. Nothing will happen but it is a good rehearsal because as the syrup reduces and begins to have a fine foam of tight little bubbles on the top, *it will* and if you miss the crucial moment, your meringue will be a failure. Keep dipping and blowing. You will find that suddenly one short sharp blow will cause fat sugar air bubbles to blow away from the back of the perforated spoon. Allow ½ a minute more. Now remember, by this time the egg whites must be very stiff indeed. Keep mixer beaters turning at full speed, or mate whipping relentlessly and pour the sugar syrup in a thin stream over the foam. Continue whipping until the top of the mixture thickens, subsides quite considerably and begins to acquire fat wrinkles. Only when this happens and the pulled-away beaters have soft but strong peaks hanging from them is the Italian Merinque ready.

We feel you will begin to get cross with us the moment you discover that the amount you must use for your *Spoom* is far less than the amount you have made. Relax, we have done this purposely. Some of the prettiest easiest, long-keeping *petits fours secs* are made with the residue and stored either for serving with your water ices various or for mixing with other stored items when you serve *petits fours* at your dinners.

The first point to accept please, is that if your made Italian Merinque does wrinkle and thicken when beaten down to blood heat it *will* wait for you! You can complete your *Spoom*, consign it to the freezer and proceed quietly to the making of *petits fours* from the remainder.

Italian Meringue Petits Fours are, basically, a restaurant pastry-cook's fill-in, perennially available from the long-storage which they accept cheerfully. Most of the items are piped, some are clapped together over flavoured butter-cream fillings, but one or two are just mixed with nuts and or *glacé* fruits and dried out in little rocky blobs—like those cornflakes and chocolate crispies the kids slosh up for themselves on wet days and while splashing chocolate over themselves and most of the kitchen simultaneously. For all our suggestions, make or pipe on to sheets of waxed paper and leave in a warm place until each lifts off easily and is quite dry underneath.

· Italian Meringue Petits Fours ·

Here is our little table of easily made types: Use a number zero plastic writing pipe in a non-sweat nylon icing bag (stockists p. 291) to pipe 2½″ long *Batons*. When set dip the tips of each one in softened chocolate chips. Store in layers on waxed papers in an airtight tin.

Use a number 2 plastic writing pipe for making both *Doigts* and *Rosettes*. For the *Doigts* colour a little meringue mix pale green with harmless green vegetable colouring. Pipe little fat, ridged fingers 2½″ long as described above. Do the same with a little pink, blue or yellow vegetable colouring. Stab each green one centrally with a scrap of angelica, the pink with *glacé* cherry, the blue with a scrap of flaked almond and the yellow with a halved walnut.

For *Rosettes* hold pipe vertically and pipe little ridged blobs or rosettes. Keep these as uniform as possible. Colour mixture or leave plain. When dried out clap some together as pairs over little spreadings of chocolate, coffee, lemon, orange or liqueur flavoured butter creams. Aim to make the filling of a contrasting colour to rosettes.

Pipe enough of these to enable you to leave some un-paired. After piping sprinkle immediately with milled pistachio, hazel or walnuts, or stab the tops with any available scraps of *glacé* fruits.

· Marquises ·

Last in this group of Water Ices come *Marquises*, for which you need for every ½ pt. of strawberry or pineapple Kirsch-flavoured frozen water ice, ¼ pt. of stiffly whipped double cream sweetened lightly with sifted icing sugar, i.e. half your chosen quantity whatever it may be. About 4 hours before serving scrape the chosen water ice mixture into a bowl, break it down with a fork, whip it into the cream mixture and return it to the freezer.

We are devoting a great deal of space to this chapter for reasons which we will now explain.

An absolutely splendid pudding goes a long way towards sending guests from the table in high humour when dramas of one kind and another have caused the preceding courses to be slightly sub-standard. With very few exceptions, party puddings can be got out of the way days, weeks and sometimes even months beforehand; and because—dare we offer it as a justification?—we have so many successful ones from our own parties that we are busting to pass on to you.

· Chocolate Refrigerator Cake ·

After a number of tries at a refrigerator cake which can also be frozen, we have finally achieved one which we think is the Best of the Lot. It is a *gâteau*, a pudding, a refrigerated or frozen item; it is not lengthy in preparation and it is very easily done. Begin by obtaining a plastic "burper"-lidded rectangular box-container measuring 12½″ × 8½″ × 2¼″ in depth. Line the base with a fitting sheet of ordinary greaseproof paper. Make, bake, cool on a rack and trim down, to the greaseproof-paper-lined size of the plastic storage box, the two Swiss roll sponge* panels which have been baked in standard Swiss roll tins. Lay the first one over greaseproof. Make the filling. Cream 8 ozs. unsalted butter until white and fluffy. Add 1¼ lbs. sifted icing sugar very gradually, together with 2 separated egg yolks, 1 teaspoon each of orange flower and of rose waters. Add 2–3 tablespoonsful of either Tia Maria or Crème de Cacao. Have ready a 10″ diameter bowl about half filled with softened chocolate chips and when it is thoroughly beaten and smooth, pour this straight on to the butter cream until the beaters of hand or rotary whisk are almost brought to a standstill by its thickness. Turn it instantly over the base panel of sponge, smooth it out right into the corners and as evenly as possible. If it has set too much by this time, achieve the necessary even smoothness by working with a metal spatula dipped in boiling water. Lay the second, trimmed-down sponge panel on top, press it down lightly, cover with a "burper" lid and put away in the freezer until the afternoon of the day that it is needed, or make only 3–4 days in advance and refrigerate.

Either way, in the afternoon of service, remove, unmould, peel off greaseproof paper and pipe stiffly whipped cream in rosettes over the entire very hard rectangle. This takes so very little time to soften that when you have completed the garnish, you keep it in refrigeration until just before serving. When the last whipped cream rosette is completed, push 3 large chocolate leaves† into the cream equidistant from each other across from short side to short side at one end. Continue with evenly sized chocolate leaves so that each one is positioned to indicate the centre of your chosen portion-sized rectangle. At the moment of service dust lightly with sifted icing sugar.

· Mont Blanc aux Marrons ·

We have discovered in the past year or two that some sort of mystique surrounds the making of a good *Mont Blanc aux Marrons*. As this is very far from the truth, we would like to clear the air. This pudding is nothing more than a border mould of chestnut *purée* with *Crème Chantilly* in the middle. The border mould, however, is very necessary; so is a number zero plain writing pipe and a nylon icing bag. Nick and peel off the outer skin from 1 lb. 2 ozs. chestnuts, taking away as much inner skin as possible without breaking them. Place in a thick fairly shallow pan, cover meanly with milk and allow to poach with the *most extreme* gentleness until tender. Strain milk into another pan and use up later for a chestnut-flavoured custard. Drain, remove all remaining inner skins and sieve chestnuts. Put 6 ozs. loaf sugar, a medium sized sherry glass of Bual or Malmsey Madeira and a couple of bits of vanilla pod into a small pan and allow to simmer over lowest possible heat until syrupy. Blend into the chestnut *purée*. Place in the icing bag with the writing pipe affixed. Oil a classic border or *savarin* mould lightly. Hold the icing bag vertically above this and squeeze being careful to doodle or wiggle as you squeeze; then the slender thread of chestnut mixture gradually falls all round the prepared interior and looks rather like a bird's nest. Turn this out onto your serving dish. Heap *Crème Chantilly* into the centre and if you are all millionairesses, do not forget to surround the whole thing with *marrons glacés*.

· Orange Cream ·

It is also a surprise to us to find how few people know that fools can be boiled—in the culinary context of course—and although *Orange Cream* is the name of the recipe we are using as an example, it is still, classically, a "Fool". Take 2 large juicy, un-blemished oranges and 1 lemon and grate the skin finely, *not* including any white pith. Put the grated skins, 6 rounded table-spoons of castor sugar, the strained juice of 4 medium oranges and ½ a medium lemon into a thick copper pan, with 4 whole eggs. Whip relentlessly over a *very* low heat until mixture begins to bubble. Remove from cooker and beat down to blood heat. Then add a liqueur glass of Kirsch and a huge heaped tablespoon of whipped double cream. Refrigerate until service please.

· Biscuit Glacé Grand Marnier ·

If you have not already met it, we would equally like to introduce you to *Biscuit Glacé Grand Marnier*—a frozen pudding which is both delicate and sophisticated. Crumble 4 ozs. *petit beurre* biscuits into a small bowl. Moisten these with 3 table-spoonsful of undiluted fresh strained orange juice and 4 table-spoons Grand Marnier. Stir them around a bit to marinade while you (a) whip ½ pt. double cream until it holds a good peak and (b) whip 2 egg whites fairly stiffly, adding as you whip 4 heaped tablespoonsful of sifted icing sugar. Continue whipping until this also holds a strong peak. Fold in 4 ozs. flaked almonds. Fold in the moistened biscuit mixture and last of all blend in the prepared cream very gently and thoroughly. Turn into an oiled mould or a series of individual oiled moulds. Cover tightly with foil and freeze.

· Cheese Cake ·

Now for a Very Special *Cheese Cake*. We created one of our own which was very good, but at last we have got our hooks on a pluperfect one and not surprisingly this is Jewish. It is not diffi-cult, just extravagant but to balance the budget it is comforting to know that it goes a very long way. Begin with a 7½" diameter sliding based cake tin. Line the sliding base with a fitting circle of greaseproof which has been liberally buttered and floured, and give the same butter and flour treatment to the sides. Then crumble up 7½ ozs. of plain digestive biscuits. Melt 6½ ozs. unsalted butter in a shallow frying pan and then work in the crumbs to achieve a paste. Press this mixture evenly over the bottom of the tin. We find that the wooden or plastic pusher provided with an electric mincing machine is ideal for the job.

Put 1½ lbs. of Sainsbury's curd cheese in a roomy bowl, break it down thoroughly. Add 2 standard eggs, the strained juice of ½ a large or a whole small lemon, the optional grated rind of ½ a small or a ¼ of a large lemon and 2 really heaped tablespoons of sifted vanilla-flavoured icing sugar. Beat well until everything is evenly blended, turn mixture into biscuit paste-lined cake tin, smooth off the top neatly and bake middle shelf, Gas Mark 4, for exactly 20 minutes. Remove from the oven, cool and refrigerate overnight. Then bang the cake tin onto a jam jar or any tin from the store cupboard so that the cheese cake comes out. Use two slices to ease cake from metal base and thus remove grease proof. Return to cake base and place on serving dish. Spread the top to ¼" depth with sour cream, cover the complete top surface with piped rosettes of fresh, whipped double cream, scatter very liberally with sifted icing sugar and finally sprinkle with optional browned flaked almonds.

· Soufflé au Chocolat ·

Harking back if we may to our earlier observations in this chapter concerning the English passion for chocolate pudding, we have great pleasure in sharing with you a new one which we think is exceptional. It is also exceptionally easy, which has a special appeal to us all. When we decide to serve it, Fanny slips from the dining room while the main course is being served. You must appreciate that this *Soufflé au Chocolat* requires 20 minutes in the oven, but it only takes moments to make and in any case we find people tend to linger contentedly over the cheese course and the last glass of red wine!

Put 4 ozs. chocolate chips or cooking chocolate into a thick pan with 2 tablespoonsful of water and let it melt extremely slowly. Beat in 2 ozs. of softened unsalted butter. Whip 4 separated egg yolks and 4 ozs. of sifted icing sugar to a white, foamy batter. Pour onto the chocolate and beat well over a tiny flame. Then bash in—and really we mean just that—bash in 5 stiffly whipped egg whites. Turn into a buttered 7" diameter *soufflé* mould and bake one shelf above centre at Gas Mark 7. These times and temperatures are totally at variance with standard *soufflé* requirements, but this is an exception and so we would not like you to think we are superseding previous directions given in earlier books. It is new, it is different, and it requires generous dollops of whipped double cream to be plopped onto the top of each serving. Then it is really dreamy and of course extremely fattening!

There is too, a much shorter way round which only calls for 8 minutes baking. Should you prefer this to our standard method, fill the given quantity of mixture into four buttered, individual, heat-resistant bowls. We have some turquoise-edged, heat-resistant sundae dishes which are exactly right in size and shape. Bake at the same temperature and in the same position for 8 minutes and serve as before. Incidentally, four extremely greedy people will be happy to have the given quantity divided among them. But to be quite frank, if a generously served, fairly rich meal has already been offered, then you are safe to divide into six.

· Soufflé aux Fruits Confits ·

There is yet a third way of serving a hot *soufflé*, which we filched from a very elegant French restaurant where the chef/proprietor believes in providing shallow ones! Try it and see if it appeals to you, using the new chocolate *soufflé* mixture or an entirely different one called *Soufflé aux Fruits Confits*. It is based on a *roux*, made with 1½ ozs. flour and 1½ ozs. butter. While this is being cooked, you heat ½ pt. of single or coffee cream in one small pan and 3½ ozs. castor sugar and ¼ pt. of sweet white wine in another. When the *roux* clears the bottom of the pan start adding the heated wine (and please do not let it boil) beating well between each addition. Then add the single boiled cream in the same way and beat in the only fairly stiffly whipped whites of 7 eggs. Butter a 2" deep oval earthenware or copper chafing dish. Sprinkle the base and sides with castor sugar. Scatter coarsely chopped, mixed crystallised fruits over this prepared base . . . your choice, remembering that halved *glacé* cherries and chopped crystallised pineapple squares are less costly than the pears, peaches, apricots and figs in those plain wooden boxes, which come from the South of France! Cover the chosen chopped fruits with half the *soufflé* mixture, scatter again with your chosen coarsely chopped fruits, top with remaining *soufflé* mixture and level off in the dish. Sift icing sugar thickly overall and bake Gas Mark 7½, one shelf above centre, for approximately 11 minutes. Just bear in mind that a *soufflé* should be crisp and dark on the outside and very moist in the centre.

· Blanc-Manger ·

To a vast number of people alive today the word *blancmange* symbolises a rather nasty, dead white "shape". In fact what we call *"blancmange"* is a classic with a fascinating history. It began life as *blanc-manger*, which was later bastardised into *blamange* and, as it advanced towards the twentieth century, shed its fine principal ingredient—almonds—until it sank into the culinary gutter and emerged in a packet!

On our traditional Christmas buffet in 1969 we served *Blanc-manger à la Princesse*.

· Blanc-Manger à la Princesse ·

For this you need ½ a gill of sweetened almond milk lightly flavoured with orange zest; 1 oz. leaf gelatine (6 leaves); 4 tablespoons cold water; 2 tumblers full whipped double or whipping cream. Have ready a bowl of ice. Dissolve the gelatine with the water over a low heat as usual. When this is syrupy and absolutely clear, add it to the almond milk. Plunge the pan into the ice and stir relentlessly until mixture begins to thicken. Then start whipping, immediately add a quarter of the prepared cream, continue adding and whipping until all has come together smoothly. Turn into a dome mould which has been thoroughly rinsed in cold water and given a thin layer lining of lemon jelly†. When set, unmould.

· Black Cherry Compôte ·

Do serve this as in Edwardian days accompanied by a bowl of *Black Cherry Compôte* lightly flavoured with Kirsch. Here we must point out that in summer the *compôte* is simply made with stoned black cherries, lightly dusted with sifted icing sugar, flavoured to your taste with the less expensive cooking kirsch, refrigerated until the moment of service and sent to table in a crystal bowl. Incidentally, this alone after a rich main course dish can be exquisite. If you want to serve it to near perfection in the winter, you must stone and bottle a jar or two of black cherries in stock sugar syrup*. We also feel guilty if we omit Fanny's gran's *coup de foudre*: those blessed cherry kernels which are cracked, peeled and added before oven bottling or sterilising.

· Sweetened Almond Milk ·

At this point we feel you will be getting cross with us because perhaps you do not happen to know what the devil we mean by sweetened almond milk. Put 4½ ozs. almonds in a small bowl, cover with boiling water, leave until the water is cool enough for you to handle them, pop the skins, put the almonds into a mortar and pound them to a smooth paste, moistening them gradually with 8½ fl. ozs. of cold water. When a totally smooth pap is achieved, place in a clean cloth and wring out every possible drop of moisture into a small saucepan. Add 3½ ozs. of loaf sugar and stir over a low heat until sugar is completely dissolved . . . and that is almond milk.

· Crème Bachique ·

While we are delving in the past, let us share a little known recipe of Tante Marie which is inscribed in so many French family "receipt" books that we lost count long ago. It is called *Crème Bachique*. Put 17½ fl. ozs. of sweet white wine (least expensive Sauternes) into a roomy pan. Add 3½ ozs. castor sugar and a pinch of cinnamon powder. Allow the mixture to come to boiling point over a moderate heat. Withdraw pan. Whip up 6 egg yolks in a roomy bowl, add the hot wine mixture gradually whipping all the time. When all is absorbed, strain through a fine sieve or *tamis* and pour into (ideally) little stone cream pots; or use individual *ramequins* or *cocottes*. Sink these carefully into a pan containing enough boiling water to come one-third up the sides of the chosen containers. Cover these with a piece of kitchen foil and allow them to poach very gently until set. Chill and serve with spirals of whipped cream on top.

Almond Soft Paste · Délices d'Amandes · Feuilles aux Amandes
Demi-lunes au Chocolat · Tartelettes aux Abricots
Maryses · Parisian Rout Cakes · Gâteau Chocolatine
Gâteau Chocolat du Prieur · Individual Chocolate Boxes
Coffee Syrup · Coffee Angel Food Cake · Kaffeekremetorte
Mokkakremetorte · Special Coffee Cream · Russian Cake
Sand Cake · Our Brown Meringues · Schauffhauser
Mum's Nut Cake · Choux Paste · Profiteroles
Vanilla Buns · Coffee Buns · Chocolate Buns
Orange Buns · Lemon Buns · Cherry Buns · Almond Buns
Praline Buns · Raspberry Buns · Gâteau St. Honoré
Dobostorte · Strawberry or Raspberry Shortcake

One of these days we intend to give up our careers and become really rich by selling *petits fours* commercially. The price charged in England for edible ones and in France for any because they are all edible, pains us and, therefore, we always make our own. There are a great number of recipes in the pudding chapter which need some form of biscuit or *petits fours* as an accompaniment. As one of the very best of these for *petits fours secs* calls for ground almonds, we must tackle the basic paste first and then run through a few suggestions to which you yourself can add.

· Almond Soft Paste ·

The mixture came to us from a German master pastrycook and is called *Almond Soft Paste*. Assemble 8¾ ozs. self-raising flour with 2¼ ozs. of ground almonds; 2¼ ozs. fine castor sugar; an egg and the grated rind of ¼ lemon. Have ready a very small quantity of water poured over an ice cube when you are feeling economical and when you are feeling grand *Noyaux*. Sift the flour and ground almonds together with the lemon rind into a mound on a very cold surface—ideally, a bit of marble. Gather up the fingers of one hand like a posy, push into the centre of the mound and carefully push out until you form a ring. Into the centre of this ring, break the egg, tip in the sugar, add a few drops of the chosen fluid and taking a small table knife in each hand, work centre ingredients to a smooth paste and gradually draw in flour from the wall which surrounds your central mixture. Continue doing this and adding drops of fluid until a paste is formed which you can just force through a large star metal or plastic pipe in a nylon icing bag.

· Délices d'Amandes ·

Cover ordinary baking sheets with waxed paper and pipe out small rosettes of the mixture, being careful to space these to allow for spreading and swelling during baking time. Some may have half a blanched sweet almond pressed onto the top, some may be sprinkled with a little crushed loaf sugar (in a fold of brown paper and with a rolling pin) and some may be left plain. All are named _Délices d'Amandes_. Bake on the middle shelf of oven Gas Mark 5 until just sufficiently set to lift out with a knife or spatula and cool on a rack. It is impossible to give an exact time as it depends upon the size of each one, but peek into the oven after the first 7 minutes. When you have made your first batch successfully, scribble the exact baking time into the margin here for future reference. Store in an airtight tin.

· Feuilles aux Amandes ·

If you wish to turn this mixture into _Feuilles aux Amandes_, roll out the Almond Soft Paste to a mean $\frac{1}{4}''$ thickness, stamp out with an ornamental leaf cutter and bake as described for preceding recipe. When these are baked and cold they can be served plain. They can be covered thinly with almond flavoured _glacé_ icing† and scattered thickly with finely chopped almonds, or they can be clapped together in pairs between a spreading of coffee flavoured butter cream (p. 249).

· Demi-lunes au Chocolat ·

Still working with the cutter and with some basic paste make _Demi-lunes au Chocolat_. Stamp out crescents with a plain pastry cutter. Bake as described for _Délices d'Amandes_. When cold pick up each one and dip the top into softened chocolate chips† and before they have had time to set, scatter with brown flaked almonds.

· Tartelettes aux Abricots ·

Before we leave this basic recipe, let us deal with glazed apricot tartlets. These _Tartelettes aux Abricots_ are a delicious tea party item or indeed can be served in place of the conventional pudding course. Roll out the almond soft paste on a lightly floured surface to $\frac{1}{8}''$ thickness, stamp in fluted rounds with a pastry cutter and press gently into buttered and floured bun tins. Place a small square of greaseproof paper over each one and fill up with dried beans. Bake at Gas Mark 6 until edges are a pale biscuit colour. Lift out papers easily with two of the four upstanding corners, trundle the beans back into their tin and do not imagine there is any waste in this procedure as we are still using the ones we started with 15 years ago. Cover the base of each cold, removed-from-its-tin tartlet with confectioners' custard*. Invert a stoned apricot cup over the custard in each one, brush the surface liberally with sieved apricot jam and surround the edges of each with little piped peaks of stiffly whipped cream. Of course, you may use tinned apricot cups if you so please, but when you want to do the real thing, halve and stone fresh apricots. Set them in a shallow pan with a vanilla pod, cover them generously with stock sugar syrup* and poach turning them very carefully so that you do not end up with little raw patches through not having given them attention during this cooking time.

· Maryses ·

Now let us tackle an entirely different *petits fours* paste which is equally versatile. Its generic name is *Maryses*. Place in a bowl 1 oz. sifted icing sugar; 4 ozs. unsalted butter and 4 ozs. sifted self-raising flour. Work with the back of a spoon until the mixture is sufficiently blended for you to whip it down to a stiff paste with a hand rotary or hand electric whisk. Pipe out in rosettes, fingers or figures of eight through a nylon icing bag with a large crown pipe affixed and bake at Gas Mark 5 until just set. Cool on a rack. Serve plain or clapped together in pairs over lemon†, orange† or chocolate (see p. 255) flavoured *glacé* icing.

All the above group will store indefinitely between layers of waxed paper in either a lidded plastic container or an ordinary tin with a well fitting lid.

· Parisian Rout Cakes ·

The same may be said of *Parisian Rout Cakes* for which just a word of warning before you start. Do not deviate from the method otherwise you will not succeed. Stick to it and it simply requires a bit of patience; 6 ozs. ground almonds; ½ oz. softened finely diced angelica; 6 ozs. castor sugar; 2 separated egg whites; ½ oz. diced *glacé* cherries; ½ oz. chopped flaked almonds and a little stock sugar syrup*. Cover baking sheets with greaseproof paper and brush the surface thoroughly but meanly with olive oil. Beat the egg whites up very lightly indeed, mix the ground almonds and castor sugar together and work in the egg whites. Place the mixture in a nylon icing bag with a small crown pipe and pipe out into small "S" shapes on the prepared papers. Then with a soft brush dipped in sugar syrup paint the entire surface with a very light touch. Wait 5 minutes and repeat to acquire a really good glaze. Sprinkle each with tiny quantities of cherries, almonds and finely diced angelica. Leave on a convenient working surface in the kitchen overnight—thus they acquire a good "skin"—and then bake in a pre-heated oven—very rare for us—but do it please, at Gas Mark 7 for 5 minutes. Cool on a rack and use or store in a tin or plastic container.

· Gateau Chocolatine ·

When it comes to *gâteaux* we have learned from all of you that no flavour has proved so popular over the last 20 years as chocolate and no *gâteaux* as popular as *Gâteau Chocolatine*. We made it at one of our "Daily Telegraph" cook-ins in 1967 and the verdict passed on it was that "it was superbly moist, rich but not sickly, could be used as a pudding as well".

We used a 6″ square solid based cake tin, base lined with buttered and floured greaseproof paper and the sides separately buttered and floured. We began by putting 2½ ozs. chocolate chips with 2 dessertspoonsful of strongly reduced, unsweetened black coffee into a pan over hot water. While waiting for the chocolate to melt in the coffee, we creamed 2½ ozs. of unsalted butter until it was white and foamy. Then we put in 2 ozs. of sifted icing sugar and 3 egg yolks in that order and whipping all the time, because we had a hand electric mixer. Then when the chocolate had completely melted, we beat it thoroughly and folded it into the butter cream using a plastic spatula. In a separate bowl we whipped a mere ¼ oz. of sifted icing sugar with the remaining 3 separated egg yolks. Weighed off a scant 2½ ozs. of well sifted flour and added the whipped whites and flour alternately again folding in with the plastic spatula. Then the mixture went into the prepared cake tin and was baked on the centre shelf at Gas Mark 4 for between 40–45 minutes. We then inverted it over a cooling rack and prepared the chocolate filling. Using the same type of chocolate chips for this, soften 4½ ozs. of them with 2 fl. ozs. of stock sugar syrup*. When smooth and well beaten, beat in a teaspoon of pure olive oil and keep over hot water but off the heat while splitting the cake into three layers. Spread the mixture over the base layer, slap the middle on top, spread again and cover with the top layer and then finally when the cake is partly assembled, you spread the sides lightly and smoothly with whipped cream. Now be careful! You must pick up the cake and hold it rather like a wheel (yes, we know it's square!) clapped between the palms of both hands and dunk all the four sides over a shallow container filled with chocolate vermicelli. When this is done, lay the cake on its d'oyley on its serving dish, cover the top completely with piped rosettes of whipped double cream and into these press rows of $1\frac{1}{4}''$ very thin chocolate squares. Use 4 squares in the front row, 3 in the next row so that they stand alternately and repeat. Then dust overall with sifted icing sugar and serve.

You will want to know how these squares—or indeed any other shapes are achieved because they are difficult to obtain and even when you can find them, very costly to buy. Pour softened chocolate into the centre of a sheet of waxed paper. Then spread it thinly over the entire sheet with a metal spatula. As soon as it is set, mark off the surface with a few guide marks made by pricking with a darning needle to indicate quite clearly where you cut to obtain the $1\frac{1}{4}''$ squares. Dip a sharp knife into boiling water, shake off the drops and cut through the dot guide lines quickly and lift off the squares.

· Gâteau Chocolat du Prieur ·

The basic chocolate sponge mixture for *Gâteau Chocolatine* is, we maintain, as versatile as the *petits fours* recipes we have given you so try it out another way. When the cake is baked—this time with the mixture spread into a narrow rectangular tin—split it into as many thin layers as possible and spread each one with the given chocolate filling, re-assembling the layers as you work. Then brush the top and sides with sieved apricot jam, scatter thickly with flaked almonds which have been browned off in the oven for a few moments and dust overall with sifted icing sugar. The almonds can sit on the floor of the oven when in use at a high temperature, or on the middle shelf at Gas Mark 2–3. This gives you *Gâteau Chocolat du Prieur*.

· Individual Chocolate Boxes ·

Let us look back over these two *gâteaux*. We are going to turn them into little individual chocolate cakes and use the basic

chocolate sponge and the little squares cut for the top of the
Gâteau Chocolatine (p. 246), for *Individual Chocolate Boxes*. You bake
the chocolate sponge mixture in a square or rectangular container which will yield you 1″ deep 1¼″ squares when you cut the
sponge up after baking and cooling. Brush the sides of each
square with sieved apricot jam and press a chocolate square
against each side, thus obtaining your miniature chocolate box.
All that remains to do is to pipe a fat rosette of *Crème Chantilly**
inside the top of each box and stab a single Chocolate Leaf† in
the centre of each one. In France these leaves are sometimes dis-
carded in favour of single coffee beans perched on the peak of
each Chantilly spiral, but this is purely a question of personal
choice.

We could fill this entire chapter with chocolate recipes and still
have masses left over, so at this point we will exert a little will-
power and move on to coffee flavoured items. But, before we
give you our first recipe, and as it is some time since we have said
it in print in a book, we feel we should stress just once more the
paramount importance of expunging from your thoughts and
vocabulary that extremely dirty word *essence*! This was once
defined by an absolutely splendid "Daily" as, "Something that
tasted like the smell of the bottom of a tatty actress's 'andbag!"

· Coffee Syrup ·

The coffee flavouring which we implore you to use in our
recipes is nothing more than the residues of black coffee left over
from any brews, accummulated in the refrigerator until you have
achieved a pint, then tipped into a saucepan, brought to the boil
and simmered relentlessly down to a very thick 4 fl. ozs. of coffee
syrup. Like this, poured into a small bottle and corked down, it
will keep for months and must be used very sparingly. Taste a
drop and see why, as the bitterness infringes on your taste buds.

· Coffee Angel Food Cake ·

So now assuming that you have some on your store shelf,
make a *Coffee Angel Food Cake*. For this you need 5 ozs. castor
sugar; 5 egg whites; 2 ozs. flour and 2 ozs. cornflour sifted
together; ¼ teaspoonful cream of tartar; 2 teaspoonsful coffee
syrup and a pinch of salt. Whip the egg whites and salt stiffly
together. Sprinkle cream of tartar lightly on the top. Draw mixture

to side of bowl. Slide sugar into the hollow and fold in gently with coffee syrup. Fold in sifted flours a little at a time. Sprinkle these lightly over the egg white. Turn into a perfectly dry, deep cake tin with sliding base, $5\frac{1}{2}''$ diameter. Bake for 33 minutes or until the top feels just spongey. Turn upside down on a rack in a warm place to cool gradually inside the tin. When cold, split and fill with coffee butter cream and also spread this over top and sides. Sprinkle thickly with icing sugar and garnish with shelled walnuts.

· Kaffeekremetorte ·

Austria and Switzerland both have a marvellous range of coffee cakes and in particular one called a *Kaffeekremetorte*. You begin by putting 3 separated egg whites in a bowl and whisking until they are stiff. Then add 3 ozs. of sifted icing sugar and whip again for exactly 3 minutes. Now stop whipping altogether and with a plastic spatula, if possible, fold in a mixture made of 3 ozs. ground almonds and $\frac{1}{2}$ oz. very fine soft white breadcrumbs. When all is smoothly blended, divide the mixture evenly between 2 standard Victoria sponge tins, which have had their sides buttered and then floured, and a fitting circle of buttered and floured greaseproof paper placed over the base. Bake on centre shelf, gas mark 5 for approximately 30 minutes, or until lightly spongey to the touch. Invert on a rack to cool. When cold, spread one of the two with butter cream* flavoured to taste with coffee syrup (p. 248). Clap the two together and mask the top and sides with stiffly whipped cream strongly flavoured with coffee syrup.

· Mokkakremetorte ·

There is another version, which is called *Mochekremetorte*. The only difference in the actual sponge is that you increase the quantity of breadcrumbs to 1 oz. and flavour the meringue mixture with coffee syrup before adding the breadcrumbs and almonds.

· Special Coffee Cream ·

Otherwise follow the preceding recipe right through and while the baked sponges are cooling on their racks, make a batch of *Special Coffee Cream*. Put 2 ozs. of vanilla flavoured sifted icing sugar, the yolks of 2 eggs and 4 fl. ozs. of coffee or single cream

into the top of a double saucepan over water, and stir over a low
heat until the mixture thickens—just like ordinary confectioners'
custard but it will not become as thick as this with any success.
Dissolve a scant ½ oz. of powdered gelatine in a maximum 3
tablespoonsful of very strongly reduced coffee syrup, and when it
is clear and syrupy pour into the still warm pan mixture. Plunge
the pan into a bowl of crushed ice, whip the mixture down to
blood heat, and gradually whip in 6 fl. ozs. of stiffly whipped
thick double cream. Taste and add extra sifted icing sugar for
sweetening if desired. Use as a filling between the two sponges
and when the two are clapped together, spread very thickly over
top and sides. Either dust with sifted icing sugar or scatter top
surface liberally with milled hazelnuts. Just one point we must
establish between us is that hazelnuts must be laid out after
shelling on a baking sheet and made hot enough in an oven at
Gas Mark 1 for the skins to be completely rubbed off before
milling. Finally, if you hark back to the recipe (p. 247) for individual Chocolate Boxes you will see that these can be made as
Individual Mocha Boxes with the same sponge, with chocolate
squares around the sides and liberal pipings of special coffee
cream on top.

Now we are going to devote our attentions to special requests
from readers and include here one or two classics for which we
have had hundreds of requests.

· Russian Cake ·

From lovers of almond paste come shoals of demands for
Russian Cake which can be made a very fine second to classic
Christmas cake. Indeed it could easily replace it if, when made and
enclosed in pale green almond paste, it is tied up centrally like a
parcel with scarlet and white ribbons.

For the sponge mixture, whip 6 standard eggs with 6 ozs.
vanilla-flavoured castor sugar over hot water until light and
foamy. Fold in 4½ ozs. sifted self-raising flour. Stir in 1½ ozs.
softened butter. Divide into two equal quantities, set one aside
and sub-divide the other. Colour one half of sub-division pink,
the other green, with harmless vegetable colouring. Bake the two
smaller quantities separately in a buttered and floured 7″ long ×
3½″ wide × 3″ deep, ordinary straight-sided bun tin at Gas Mark 4
on the middle shelf until just springy to the touch. Bake the un-

coloured mixture in a 7″ square tin, thus achieving three pieces of equal width. When cold, cut two 1¾″ wide fingers from the plain sponge and one each from the pink and green. Clean, burnish and lightly dust the 3½″ wide bun tin with cornflour. Line completely with fairly thinly rolled out pale green almond paste (p. 243), and brush the interior lightly with sieved apricot jam. Cover the base with one pink finger and one plain one, brush these with the apricot mixture and place the remaining green finger over the plain one and the plain over the pink. Cover with almond paste and turn out ready to cut into slices. (Eat up sponge discards separately or use to make small trifle).

· Sand Cake ·

We have a shoal of vociferous demands for Sand Cake, one of the classics of the 3-tiered Victorian cake stand and sadly neglected in even some of the best *pâtisseries*.

Cream 8 ozs. of butter very thoroughly and then beat in 5 ozs. sifted icing sugar. Weigh off 3 ozs. sifted flour and 3 ozs. potato flour (*féculas de pommes*) and sift these two together. Add a third of this flour mixture to the butter cream, then 2 separated standard egg yolks; repeat twice more with remaining flour, making 6 separated egg yolks in all. Fold in the stiffly whipped whites of the 6 eggs and turn into a 9″ × 5¼″ × 2½″ deep rectangular cake tin. Bake in a pre-heated oven, middle shelf, at Gas Mark 4 for 55 minutes. Invert on a cooling rack and dust very thickly with sifted icing sugar for standard service.

Victorians seemed undecided about the addition of the finely grated zest of 1 medium lemon which we think improves this delicate, close-textured sponge cake; you will just have to try both and form your own conclusions.

· Our Brown Meringues ·

To complete our request trilogy we dutifully record *"Our Brown Meringues"*. These will fulfil the requirements of those who want a brown meringue with a gooey centre, which is good enough to serve either as a cake or a pudding. Separate 5 standard egg whites and put them in a large bowl. Stand beside them 6 ozs. soft brown sugar and a separate 2 ozs. of soft brown sugar. This is sometimes called "pieces sugar" and has nothing whatsoever to do with that sweet straw coloured grit which we call an abomination (with apologies if this displeases you). Now prepare one or more baking sheets which must be covered with oiled greaseproof paper and there should be more energy than oil used, as if you are liberal with the oil you will have a skiddy surface and as you pipe out the meringue mixture, it will take off across the paper. Whip the egg whites by themselves until they are just stiff. Sprinkle the 2 ozs. of sugar across the surface, whip steadily for a further 3½ minutes, stop whipping altogether and fold in the remaining 6 ozs. of sugar. Fill the mixture into a large nylon icing bag with a no. 7 crown pipe affixed and pipe out 2½–3" base diameter spirals with a neat peak on each one, remembering not to cram them too closely together. Bake at Gas Mark ¾ middle shelf of oven until the meringue lifts easily from the paper and has a firm unbroken base. All these need is a generous dollop of stiffly whipped unsweetened cream between two meringues clapped together. If you want to be fancy you can blend coarsely grated bitter chocolate, from a sweet shop, into the cream; or place slices of coffee ice cream into individual containers, put one brown meringue on top of each, spread with whipped cream and sprinkle with crushed coffee beans.

· Schauffhauser ·

If you are one of the many who serve on a Charity Committee tea circuit, you may be glad of a recipe for *Schauffhauser* which, like meringues, keep best in an earthenware container which has a well fitting lid. They are easy to make and there are seldom any left when we offer them to friends. Whip 3 separated egg whites very stiffly indeed, add 4 ozs. castor sugar by sprinkling it over, not slinging it in in a lump so that it crushes out some of the air particles that you have captured so laboriously. When the sprinkling is completed whip fast for a further 3 minutes. Stop whipping. Fold in a scant coffeespoonful of ratafia—the real one not the essence—then 3 ozs. of ground almonds (sprinkle these on lightly too) and finally, ½ oz. of sifted flour. When blended drop the mixture from a teaspoon widely spaced onto rice paper (stockists p. 292) on a flat metal baking sheet and bake at Gas Mark 2, centre shelf, for exactly one hour. Cool on a rack, then just trim off the ragged fringes of rice paper with a small pair of scissors before cooling, and serve plain or clapped together in pairs with coffee flavoured or ratafia flavoured butter cream*.

· Mum's Nut Cake ·

Should you prefer the flavour of walnuts to almonds, we have a rather splendid recipe which we simply call *Mum's Nut Cake*. This is a good keeper in a lidded plastic box or cake tin, but it does call for ground rice, so do not start assembling the ingredients until you know that you have some of this on your store shelf. Then gather together 8 ozs. milled walnuts; 4 ozs. preferably unsalted butter; 5 ozs. sifted icing sugar; 3 separated standard eggs; 2 tablespoons strained orange juice; 2 ozs. ground rice. Cream butter; cream in sugar with orange juice, adding gradually. Work up ground rice and nuts together. Add a little of this mixture, then an egg yolk, continuing until all are absorbed. Finally, fold in stiffly whipped egg whites. Spread evenly over Swiss roll tin which has been lined out with buttered and floured greaseproof. Bake for 12 minutes, middle shelf, Gas Mark 4. Cool on a rack, divide into three equal panels. Spread with chocolate filling, top-spread with remainder and store. For the filling dissolve 2 ozs. granulated sugar in 3 tablespoons hot water. Add 4 ozs. chocolate chips. Stir over low heat until smooth and blended. Add ½ oz. butter in tiny flakes. Note: a few drops of rum will not come amiss as an addition.

· Choux Paste ·

It could never be said that we have given you a useful cross-section in this chapter if we failed to include *Choux Paste*. The time has come to remind you that the basic recipe for *Choux* paste made with water, which you will find in the *Cook's Book*, is only the beginning of the story. There are in all seven *Choux* pastes, including the savoury ones, those made with orange juice and coffee and a cream and sugar one which we think is the most delicate of them all. You may use this for eclairs and cream buns, and also piped out plain in little blobs with a ½" writing pipe.

You will need 3 ozs. flour; 1 oz. butter; 2½ eggs (we will explain this in a moment); 1 large piece of lump sugar and 5 fl. ozs. milk. The average standard egg weighs 2 ozs. Weigh one. Crack into a cup or small bowl, beat up lightly with a fork until the globules have broken down and weigh off a scant 1 oz.—just allowing a fraction for the shell. Put the butter, milk and sugar into a thick pan and bring milk to boiling point over a low enough heat to allow the butter to be completely melted by the time the milk boils. Toss in the flour—still over the heat—allow the milk to foam over it, snatch it from the heat and beat very thoroughly indeed with a wooden spoon. Add the ½ egg and beat again with the wooden spoon. Switch over after this to a rotary or hand electric mixer. Whip in the first of the two remaining eggs until you pass through the stage where the mixture is in little globules and rather slimey. Forge on until you reach a very smooth and very thick paste, add the remaining egg, repeat the procedure, cover with a plate or saucer and leave until absolutely cold. On no account refrigerate. It is now ready to pipe and bake in whatever manner is required for the items we are going to suggest.

· Profiteroles ·

In the first section we will deal with individual *Profiteroles* which can be made in graduated sizes by varying the diameter of the plain writing pipe employed for laying them out on a waxed-paper-covered or oiled greaseproof covered baking sheet. For very small ones use a ¼″ plain writing pipe; for medium a ½″ and large ¾–1″ plain writing pipes. Before attempting to pipe them have ready at your side a tumbler of cold water with a small table knife immersed in it. When the bag with chosen pipe is not more than half full with the mixture, twist the empty end so that it does not ooze out the wrong way when you are piping. Hold the pipe vertically above the prepared baking sheet and lop off each little blob or stump with the knife dipped in cold water and the drops shaken off—this gives you a very neat finish. Of course, the same procedure is followed for the other two sizes. With eclairs, pipe horizontally against the blade of the cold, wet knife and pull back from it to the desired length and again lop off with the knife. This gives you eclairs in the aforementioned sizes.

When you come to the baking, remember that like meringues all variants of *choux* paste are like little pieces of blotting paper to humidity in the atmosphere. Therefore, they must be *thoroughly* baked and not removed—as all students try to do the first time they make them in our kitchen—while they are still a pale golden beige. The average time for baking eclairs or chocolate buns is 11–15 minutes for small ones; 25 minutes for medium sized and 33–38 minutes for the large ones. They are always baked one shelf above centre at Gas Mark 7½.

Having dealt with what we call "the basics" we shall now dispose of the chat and give you a cold-blooded break-down on a wide range.

The following table sets out standard varieties of either *profiteroles* or *choux* buns as used by first-class French pastrycooks. In each one the filling is confectioners' custard.

· Vanilla Buns ·

(*Choux glacés à la vanille ou Profiteroles glacées à la vanille.*)
Use plain vanilla confectioners' custard to fill cases. Ice them with *glacé* icing† made with vanilla-flavoured icing sugar.

· Coffee Buns ·

(*Choux glacés à la comtesse ou Profiteroles glacées à la comtesse.*)
Add strongly reduced, unsweetened coffee syrup, (p. 248) to confectioners' custard. Ice with *glacé* icing† using coffee syrup instead of water.

· Chocolate Buns ·

(*Choux glacés au chocolat ou Profiteroles glacées au chocolat.*)
Fill with chocolate-flavoured confectioners' custard. Ice with chocolate *glacé* icing. Put 4 ozs. chocolate chips into a small pan with 2 tablespoonsful stock sugar syrup.* Allow to soften very slowly stirring with a wooden spoon and adding extra teaspoonsful of sugar syrup with great restraint until you achieve a thick, creamy, pouring mixture. If nervous, test with a teaspoonful over the back of a tablespoon. If, when you shake the spoon, the mixture sets smooth without all running off, go ahead and use. If it does run off, add a few more chocolate chips and stir them till they have thickened mixture smoothly.

· Orange Buns ·

(*Choux glacés à l'orange ou Profiteroles glacées à l'orange.*)
Add orange Curaçao to confectioners' custard. Ice with *glacé* icing using orange juice instead of water.

· Lemon Buns ·

(*Choux glacés au citron ou Profiteroles glacées au citron.*)
Add the grated rind of 1 lemon to confectioners' custard. Ice with *glacé* icing using strained lemon juice instead of water.

Four of the five examples have their own classic garnishings:

Coffee Buns. Crushed coffee beans on top.

Chocolate Buns. Grated milk chocolate or milk chocolate *couverture* sprinkled on top.

Orange Buns. Small segments of crystallised orange arranged on top.

Lemon Buns. Small segments of crystallised lemon arranged on top.

These are simple variants. In the next group we will deal with more elaborate ones.

· Cherry Buns ·

(Choux glacés à la Montmorency ou Profiteroles glacées à la Montmorency.)

Use cherry brandy flavoured confectioners' custard, with a single cherry on stalk preserved in cherry brandy set on the top of *glacé* icing which is also flavoured with cherry brandy.

· Almond Buns ·

(Choux glacés aux amandes ou Profiteroles glacées aux amandes.)

Use ratafia flavoured confectioners' custard and *glacé* icing; browned flaked almonds sprinkled on top.

· Praline Buns ·

(Choux glacés pralinés ou Profiteroles glacées pralinées.)

Use praline* worked into confectioners' custard and Praline Icing. For this place 1 unbeaten egg white with 1½ ozs. sifted icing sugar in a small basin and stir vigorously until mixture foams a little. Add 2 ozs. finely chopped almonds and stir again. Cover with a scrap of kitchen foil and leave for 30 minutes. Then use to ice buns and sprinkle praline powder on top.

· Raspberry Buns ·

(Choux glacés aux framboises ou Profiteroles glacées aux framboises.)

Use half the weight of sieved, fresh, unsweetened raspberries stirred into confectioners' custard. *Glacé* icing made with *Framboise* (stockists p. 291) and water. One fresh raspberry and a minute sprig of dried maidenhair fern pressed on top of each.

· Gâteau St. Honoré ·

Classic *Gâteau St. Honoré* made with the same *choux* paste can be a nuisance to do, because like several other items made with *choux* paste, it has to be made on the day and ideally after luncheon if it is for dinner, and so although we include the necessary one in the pudding chapter (p. 213) we thought you would like to know how a very brilliant cook makes it for inclusion on her pudding trolley in a form which enables her to whip it up in her kitchen in a few moments. The cook is Madeleine Stratton, who, in our opinion, is among one of the best *saucières* in England.

We were leaning up against the marble top of her pastry bay gossiping with her while she cooked through an extremely busy luncheon session. We were suddenly ordered out of the way when an order came through for her *special Gâteau St. Honoré*. She ran a sharp knife through the centre of the puffy circle of *choux* paste which had been cooling on a rack. Laying the top half aside, she heaped the base half with enormous dollops of *Crème Chantilly** then covered that with the top half. She tipped 2 cups of granulated sugar into a very thick saucepan and this she placed over a very low heat and we continued gossiping until the sugar had begun to melt and turned brown in the centre of the pan. We then completed our talk while she shook the pan gently until the whole mass turned to golden brown caramel. Then working with a large, flattish metal spoon she skimmed the entire surface and sides with caramel so finely that it ended up wearing an overcoat of sugar like a skating rink, which you pour over *Crème Brulée*. Sitting on the rack were 12 little *profiteroles*. She filled each with *Crème Chantilly*, dunked them completely in the remaining caramel mixture and arranged them around the edge.

"*Gâteau St. Honoré* for 8," shouted a waiter coming through the swing doors. Madeleine handed him the plate, turned to us and said, "What about a coffee." Try it sometime you will find it as easy as it sounds.

· Dobostorte ·

Do you know Hungarian *Dobostorte*, which has the vulgar name of "squashed cake" in this family for reasons which you will doubtless appreciate as we go along. Let us warn you that you will need four 4½–5″ diameter sliding base cake tins if you are to use all the mixture simultaneously for baking. Otherwise you take a quarter for each tin for this diameter, cover the bottom with buttered and floured greaseproof paper; butter and flour the sides and bake the four in rotation at Gas Mark 5, one shelf above centre for approximately 9 minutes.

Separate 6 standard eggs; whip the whites until stiff; fold in 2½ ozs. sifted icing sugar and whisk again for about 2¼ minutes. Add 2½ ozs. sifted icing sugar to the yolks; whip this until very nearly white. Add the meringue mixture gradually to this batter alternating the gradual additions of 4 ozs. very carefully sifted flour. Cool each baked disc on a rack and as soon as it is cold lay it on a sheet of wax paper large enough to accommodate all four. Cover these with a further sheet of wax paper and put three or four heavy books on top. Hence "squashed cake!"

While the squashing is in progress prepare the filling, by melting 2 ozs. chocolate chips in a small pan over hot water; when these have collapsed beat well off the heat and beat in 2 ozs. sifted icing sugar and 2 standard eggs. Return pan to its outer pan of hot water and whip until very thick and creamy. Plunge the mixture pan into ice and whip down to blood heat. In a separate bowl cream 2 ozs. of unsalted butter and gradually whip in your chocolate cream mixture. Lastly, stir in 1 oz. of ground or milled (toasted until the skins rub off) hazelnuts. Spread the rounds, one above the other, with the cream, which should be equal in depth to each squashed layer. Spread hot caramel quickly over the last, top layer with a knife dipped in boiling water and with the same knife mark the surface off immediately into 6 portions.

· Strawberry or Raspberry Shortcake ·

Finally, and in case you should want to show off on any summer occasion to any American friends, here is a recipe for *Strawberry or Rasberry Shortcake* which, we hope you will agree, is a good deal better than average. Take 6 ozs. of thoroughly sieved flour and put it in a bowl with 6 ozs. of the very best butter and 4 ozs. of castor sugar. Work this mixture up with the tips of your fingers until it forms a smooth paste. Roll this into a ball; turn onto a lightly floured cold working surface, dust the top surface lightly with flour and roll the ball in this for a moment or two. Have ready two shallow 7" diameter sponge tins, which have been base lined with buttered and floured greaseproof paper and the sides buttered and floured. Divide your paste into two equal parts and roll these out gently until they are sufficiently thin to yield two 7″ circles. Place one in each tin and flatten out gently with your fingers until each one covers the whole area and is reasonably smooth on top. Bake centre shelf of oven at Gas Mark 3 until the mixture is only evenly coloured pale beige and just set, and leave in tin for 5 minutes. Turn the first one out onto the chosen dish for service; turn the second one out onto a rack to finish cooling. When the first one is cold, cover the entire surface very liberally indeed with whole small strawberries or raspberries. Dust lightly with sifted icing sugar. Cover this with halved small strawberries, cut side uppermost, or whole raspberries if you please. Dust again with sifted icing sugar. Place the top, cooled shortcake on top and cover this with small strawberries or raspberries and pipe fat rosettes of cream all over in the little spaces between the fruit. Dust again with sifted icing sugar and if you think this amount of cream is inadequate, have a separate bowl of cream when serving.

nineteen · IRONING OUT THE CREASES

With a few notable exceptions wine and food are inseparable and the one is incomplete without the other. We stand between the Scylla group of those who maintain food should take precedence over wine; and the Charybdis group which stubbornly insists wine should take precedence over food. Both we insist should be equal and complementary to one another like the partners in any really successful marriage.

All this is indeed implicit in the French "*Un répas sans vin est un journée sans soleil*"—because equally no Frenchman would allow the possibility of a day without any food!

Please accept, therefore, that in all the points we will try to make in this chapter, we are striving for *balance*, shying away from precedence and stubbornly allocating equal importance to both Ceres and Bacchus.

"Wine taken in moderation irons out the creases in our daily lives." *John Cradock*

However carefully you strive to maintain a perfect and balanced marriage between the dishes you select for entertaining and the wines you choose, it will all fail if you cannot exert two small acts of control over two barbaric customs which, of course, have come from the United States of America. We refer to the obscene habit of smoking between courses and the palate ruining habit of drinking hard liquor immediately before a meal.

This does not pre-suppose that the tired business man cannot have a whisky and soda in his bath at 6 o'clock in the evening to revive him and then appreciate his own wines at a dinner which does not start until eight; but it does mean that from 7.30 to 8 he offers to his guests and drinks himself one of the dry fortified wines or a light still or sparkling aperitif wine, all or any of which will be thoroughly chilled.

On this question of chilling do please get "with it" and hand

over any of those ridiculous "trad" wine coolers which still
remain in your possession. They can be turned into quite good
flower containers but they are monstrous for wines. As we try to
avoid making categorical statements of this kind without qualify-
ing, let us at this juncture ask you to try a small experiment with a
wine cooler. Put in a bottle of hock, pack round with ice and
water and measure how much of the bottle's contents is standing
clear of both remaining unchilled while the part which is immersed gets progressively colder and colder! Then you will see
why we plead with you to use your modern domestic refrigerator
and chill such wines as require this treatment either upright in the
door or prone on the shelves with, at *this* stage, all corks un-
drawn; thus no-one will get a frozen glass or a lukewarm one
from the same bottle any more.

· APERITIF SUGGESTIONS WHICH WILL NOT KILL THE PALATE ·

Madeiras · Sercial or Verdelho·
Port · Dry white rapidly overtaking sherry in popularity·
Sherries · Fino (dry); Amontillado (medium dry)·

The above group are all fortified wines so called because they
are fortified with brandy during the making. Here we must kill a
legend which still flourishes among the pretentious and uninformed. Fanny actually heard a young man in a television studio
among a gathering of older men laying down the law on the subject of fortified wines in general and Madeira in particular. Said
he, "I don't think Madeiras are worth buying because they are so
treacherous in bottle; they go off at the drop of a tiny hat." In
fact, Madeiras last indefinitely in bottle and in 1954 we drank a
Madeira of which our host, Mr. Graham Blandy of the Quinta Du
Palheiro in Funchal, Madeira he said "This wine was in bottle three
years before Marie Antoinette was beheaded."

Before we pass on to the next group, there is a small point we
would like to make regarding dry white port. In port's home in
the north of Portugal, the Douro, this is sometimes called
"Breakfast wine" when served in the morning over crushed ice in
a tall glass as a long and cooling drink. You might like to try this
sometime on the odd day of summer with which we are endowed
in England.

· TABLE WINES AS APERITIFS ·

There are a number of dry, still, white table wines which make excellent aperitifs and they have the added advantage that you can go on serving them with many *hors d'oeuvre* or fish courses at the table. Top of the list is a dry Champagne, one of the two table wines which can be drunk throughout any meal by those who can (a) afford and (b) like this kind of partnering. If, on the other hand, you want to follow this one wine practice and are not endowed with a Champagne income, you may pursue the same course perfectly correctly with a modest and modestly priced *vin rosé*. For just a few other typical examples, test the little group we offer and see if they fulfil the requirements we claim for them because, of course, in the final account—and this no-one must ever lose sight of when writing about wines—if you do not care for a wine suggestion, no matter how authoritative its recommendation, it is no use to you. We have always maintained and always will that the *wine you like* is the right wine for you.

Sancerre, Vouvray and Muscadet all come from the Loire or *Château* area of France. Alternatively, see how you get on with Italian Soaves or Orvietos or set up a sampling of Alsatian Rieslings, Yugoslav Rieslings, light Moselles or Spanish Chablis types from the Rioja. When able to fly high you cannot beat one of the great white Burgundies which will, of course, fulfil your pre-dinner *hors d'oeuvre* or fish course requirements.

· HORS D'OEUVRE ·

After our preceding remarks it still becomes necessary to qualify where this course is concerned . . . for example, the oyster of which the late H. H. Monro (Saki) observed so rightly as being "more beautiful than any religion", but they would not be if taken with a dry, white port or a nice drop of Verdelho. Give them a Chablis or a white Burgundy such as a Pouilly Fuissé or if you can ever get hold of it, best of all the still Champagne called *Champagne Natur*. Melon, on the other hand, will be happier with one of the dry fortified wines and if you can afford real grey caviar, you can surely go a bomb for once and team it up with dry Champagne. Conversely, when you are offering a really big assorted *hors d'oeuvre* which contains items with vinegar and maybe little dusts of paprika as well as little *soupçons* of curry flavouring, go right down the vinous tree and pluck a *rosé* from the very lowest branches.

· FISH ·

Time and again we hear the riotous exclamation, "Fish—well, that will have to be a white wine." Well, it will not have to be anything of the sort. It all depends on the fish because while the average fish dish will marry superbly with a dryish white wine, a salmon for example demands a lusty *Montrachets* or *Meursault* from Burgundy but equally well can be drunk with a light claret which, of course, you do *not* chill but serve at room temperature.

Consider the case of *Sole au Chambertin*—Chambertin being one of the greatest of the red Burgundies—or indeed *Sole Bourguignonne* which speaks for itself. You would scarcely serve a dry, white wine with a dish poached in red Burgundy if you were striving for a happy table marriage, would you? Again, if you were making a *Matelotte d'Anguilles* (eels cooked in a red wine of Mâcon) precisely the same type of ruling will apply. So, when you make out your menu you either tell yourself or your husband/cellarer that you are cooking fish in white or red wine and will, therefore, require a complementary one to whichever it is. Do so sufficiently in advance for the poor wretch to have time to buy it and it to settle down before serving.

· EGGS ·

Very tricky!

Two schools of thought here. One argues that wine and eggs cannot partner each other successfully. We hotly dispute this assertion because if you make an exquisite dish of eggs poached in red Burgundy and cream, you would scarcely consider serving it with a Guinness! However, as John has more decorations and has taught Fanny all she knows about wine, let him speak for himself. He suggests that if you, like Frenchmen of modest income, import pipes of *vin ordinaire* from France and bottle it up in your own cellar, you can happily knock a glassful back with a dish of scrambled eggs but it would be safer for your reputation if you refrain from doing so at a dinner party. He says the strong incidence of cheese in a *Soufflé au Parmesan* totally justifies a bottle of thoroughly chilled claret (Bordeaux) or one of the lighter red Burgundies. We were dictating this bit in the kitchen and a young male assistant interpolated, "Tell them to use their loaf, like you tell me," he grunted.

Well, it is commonsense is it not? Cheese is red wine's greatest partner—*quad erat demonstrandum.*

· POULTRY ·

As poultry is a white meat you can make a perfect partnership with a dry, white wine, but so you can with some of the lighter red wines notably those from the Bordeaux area of France. This is the home of the "clarets" as they are called in England. Indeed claret is often referred to as the Queen of Wines because it is gracious, delicate and of infinite variety (typical woman!). The main area is the Médoc sited on the left bank of the River Gironde. The vine-yards stretch from St. Estephe in the north to Margaux in the south and it is true to say, as a generalisation, that the further south you go in this region, the lighter the wine becomes. We would advise the moderate spender to begin with generic or district names such as St. Estephe, Pauillac, St. Julien, and Mar-gaux and gradually progress to the single *château* wines from those villages. To the south of Bordeaux lies the capital Graves which produces some very fine red wines while to the east you have the more robust red Bordeaux from Pomerol and St. Emilion.

The Loire country also has some lightish red wines at moderate prices such as those of Chinon or St. Nicholas de Bourgueil while Italy can offer a number of reasonable reds, the best known being those of Chianti or the Valpolicella.

· MEAT AND GAME ·

What we suggest in the preceding poultry chapter is equally applicable to veal, pork, young lamb and even pheasant which has not been hung, but when it comes to beef, partridge, grouse and venison you need a lustier red Bordeaux from St. Emilion or Pomerol or, if the price is not too high for you, move from Bordeaux into Burgundy. Once again, for more modest spending, restrict yourself to the district or generic names. Typical examples are Beaune, Pommard, Nuits St. Georges and Volnay. If you are prepared to spend a little more, then extend your range to include single vineyard names, Aloxe-Corton des Brulieres, Corton Musigny, Richebourg, Clos de Vougeot, Echézeaux and right up to the fabulous Romanée-Conti.

There are also good medium priced wines to be found in Beaujolais but pray do not think you are giving yourself or anyone else the slightest hope of vinous pleasure if you allow yourself to be conned into buying an old one by an unscrupulous seller of wines as opposed to a classic wine merchant! Red Beaujolais (for there is a delicious very little known white Beaujolais as well) must always be drunk young and never more than 4 years old. Please not only when it comes to this but with all your wine buying, be careful where you buy. It is no use going to a bucket shop type who offer bargain offers with fancy labels; it will always pay you if you are not knowledgeable on your wines, to put yourself in the hands of a reputable, long established wine merchant.

While you are about it and when you get your next bottle of red Beaujolais, try the French way of drinking it and serve chilled instead of at room temperature provided it *is* a good one and not a very thin one. You should find that this procedure improves it considerably. Once again, may we stress however, that this is one of those exceptions to the rule that red wines are *chambré*-ed or brought up to room temperature and white wines are chilled as we have already explained.

Now let us go back for a minute to the phrase we employed just now "single vineyard" wines. These fall into two distinct groups: those which are shipped to England in bulk and bottled over here —a less costly procedure and, therefore, one which reduces the selling price of the wine—and those of higher price which are the wines bottled in the vineyard. The term applied classically in the Bordeaux area to this latter is "*Château* bottled" and in Burgundy "*Domaine* bottled".

At this point let us pause to consider the service of red wines like these that we have suggested. They should be brought up from the cellar and placed in the dining room up to 24 hours before service so that they can gradually attain the temperature of the room. Remind yourself that wine is a living thing and so must be allowed to breathe and absorb the oxygen in the air which improves it fantastically. Therefore, draw corks up to an hour beforehand for young wines and allow progressively *less* time for breathing for older wines. When you come to the really great old wines, these are fragile in comparison with the youngsters and, therefore, can only breathe for a short period without exhausting themselves.

· CHEESES ·

We have said this so often in print that we are diffident about saying it again, but if you happen to be of those few remaining cook/hostesses in Britain who still serves cheese after the pudding, pause and give thought to what you are doing.

If there remains in each glass some of the red wine you have chosen to accompany your main course—and particularly so if it is any age in bottle you are calling upon it to exhaust itself with oxygen while you eat the pudding and drink an accompanying sweet white wine. Moreover, you are asking the poor unfortunate tastebuds to switch over to the balance of the sweet wine and the sweet dish and then switch back again to the depth and character of red wine which was capable of supporting meat, game or poultry. The French do not do this and anyone who knows anything about this subject will acknowledge that France is the centre of the gatronomic world. They finish their red wine with a mouthfulsof cheese or when opportunity allows broach an even lustier red wine than the one drunk with the main course to stand toe to toe with such splendid cheeses as Roquefort, Bleu Bresse, Italy's Gorgonzola or England's Blue Stilton. Then and only then do they make the very big change to the delicate sweet wines and their accompanying *entremets*.

Pudding wines should be sweet. You can have a sweet (or rich) Champagne or the great *Château d'Yquem*, one of the great German wines or again, come down to earth, a district wine like a Barsac or Sauternes. Alternatives are the sweet fortified wines; a Bual or Malmsey Madeira or a brown or cream sherry. Even then there is an area for controversy, for like eggs, wine does not find it easy to get on with chocolate and there are many wine "experts" who maintain that a good marriage cannot be made between the two. We overcame this difficulty by serving one of the fortified wines such as either Bual, Malmsey or a cream or brown sherry as set out above. All pudding wines, whether fortified or otherwise, should be served well chilled.

· PORT ·

One of the things which infuriate port savants is the misconception that port must be served from decanters. In fact, it can be served direct from the bottle and you need not invest in costly

vintage port. The majority of people nowadays settle, quite
rightly, for a tawny port. Tradition rules that this is launched by
the host and passed from hand to hand clockwise around the table
until it returns to him, each person helps themselves and it is at
his discretion to send it on second and even third tours.

It is, however, a heinous offence for any guest to leave the port
either in bottle or decanter, stuck in front of them and not keep it
circulated. Should you ever find yourself in the home of port, the
Douro, you may be astonished at having the man next to you
filling your glass, then his own. This is the tradition, whereas in
England, women who stay for the port help themselves and pass
on just the same as the men, and here again back to the vexed
question of the cigarette.

The ruling in Oporto is that a vintage port completes the first
circuit before cigarettes or cigars are offered but with a tawny port,
the bottle or decanter, the cigarettes and cigar boxes are launched
simultaneously.

· LIQUEURS AND COGNAC ·

Only one small point here. We all know they are served with
coffee and we all know that liqueurs are served in very small
liqueur glasses. What some people still do not seem to have
understood is that unless the cognac is of enormous stature and
distinction, small brandy *ballons* should be used and it is ostenta-
tious to put quite a modest cognac or indeed any brandy into a
container suited to a ladies' floristry club table decoration. Moreover, it is absolutely shattering that anyone should ever heat a
brandy *ballon* over a spirit stove unless they are intending to foist
cheap cooking brandy on their guests, in which case by all means
heat it up. The procedure will, to some degree, mollify the crudity
of this raw spirit whereas it will wreck a good cognac. All that is
needed is the warmth of the human hand. You will notice that as
we have been talking to you, we have used the word cognac as
distinct from brandy. The reason is quite simple to understand
and indeed today a matter of law. No brandy may be designated
cognac unless it comes from Cognac in France. While we are
about it please remember all we have said about cognac is
applicable to *Armagnac* and the *Marcs*.

Armagnac is matured in black oak casks. Cognac is matured in
light oak. Marc is a distillation which crops up in many areas of

France. There is a Marc de Provence, a Marc de Bourgogne and so on. Incidentally, you may like to know that there are many who maintain that a really superb Armagnac is at least the equal to a Cognac of matching quality.

· GLASSES ·

Before we embark on specifics, we must point out that to the wine lover there are three separate and distinct pleasures in drinking a glass of good wine: the nose, scent or bouquet, the colour and the flavour. If a glass has a wide top to it, the nose, scent or bouquet will be dissipated in the upper air before you can enjoy it. If a glass is cut or coloured it is impossible to appreciate the colour, so wave goodbye to all your fancy glass if you want to be a disciple of the great God Bacchus, but take heart because this is not a costly affair.

You can serve the greatest company in the world with the finest wines in the world in plain, tulip shaped glasses that will cost you as little as 2/– each. It will not be possible to fault you. Naturally, you can have special glasses for sherry, Champagne, port, hock, white wine, claret, Burgundy *et al* if you can afford them, but you can get by with anyone with a set of 5 fl. oz. tulips for serving Madeira, sherry and port and a set of 6⅔ fl. oz. for all your table wines.

Finally, never fill a glass more than two-thirds full as one of the joys of wine drinking is to swirl the wine gently round the glass, a movement which helps to bring out the bouquet or smell. If you fill the glass to the brim such a movement would slop wine all over the table to the consternation of yourself as either guest or hostess.

Tomato Wheels · Tomato Water Lily
Globe Artichoke Centre Piece
Chrysanthemum Head · Egg and Parsley Border
Lemon and Parsley Border · Twisted Cucumber Slices
'Pineappled' Bread Socle · Bread Border
Fried Bread and Royal Icing Initials
Miniature Bread Vol-au-Vents
Biscuits as Garnish · Pinking Scissors · Stanley Knife
Table Fork · Butter Pagoda · Shaded Piping · Our Fondant
Almond Paste · Rolling Pin Cake · Traditional Royal Icing
Professional Royal Icing

This is the chapter over which we have had to exert the utmost restraint. We are a couple of garnish addicts who are aided and abetted today in all our work by three young men called Peter, Frank and René, who work with us. When for a fleeting moment they are devoid of ideas for something new which simply must be tried immediately, our Editor floats into the kitchen on the phrase, "I had a marvellous idea in the train on the way down to you . . ." In consequence a working day which would otherwise be concluded at the fairly reasonable hour of 9.00 p.m. is stretched to the utmost (which makes it about 1.00 in the morning)!

In a sense we are also aided and abetted by "The Daily Telegraph" because as we write this, in the kitchen, we are fulfilling for the twentieth year our undertaking to this newspaper to produce "some new garnish and decoration ideas for Christmas". Frank has turned one of our sinks into a working surface with a bit of laminated plastic and is evolving an evergreen garland which will do triple duty on "Our Page", in a Christmas stage show and at our traditional Christmas party encircling a giant Christmas pudding. Just to defy superstition we have found some really remarkable imitation arums (stockists p. 291) which we shall mingle with holly berries between the dark shiny leaves. René is painting a giant flower pot with flat white paint and smothering it and himself with silver glitter dust for a glitter tree with leaf-stripped willow stems, flat painted, glitter dusted and bound together with strong string. We shall drive the "bunch" into a hollow painted and glittered rod and when this is driven into the wet-sand-filled-pot, we shall stick the minutest silver balls to every other willow tip—a chore which will keep us busy for some hours.

Fanny is doing her usual one finger act with the typewriter, _standing up_ against one of her island units prodding out the information on how she has just iced a large cake and decorated it with a rolling pin and a set of fluted pastry cutters. Peter, with the tip of his tongue protruding and a look of enormous concentration on his face, is threading strands of unstoned dates onto brown buttonhole twist for a Christmas dinner table centre piece and the deafening screech of Johnnie's electric saw confirms that he is cutting out cake boards in heart and panel shapes which will in due course be covered with gold and silver papers for our Log and Rolling Pin Cakes.

We faced these truths about ourselves. Johnnie pointed out to Fanny, "Given the opportunity you will spend sixteen hours over a party *pièce montée*, which is demolished in as many minutes. What's more," as always on the rare occasions he gets on his high horse, he warmed to this theme, "the average cook-hostess hasn't got the time and couldn't justify spending it anyway on the grounds she could earn money from so doing—as you can!"

So *no elaborate garnish* was made the governing principle in this chapter, with a further rider from Johnnie to Fanny, "Exclude everything that *you* could do in three hundred hours like those edible lagoons and meringue Taj Mahals on our *Table d'Honneur* at Olympia for the Queen and Prince Philip." Therefore, we have limited ourselves to some suggestions for quick and easy garnishes suitable for party tables from the formal dinner to trays of *canapés*.

So let us start with Canapés. Out with us are those corny old apples stabbed with cubes of cheese on cocktail sticks. Out too are radish waterlilies, and apples, oranges and lemons wired from the back onto sprays of laurel leaves. Frankly, we are sick of the sight of them.

· Tomato Wheels ·

In their place we suggest *Tomato Wheels* in the four corners of a vividly coloured, fibre glass rectangular tray. The colours of these are excellent: there is a smokey greeny grey one, which is very distinguished looking, there are scarlet and emerald green ones which are ideal at Christmas, and a blue which looks almost medieval despite the rather nasty sounding modern substance from which these trays are made.

For our corner decoration, take four very fat, firm tomatoes, or use just one as a centre piece. Rehearse what we are going to explain before you go off madly and are not absolutely clear as to what has to be done. Turn each tomato bottom upwards. If it does not stand perfectly steadily, cut a small slice from the top — which is now the base. Then with a small, very sharp, pointed knife cut across the top and down as if you were going to cut the tomato in halves, but stop about $\frac{1}{2}''$ from the base. Reverse your knife and cut again, exactly as before; check knife position to make sure this second cut would divide the halves centrally and make four quarters if done right through. Do not!! Stop again $\frac{1}{2}''$ from tomato base. Now reverse the little knife in your hand so that the cutting edge is uppermost. Drive the tip into the middle of each (still attached) tomato quarter and level with the base of the previous cuts and push the knife up to the top. Do this on each quarter and you will now have eight petals with their skins untorn. Press from the top with knife blade after making the first two cuts and scraps of ragged edge will almost surely be your reward!

Now pare away some of the flesh from the inside of the petals, being careful not to force the petals outwards more than a fraction. Fill an icing bag (no. 7 crown pipe affixed) with any savoury cream mixture from *pâté* to cream cheese, tuna in mayonnaise or Liptauer cheese (p. 208) and pipe a fat uprising rosette, thus forcing the petals outwards and causing the piped filling to show through the interstices. Take eight $1\frac{1}{4}''$ diameter fluted circles stamped out with a pastry cutter from $\frac{1}{8}''$-thick slices of Gruyère, Emmenthal, or even processed cheese. Push one side of each into the filling between two petals and lo-and-behold a highly decorative, completely edible Tomato Wheel.

· Tomato Water Lily ·

Escoffier has a similar, very pretty trick with medium to large firm tomatoes, by which he turned each one into an edible container for a buffet or table salad presentation. These are only difficult to make if the tomatoes have a tendency to over-ripeness, so make sure they are really firm and that you have a really sharp, pointed-tip knife, then all should be well. Cut as for Tomato Wheels and then, very gently, disengage these petals from the centre core pips and flesh either with the tip of a knife (which is risky as you may cut across the petal behind your knife) or, as we find easiest, with a crafty thumb! Either of our old friends *Caviare* Cream† or Liver *Pâté* Cream (p. 50) look and taste very satisfactory if piped through a nylon icing bag (with a no. 7 crown pipe) into the centre of each tomato, which should now resemble a bright red water lily. There are doubtless many other fillings you might prefer, but you should try liquidised or sieved hard-boiled eggs, seasoned with a drop or two of anchovy *purée* and beaten to a creamy consistency with real thick mayonnaise. If liked, a little whipped cream may be added. As individual items on an *hors d'oeuvre* table you could also use *Tchina* (p. 51).

Another good variant is to use these edible containers for individual salads. For these, begin by lining out each water lily with very finely torn pieces of cos or cabbage lettuce, mixed perhaps with a few washed picked watercress petals. Then fill each with Russian salad which you all know very well and use sliced cucumber for the final treatment. This is in fact just what we did with cheese rounds for Tomato Wheels; you merely substitute unpeeled cucumber slices. The effect is not only charming, but very fresh and appetising looking. Just do not set them out on paper d'oyleys, because if a tiny amount of the tomato juice seeps out it will deface the d'oyley; it is far better to place them fairly closely together, refrigerate until the moment of service, then stand each one on a leaf of lettuce and thus arrange on the serving dish.

· Globe Artichoke Centre Piece ·

Use a globe artichoke for a centre piece. Cut the stalk back hard to the base. Set in position and at the last moment (have them ready floating in a soup plate with very little water) stick a single detached red/pink/white geranium blossom inside each upward-pointing leaf so that the tiny stem vanishes and the petals just peek over each leaf tip. Drive a cocktail stick into top centre and wiggle it round to make a hole large enough to take three to five blossoms in a cluster. At Christmas time do the same trick using artificial holly berries.

· Chrysanthemum Head ·

Make a Chinese decoration with spring onions. Trim fat ones down neatly to about 4–5" in length. Lay flat on the table and with a very sharp small knife cut the bulb end into a tassel to a length of about 2–2½". Toss these into ice and water and refrigerate until the white curls up. Tie the stems together with thick cotton or very fine string, shake, and you will find yourself holding a very

credible *Chrysanthemum Head*. Put into any tiny water-filled container which the petals will conceal and you have a third centre
piece for *canapés*. This one is also effective driven into the funnel
hole on a cold raised pie on a buffet.

Although it is true to say that a vast amount of easy garnish is
out of reach for those who simply cannot use icing pipes, there is
a tremendous amount which can be done with only a small,
sharp, point-ended French kitchen knife. If you add in the use of
harmless vegetable colourings, you can work wonders very fast.

Have you ever dyed eggs? Not the kind we all know from our
own childhood which used to be hidden for us to find each Easter
morning, but hard-boiled shelled eggs which you intend stuffing
and serving, halved as edible garnish to large fish items for a
buffet, or as finger food when something more substantial than a
minute *canapé* is needed for a drinks party.

Once the eggs are shelled, under a thin stream of water, to
force shell and inner skin away and avoid those defacing little nail-
marks, two-thirds fill a roomy bowl with cold water and add harmless vegetable colouring drop by drop stirring thoroughly until
the water takes on a fairly dark, but not thick and dark tone of
pink, blue, green, yellow, etc. Slide in the eggs and leave them for
a couple of hours or overnight. Then halve them across centrally
or lengthwise. The whites will have become a gorgeous shiny
green (the best colour for this *truc*). Now whatever filling or
mounded topping you intend using, cut a tiny sliver neatly from
the underside of each egg-half so that it stands steadily and does
not slither about. Guard these scraps carefully. Sieve the hard
yolks, add cream cheese, a flick of anchovy *purée* and enough
cream to make a thick piping mixture; or use mayonnaise, lemon
juice and pepper, or liquidised sardines and cream or mayonnaise
—the permutations are infinite! Put the mixture into an icing bag
with an ornamental pipe affixed and pipe a fat squiggle on top of
each hollowed out egg-white case. Then push the tiny base-
slivers of green egg white into the top of each finished egg and
sprinkle the filling with powdered paprika.

· Egg and Parsley Border ·

Say you want a border for a dish of these, or of sole fillets
coiled, poached and set out on an oval flat metal dish and masked
with *chaudfroid* or mayonnaise, cut un-dyed hard-boiled eggs into

neat $\frac{1}{4}''$ thick slices. Pull tiny sprigs from fresh parsley heads and arrange around the dish rim one egg round and one parsley sprig alternately. It is so easy you will scarcely credit how effective it is until you have tested for yourselves. If before setting each egg slice in position you slide it through aspic at-the-syrupy-stage, you can do this one the night before serving, refrigerate and find it unimpaired the next evening when you eye your cold fish course or buffet item with trepidation!

· Lemon and Parsley Border ·

You can do another very effective one with halved $\frac{1}{4}''$ thick slices of lemon. Put these half-circles, cut side inwards, around a dish rim so as to achieve a yellow scolloped effect, use parsley as explained for Egg and Parsley Border or if preferred use minute sprigs of fresh fennel.

· Twisted Cucumber Slices ·

Suppose you are serving a whole, skinned salmon. Take thin, unskinned slices of cucumber and cut through in one place on each slice from edge to centre—no further. Twist the two sides of this cut, one left and one right which turns the slice into a twist which stands erect when you set a row of them down the spine-bone of the fish; or use on glasses containing shell fish cocktails and hang a twisted slice over the rim of each glass.

· "Pineappled" Bread Socle ·

All the things we have mentioned so far with the sole exception of the artichoke are in everyday use and bread too is ordinary. So now let us explore the potentials of an ordinary sandwich loaf. Cut off all crusts evenly and carefully and then with a large sharp knife transform it into a fried bread base for a glazed tongue, a duck, a ballottine or even a panel of *pâté* and thereby enable yourself to give it elevation on your buffet, a matter of vital importance. The first process is known as "pineappling". Take a large sharp knife and make $\frac{3}{4}''$ apart, $\frac{1}{4}''$ deep vertical cuts diagonally to the corners of the crustless loaf on each of the four sides (leaving top and bottom plain). Then slope the knife slightly and make another series of cuts very close to the previous lot, thus achieving grooves. Now repeat the process diagonally across your first set of cuts and the job is done. Heat oil in your deep fryer until very hot indeed and fry the "pineappled" bread to a good rich golden brown all round. Cool on a rack, wrap up tightly in kitchen foil and keep for at least 48 hours so that you can get the job done in the time.

· Bread Border ·

Fence in a plain dishful of cold game, meat or poultry portions and thus transform a rather dull, flat presentation into an effective buffet item. Use either plain or fluted pastry cutters for this one. Cut generous $\frac{1}{4}$" thick slices from a sandwich loaf. With a 3" plain or fluted pastry cutter stamp out the number of circles you think you will require to go right round the edge of your chosen dish. Then take a 2$\frac{1}{2}$" matching cutter, stamp out the centres and finally cut a 1" straight edge on each of these rings, so that when you come to arrange them round the edge they will stand erect without toppling over, but do not check this until you have fried them or they will all break to bits. If using for decoration only, just fry both rings and the 2$\frac{1}{2}$" diameter circles to a rich golden brown. If you intend them to be eaten, pass them through beaten egg and milk in the proportions of 1 standard egg to $\frac{1}{4}$pt. milk. Pipe a rosette of chosen herb butter* a $\frac{1}{4}$" in from your dish edge and press the flat end of your ring into it. Repeat all round dish leaving $\frac{1}{2}$" between each ring. When this is completed, pipe an even smaller rosette in the space left between each ring and press a circle into it at right angles to the rings. Finally, if you want to be really fancy (quickly) dab a little tuft of parsley head against the outside of each squashed rosette where the herb butter has been pushed out by rings. Do not do the same for the circles—this would be too much.

We also use these rings for a swiftly achieved border to a *Savoury Cocktail Gâteau**. After you have completed the filling of the layers and the reassembling into a round *gâteau* shape you normally spread the sides with a savoury or herb butter and then trundle the cake like a wheel through either milled nuts or mixed grated cheese and milled fresh parsley. Skip this trundling bit and when the sides are butter spread, trundle fried bread rings up against them angling each one slightly so that the final effect is of a fan-like series of rings. This treatment is most effective when done with flute-edged rings rather than plain ones.

· Fried Bread and Royal Icing Initials ·

Once when we did a wedding buffet for a cousin, we gave each savoury item fried bread initials. The couple's Christian names were Sarah and James, so we simply cut a crustless bread slice ($\frac{1}{2}$" thick) into 3" high plain S and J and made them stand erect by pressing them into a small strip of piped savoury butter covered over with fine tufting of parsley heads. On the sweet items we cut the initials out in tragacanth—stiffened, professional royal icing coloured appropriately to the food on the plate and made them stand erect by a strip piping of ordinary royal which hardened sufficiently to grip them when set.

· Miniature Bread Vol-au-Vents ·

It would be an insult to your intelligence to waste words on stamping out fancy shapes with fancy cutters, but there is a faint possibility some of you have never encountered *Miniature Bread Vol-au-Vents*, a little gem that alas is not our own but the creation of the incomparable Mrs. A. B. Marshall, quite the simplest *canapé* container which is its own garnish when made and filled. Stamp out from $1\frac{1}{2}$" thick pieces of crustless bread the requisite number of 2" diameter rounds and press down into the centre *to half-way only* a cylinder 1" diameter cutter. Then it is up to you as to whether you fry them crisply in slightly smoking hot oil as they are or pass each one rapidly through a classic egg and milk mixture first. Drain on a rack and with the tip of a pointed knife ease out the little centre pieces which leaves you with a golden brown "lid" and a little hollow case identical with a *bouchée* or baby *vol-au-vent* of bread instead of puff paste. These can be filled with anything from *caviare* cream† to finely chopped hard-boiled egg in mayonnaise!

Nor does this exhaust the resources of this clever little *truc*. We used them on television recently as we will now describe. One large classic rectangular metal flat, an outer border of the shaded rope piping (p. 282) in well-seasoned duchess potato mixture*, one inner rectangle of carrots cut with an oval Parisian cutter and steamed for a few moments and one innermost rectangle of these little *bouchées* filled with *petits pois* and parsley-laced cream. You see if you take the trouble to pass them through the egg and milk mixture, you can make them a day in advance for serving hot.

Parcel any number up in foil and refrigerate ready for slipping into a warm oven to heat through, be filled with the cream/peas mixture and put in position.

Alternatively you can arrange the cases on a d'oyley or napkin covered dish. Pipe in your chosen savoury filling until it rises well above the top of each little case. Slap the little bread centres back at an angle (to show off the filling inside) and just before service sprinkle the filling part with chopped nuts, powdered paprika, chopped or milled parsley or finely grated cheese according to what you regard as most complementary to the flavour of the chosen filling.

· Biscuits as Garnish ·

Bought biscuits can be made to work for you in the garnish field too. Nothing looks more effective as a "fence", around the snow-covered "garden" of a Chocolate or Gingerbread House than halved chocolate coated fingers—the very slim ones please. You merely cut off the tips at one end, dab these with a minute scrap of butter or royal icing and stand them up all round the cake board. They can also be called upon to give you speedy and effective elevation to a long rectangle of chocolate or coffee *gateau*. Cover the cake top with chocolate butter cream. Rough it up to simulate tree-bark. Push whole uncut little chocolate stick biscuits into the top, criss-crossing them one third from their top tips so that they march down the *gateau* like an edible guard of honour. Dust overall with sifted icing sugar. You can, of course, do precisely the same thing with pretzel sticks to form a guard of honour on the top of a long rectangle or panel of savoury *gateau*.

Those little savoury biscuits, which look like tiny balls and are filled with a cheesy mixture, make a splendid top rim decoration. Just range them around the top of a savoury *gateau*, spear severa. onto an ornamental skewer and drive the skewer into the centre

· Pinking Scissors ·

We have been totally unorthodox in our use of kitchen "aids" as far back as we can remember and one of the most successful mis-uses has been of pinking scissors. With these you can cut strips, leaves, flower petals rings, circles, diamonds, etc., in cucumber skin, lengthwise-split green onion stem, de-pipped and pithed pimentoes, tomato skin, and when you want to simulate truffles—the skin of those purple/black aubergines or egg plants. We think we have said enough about it to start you thinking about pinked items of your own, if we add that this is the quickest way in the world of achieving a very expert looking serrated edge to halved hard-boiled eggs or halved, hollowed tomatoes for filling with savoury mixtures. Like a fly round a jamjar just tear round the rim . . . with your pinking scissors, which we know well enough right minded women use for dressmaking!

· Stanley Knife ·

It is the same with a Stanley Knife, a house decorator's tool of inestimable value. When we first saw a decorator using one for shaving off the edges of linoleum insets with which he was dropping palm tree components flush into a linoleum-covered bathroom wall (more typical lunacy), we shot out and bought one. Since then our cold roast legs of pork look absolutely marvellous on cold Sunday luncheon buffets. We simply score the rind into small squares—very deeply—and roast the pork our usual way*. The cut cubes rise, richly blistered with the final two bastings at great heat and the fatty grooves are darkened with the coagulated juices from the pork flesh. It gives a splendid effect to the finished leg. If one little section has not responded quite as darkly and richly as the rest, we merely heat a steel knitting needle (with a cork on one end to avoid burnt fingers) over a strong flame until it glows redly, lay it in the delinquent grooves which swear loudly in response and turn chestnut brown with affront!

· Table Fork ·

A most neglected garnish implement—in our view—is an ordinary table fork. To illustrate what can be done with it, let us explain to you the way we devised a Christmas or Easter Log Cake or *Buche de Noël* for people who simply cannot cope with icing pipes. Bake your traditional Christmas cake mixture in two long, 2 lb. stone jam jars and join them together lengthwise with a circle of almond paste or else invest in a log mould (stockists p. 291) and bake your cake in it. Be sure to line the insides carefully with kitchen foil and iron out any creases with your thumb. When the cake is baked and cooled, roll out a slab of almond paste and cut it to the length of the cake and the width of the circumference. Brush the top half of the cake-roll with sieved apricot jam. Roll it on to the almond paste, continue brushing and rolling until the cake is neatly and securely jam-stuck to the almond paste. Place on its cake board with joins underneath. Gather up a few scraps of almond paste trimming. Work up between the palms until smooth again. Roll out into a flattish, say 1½″ diameter, sausage. Cut from it a 3″ length making sloping cuts at each end. Brush one cut with apricot jam and press it firmly to the top of the cake to simulate a branch. Make more if you think the cake needs it. Make up your royal icing (p. 288), slap it onto the cake top all down the length and very thickly and pull it over the entire cake with a fork, roughing up the surface as you work to make little snowy "peaks". Before the icing has time to set, push scarlet or green cake candles into the top of the cake from end to end, being sure that the spaces between them are even, otherwise it will look a mess. Now slap more icing thickly onto the ends and rough these up with a fork and that is the cake iced for Christmas.

The only difference between this one and an Easter log or *Buche de Pâques* is that you cover a Swiss roll with lots of pale lemon flavoured and coloured thick butter cream and rough it up in precisely the same way as you did the royal.

· Butter Pagoda ·

You only need a fork to make the most impressive and delicate *Butter Pagoda*. We make small ones for the dinner or luncheon table and large ones for buffets. Shape fairly soft butter into a 4″ cone (diameter) on a wooden board with two small table knives. Get that cone really neat as otherwise you will be stuck with a lopsided appearance when the cone is fork-finished. Chill your cone until it is fairly firm in ordinary mild refrigeration. Then work with a small pan of hot water beside you and a small table fork. Dip fork into water, shake off drops and drive prongs into the butter for about ⅛″, 1″ above base and with the back of the prongs uppermost. As soon as the fork is in, raise the handle to a vertical position and drive the prongs down for about 1″. Then pull the fork handle outwards from the cone just as if you were pulling a lever down. This will give you a curly, prong-ridged petal which is thicker at the base. Leave a space of ¾″ and repeat until you have a ring of these petals completed. Go 1½″ up the cone and do exactly the same thing but be certain that your fork goes in above each $\frac{3}{4}''$ gap, thus each set of curling petals, as you work round, curls in between the preceding set outwards and over. Make each tier's petals slightly shorter as you rise to the peak of the cone. When you are within $\frac{1}{2}''$ of the top, drive the fork prongs straight through the peak for that $\frac{1}{2}''$ and exert a little pressure to left and right to form two facing, outward-curling baby petals at the peak. Run a couple of knives underneath the base of the Pagoda, as it has now become, and lift it onto a small plate or silver salver. Just before service put a ring of parsley heads around the base and dab a tiny tuft of parsley in between the two topmost petals. Before we leave this, here comes the word of warning. If this butter gets too soft while waiting and after completion, those petals will collapse, so keep in refrigeration until the moment of service and all will be well!

· Shaded Piping ·

For many years we have made shaded royal icing and butter cream flowers using special petal pipes affixed to non-porous nylon icing bags, but this can be interpreted with far greater ease and standard icing pipes in a whole range of savoury as well as sweet mixtures such as duchess potato, gelatine-stiffened mayonnaise, stiffly whipped cream or herb butters.

The pipe for our new discovery is the standard no. 7 crown (stockists p. 291). All you need do is divide your chosen mixture into three equal parts; leave one its natural colour and colour up the other two with two complementary additions of harmless vegetable colouring—example: pale green and fairly strong yellow with natural duchess potato. Put your pipe into your icing bag and flatten it out on the table, put your hand underneath inside holding up the top half so that you can see the pipe at the opposite end, smear the base half which is lying on the table with, say, the green coloured mixture, put a matching layer of the natural on the top and spread a final yellow layer over this. Twist the bag so that the mixture comes to the tip of the pipe and pipe a simple rope over and over, pulling the pipe towards you as you go. Do this round the edge of an ordinary oval platter and you will have the most elegant ridged rope, in which by some miracle the natural peeps right through the rope coils with marvellous precision right down the centre, and the left hand side shades into green, while the right shades into yellow.

Cooks will only need to reflect on this for a moment to realise the almost endless permutations and combinations which arise from this simple treatment. Conversely, if you use the pipe quite straight and push it half back over the top of each preceding push, you get a mounded line: green on top, natural in the middle and yellow on the base; a rosette or peak finds the natural in the middle, a zig-zag green comes out on top, natural on both sides underneath it—don't ask us why—and yellow on both sides at the base. For those three colours, read any variations and any sized crown pipe from the most minute which is suited to delicate decorations on a sweet or savoury *gâteau*, or on cocktail *canapés* of endless different shapes and flavourings. What it does to your reputation is quite remarkable because if your guests have not made this childishly simple discovery for themselves, they will never work out how you have done it!

Finally, odd as it may sound, this is a boon to the inexperienced at handling icing pipes because the most elementary movements which *look* elementary in single colours produce dazzling results in shading; so we only need to add now that the colourings we have obtained in Britain, all harmless, are as follows:

Caramel	yields	beige to brown.
Mauve	yields	pale mauve to purple.
Blue	yields	palest pastel blue to dark, bright and strong.
Cochineal	yields	palest "pretty" pink to a rather hefty red.
Carmine	yields	a delicate pale pink to a subtle dark red.
Saffron	yields	pale yellow to a pretty powerful near mustard.
Green	yields	palest green to one which becomes brassy when used liberally.

Add a touch of carmine to fairly strong yellow and you will get a good orange.

Add a touch of blue to a medium green and you get a very respectable darkish turquoise.

Add a drop of carmine to any anaemic savoury sauce and then develop the tone with caramel and you will get a rich reddy brown.

And that we think is enough to start you off. Just remember one thing—do not fall into the trap from which we have emerged with chagrin. When working in, say, sweet butter cream and royal icing, accept that you cannot match them pink for pink, blue for blue or anything for anything else because one has a yellow butter base and the other a stark white base of sifted icing sugar. You are all right on a contrast with these two mediums together, provided you have pre-determined what additions produces what results.

At the moment of dictating this, Our Editor trapped us. She looked up with an expression of inordinate vanity, "I've got an absolutely super idea—meringue mixture!" the wretch announced and that wrecked the entire day. The team stampeded to the kitchen. We were due on television the next day and our *mise en place* was incomplete; but you will understand the nature of our beasts more completely if we confess that until we had an array of enchanting shaded meringues piped with the same no. 7 crown pipe and cooked exactly as our standard recipe*, and had rushed round showing them to some carpenters who were not in the least amused, and thought we were all raving mad, the *mise en place* waited. We went to bed very late indeed; but please try this if you want to experience the same elation as we did.

To anyone who uses icing pipes in nylon or paper icing bags it is incomprehensible how anyone else can find them difficult to handle; the fact remains that there are thousands of extremely good cook-hostesses to whom they are anathema. For this reason we set about finding out if it was possible to make really effective iced cakes, whose finished appearances suggested skill and massive time expenditure on the part of the executant, and which, in fact, could be done in a very short time; we emerged more than slightly dusted with sifted icing sugar but flushed with triumph when we had proved to our own satisfaction that it was possible and that all that was needed for the simplest was a rolling pin and a set of graduated, fluted pastry cutters (stockists p. 292). The medium for this kind of icing is fondant, of which there are many variants, but the great virtue of the one set out below is that it can be rolled out like pastry paste, and also like pastry paste, rolled up thereafter on the rolling pin and unrolled over the top of the cake!

· Our Fondant ·

The following quantities cover a 5–5½ lb. cake thickly. 3 lbs. sifted icing sugar; 6 ozs. liquid glucose (stockists p. 291); 3 separated standard egg whites; chosen flavouring and chosen colouring.

Soften glucose in a small pan over boiling water. Place icing sugar in a roomy bowl and make a well in the centre, add unbeaten egg whites and glucose when runny, chosen flavouring and a few drops of chosen colouring. Start working up with a wooden spoon until mixture achieves a stiff consistency of a good rolling pastry paste. Remember to add additional drops of colouring as you work up if first drops make mixture too pale. Turn fondant dough on to a cold surface dusted with cornflour through a sieve (do not use flour as during long keeping this ferments underneath and can cause icing to rise). Roll out fondant dough mixture like pastry paste with rolling pin dusted very lightly with cornflour.

Do not hesitate to add drops of water to finished ball of fondant if this tends to crack when a small test piece is rolled out. Just remember to work any such additions down thoroughly and roll lightly again in sifted cornflour before using or mixture will stick to pin.

Before we explain the above recipe to you, let us go to work together on the assumption that you will need to cover your rich fruit cake with almond paste before applying the old "fly-away" royal icing or the fondant; but please accept that if you make that (to us) horrible marzipan stuff, or if you use egg yolks, or castor or granulated sugar, or almond essence, or any other of what we call the "nasties" which are so often and naughtily recommended —that is what your paste will taste like! Please in your own interest, make the real thing; and multiply our given quantities to suit your requirements.

· Almond Paste ·

Mix 8 ozs. ground almonds and 1 lb. sifted icing sugar together until thoroughly blended in roomy bowl. Make well in centre; add a coffeespoon of both rose and orange flower waters; a few drops of true almond flavouring and raw unbeaten separated egg white (maximum 1 small). Start working up with wooden spoon or knife to form a stiff paste. If this ends up crumbly, make fractional additions of egg white until you can knead it smoothly on a very lightly oiled cold surface; set aside. Dust cold surface fairly generously with sifted cornflour and go to work on the assembly, for which there is one swift, easy method only for achieving a perfectly smooth and even cake-covering*.

· Rolling Pin Cake ·

Brush almond paste surface all over lightly with raw un-beaten egg white, make up fondant (p. 284). Measure diameter of cake (e.g. $8\frac{1}{2}''$), measure depth of cake (e.g. $3''$) and double this (e.g. $6''$), add diameter (e.g. total $14\frac{1}{2}''$) and roll fondant out to thick circle measuring just a shade less. Do this whether using almond paste or not. Roll up fondant circle on rolling pin and unroll over the prepared cake (cornfloury side underneath). Then very slowly and gently press in the sides trim off any surplus which overlaps the board and your cake will be smoothly, per-fectly iced, *all over* in just about the time it takes us to record this sentence.

At this stage it is, of course, as plain as a pikestaff, but, you have surplus fondant and it is with this that you decorate. For a $9''$ finished-diameter cake stamp out a $6\frac{1}{2}''$ circle with a fluted circular pastry cutter. Brush the underside meanly with raw un-beaten egg white and lay centrally on cake top. Stamp out three more fluted circles with (a) a $3\frac{1}{2}''$ cutter, (b) a $2''$ cutter and (c) a $1\frac{1}{2}''$ cutter. Egg brush the underside of each and set them centrally one above the other, first (a), then (b) and then (c). Drive a $3\frac{1}{2}''$ long Christmas tree candle through the top one. Stamp out seven $\frac{3}{4}''$ circles and arrange them around the rim of the $6\frac{1}{2}''$ circle and press a tiny cake candle into each. Last of all, for the top cut, stamp 15 slender crescents with the $1\frac{1}{2}''$ cutter and arrange them around the top edge of the cake. Further side decorations are purely optional, but, if desired, stamp out eight "leaves" or other slender tapering shapes with a cutter. Brush the undersides with egg white and press them around the cake sides. Wrap remaining fondant in a damp cloth until needed.

Banish those paper cake frills altogether. Multiply the cir-cumference of your cake by $2\frac{1}{2}$ and join $2''$ wide strips of net or tulle in chosen colour to make two long strips. Cut two; lay one above the other; run a double thread all the way round one edge of the two strips together; draw them up to the size of the cake; drop frill over cake to base and press gathered edge into sides all round. These frills tend to jump a little, so re-roll your remaining fondant and stamp out fifteen more "crescents" from a $2''$ fluted cutter and lay them on the gathered tulle or net at the cake base all the way round. They will hold it down and enhance its appear-

ance still more. For your encouragement the time taken to cover
cake with fondant, stamp out and affix all cut-outs and the frills
was 40 minutes the first time and 30 minutes thereafter.

Of course, being us, this Rolling Pin Cake merely spurred us on
to further inventions.

Assume now that you want to ice a favourite sponge-*gâteau*
mixture baked in a traditional round tin which is normally split,
centre-filled with a butter cream mixture and clapped together
again. Cut out the splitting/filling bit altogether. Pile your chosen
butter cream on the top and level it off neatly and carefully, with a
knife or metal spatula dipped in hot water and wiped quickly
before using. Work a smooth top and draw sufficient of the chosen
filling mixture down the shallow sides so that the cake is completely and only fairly smoothly masked with it. Slip it in the
refrigerator for long enough to harden the spread mixture. Then
give it a final, easy smoothing with the hot knife or spatula.

Now make a batch of fondant: 2 lb. batch for a 12" diameter
cake, 1½ lb. batch for 10" diameter and 1 lb. batch for ⅞" diameter.
Divide this into four equal parts. Colour three of them, say pale
green, pale pink and pale mauve and leave the fourth uncoloured,
i.e. white. Keep in separate bowls covered with damp cloths. Cut a
greaseproof paper circle of the diameter of your cake top plus the
depth of both sides. Example: for a 10" diameter sponge top with
1½" deep sides cut a 13" diameter circle. Divide this into four
quarters. Roll out each fondant ball in turn on a sifted cornflour
base until you can cut out a quarter using the greaseproof pattern
and slip each one in turn into position on cake top. We slid a rim-
less cake tin base cake tin under each section for easy lifting—a
good substitute is the base of a large food can. Press sides in
gently. It tends to stretch a little so trim off base edge carefully and
ensure a perfect join at the intersections by running rolling pin
lightly rubbed with cornflour gently over surface. Now cut two
2½" strips of tulle three times the length of the measured cake's
circumference in chosen colour. Overlap the double joins, run a
thread along one edge, gather up to fit cake's base and push
raw edges in with tip of table knife while fondant is still moist.

You can leave top without any further decoration, or you can
cover slightly wibbly joins with narrowest baby ribbon, or with
narrow strips cut from fondant trimmings using them plain, or
pricking tops with prongs of small fork or nipping along each

strip with pastry crimpers. You can put one big candle in the centre, or matching coloured candles in each section around the top edge. If you are really ambitious and *can* use a plain fine writing pipe, you can pipe free-hand trails or simple sprays in matching coloured butter cream over each differently coloured section.

There is a little more to this tale, however, we gave a friend of ours, who belongs to the cannot-use-an-icing-pipe-brigade, an almond paste covered rich fruit cake and stood over her acting as callers while she made her fondant, rolled it out, rolled it up and unrolled it over the cake. No problems whatever. She was elated, but we were not, because *en route* she had picked up little bits of this and that on her rolling pin and the finished surface was by no means perfect! We looked at each other and John suggested, "Why not assume that in these circumstances she *must* use a fine plain writing pipe?"

"But I can't," she wailed, "that is why you have given me this to do!"

"We know that," said John firmly stuffing a bit of royal icing, that we had been using, into an icing bag. "Look," he twisted the bag and held it vertically over our working surface. "Just doodle," he suggested adding action to words. John then invited our friend to try when she had seen what he had done and in moments she had mastered a wibbly serpentine turn-and-turn about doodle or squiggle, which so pleased her that she moved straight on to the cake and doodled all over it. The result was enchanting and it looked like simple lace work. We tell you this merely because this sparked off yet another idea which can be done with or without the doodling.

· Traditional Royal Icing ·

To make *Traditional Royal Icing*, whip 3 egg whites, the strained juice of 1 medium lemon and 2 drops of blue vegetable colouring for 30 seconds if using an electric mixer or rotary whisk or beat vigorously for 5–6 minutes with a wooden spoon. Continue whipping or beating while adding sifted icing sugar (approximately 1½ lbs.) and continue until mixture is smooth and holds a floppy peak for covering the cake. Add more icing sugar to achieve an erect peak for piping. If you now work in a teaspoon of glycerine, your classically firm royal icing should not crack and fly in all directions!

· Professional Royal Icing ·

You might also like to have our recipe for *Professional Royal
Icing*. Dissolve 2 rounded teaspoons of albumen powder (stockists
p. 291) in 3 fl. ozs. water at blood heat. Add 1½ lbs. sifted icing
sugar beating well between each addition until the mixture holds
either a floppy or erect peak. If using an electric mixer be sure to
beat slowly and so the majority of the beating in the early stages
when the mixture is very loose. Remember to keep covered with
a damp cloth while working so that no skin forms on top of the
icing.

Albumen Powder	Hartley Smith School of Cake Decorating, 34 Hampstead Road, London, N.W.1.
Almond Paste	Hartley Smith School of Cake Decorating.
Arum Lilies	J. J. Blackburn & Co., 26 Wellington Street, London, W.C.2.
Cèpes (*tinned*)	Louis Roche Ltd., 14 Old Compton Street, London, W.1.
Cornet	Elizabeth David Ltd., 46 Bourne Street, London, S.W.1.
Cream Cheese	Branches of J. Sainsbury Ltd.
Fraise de Bois	Thompson & Morgan Ltd., London Road, Ipswich, Suffolk.
Framboise	Peter Dominic Ltd., 2 Orange Street, London, W.C.2.
Graef International Slicer	Name of local stockist available from Ideal Home Institute, Household Equipment, Central Chambers, Hendon Central, London, N.W.4.
Gumtragacanth	Hartley Smith School of Cake Decorating.
Icing Pipes (*set*) *for use with paper icing bags*	Creeds (Southern) Ltd., 6 Bruce Grove, Tottenham, London, N.17. Creeds (Northern) Ltd., 1 Stanley Road, Birkenhead, Cheshire.
Ice Cream Ball Cutters	Elizabeth David Ltd.
Liquid Glucose	Most branches of Boots the Chemists.
Log Mould	G. F. E. Bartlett & Son Ltd., Maylands Avenue, Hemel Hempstead, Herts.

Metal Icing Scraper	Hartley Smith School of Cake Decorating.
Miniature Pie/ Tartlet Tins	Elizabeth David Ltd.
Pastry Cutters (*graduated, fluted*)	Elizabeth David Ltd.
Puff Pastry (*Jus-Rol*)	Obtainable throughout the country at good stores which sell frozen foods.
Rice Paper	Selfridges Ltd., Oxford Street, London, W.1.
Romaine (*seed—also known as Corn Salad*)	Thompson & Morgan Ltd., London Road, Ipswich, Suffolk.
Roman Pot	Name of local stockists available from Ideal Home Institute, Household Equipment.
Special Half-day Demonstration of Work for Christmas	Hartley Smith School of Cake Decorating.
Turntable	Hartley Smith School of Cake Decorating.
Unsweetened Chestnut Purée	Selfridges Ltd.
Vesiga	Fortnum & Mason Ltd., 181 Piccadilly, London, W.1.
Vegetable Colouring	Obtainable throughout the country at all good food shops.

INDEX

A

B